SP4: Gene Crowder

You are great American —

Tadeusz Gaweda
8-8-15
Fayetteville, NC

I Love America
The Memoirs of Command Sergeant Major Tadeusz Gaweda, U.S. Army (Ret.)

by
Tadeusz Gaweda
with Charles E. Glover

DORRANCE PUBLISHING CO., INC.
PITTSBURGH, PENNSYLVANIA 15222

The contents of this work including, but not limited to, the accuracy of events, people, and places depicted; opinions expressed; permission to use previously published materials included; and any advice given or actions advocated are solely the responsibility of the author, who assumes all liability for said work and indemnifies the publisher against any claims stemming from publication of the work.

All Rights Reserved
Copyright © 1999 by Tadeusz Gaweda
No part of this book may be reproduced or transmitted in any form or by any means, electronic or mechanical, including photocopying, recording, or by any information storage and retrieval system without permission in writing from the author.

ISBN-10: 0-8059-4597-0
ISBN-13: 978-0-8059-4597-3

Printed in the United States of America

Third Printing

For information or to order additional books, please write:
Dorrance Publishing Co., Inc.
701 Smithfield Street, Third Floor
Pittsburgh, Pennsylvania 15222
U.S.A.
1-800-788-7654
Or visit our website and online catalogue at www.dorrancebookstore.com

To the members of the armed forces of the United States of America, past, present and future.

Contents

Acknowledgments 7
Introduction 11
  1. Darkness to Daylight 15
  2. Through the Iron Curtain 28
  3. Working in America 39
  4. In the Army Now 43
  5. To Germany, With Love 52
  6. Field Soldier 62
  7. "This is the 82nd Airborne, All is Well" 70
  8. Christmas Good-byes 77
  9. Vietnam 80
10. Interlude 94
11. Vietnam II, MACVSOG 102
12. Troubleshooter 115
13. Return to Fort Bragg 123
14. Command Sergeant Major 128
15. The Legend Grows 139
16. Korea III 146
17. Signal Duty and Another Gender 159
18. Homecoming for Edith 171
19. Battalion to Brigade 178
20. Korea, Last Tour 184
21. Grenada 197
22. Armed Forces Day, Chicago 208
23. Corps Sergeant Major 211
24. Citizen Gaweda 224
25. A New Boss 228
26. Best of Days, Worst of Days 240
Epilogue 247
Glossary 257
Index 261

Acknowledgments

My everlasting gratitude goes to my devoted wife, Edith, the love of my life, who provided unceasing encouragement throughout this literary effort, and who also did my typing. I am especially indebted to Mr. Alan W. Garner, president of Wells & West Productions, and Mr. Charles E. Glover, my collaborator, who did most of the work.

I am also thankful for the moral support provided by my sons, George and Gregory; their respective wives, Peggy and Amy; and my granddaughter, Ginny. I am particularly grateful to my older brother, Eddie, who provided so much background material about our family's forced expulsion from Poland and our subsequent internment in a German work camp. My sisters, Mrs. Pelagia Glabik and Mrs. Wanda Matrejek, also deserve recognition.

And, finally, I salute and thank the scores of friends and colleagues who contributed to this book. They are:

Gen. James J. Lindsay (U.S. Army, ret.); Lt. Col. Ted Danielson (U.S. Army, ret.); Sgt. First Class Thomas Beckworth (U.S. Army, ret.); Col. Robert N. Seigle (U.S. Army, ret.); Lt. Col. Maurice (Moe) Winter (U.S. Army, ret.); Col. Heath Twichell (U.S. Army, ret.); Brig. Gen. Richard Potter (U.S. Army, ret.); Col. William Orlov (U.S. Army, ret.); the late Col. Alvin Ornstein; Col. Timothy Scully, U.S. Army; Sgt. Major

Ernest Smitka (U.S. Army, ret.); Command Sgt. Maj. Glenn Forsythe (U.S. Army, ret.); Command Sgt. Maj. Henry M. Spell (U.S. Army, ret.); Col. Henry Ruth, U.S. Army; Command Sgt. Maj. Robert D. O'Brien (U.S. Army, ret.); First Sgt. Micheal Dacyszyn (U.S. Army, ret.); Sgt. Maj. Joe Turner (U.S. Army, ret.); Maj. Gen. Leroy Suddath (U.S. Army, ret.); Command Sgt. Maj. Richard C. Burnell (U.S. Army, ret.); Command Sgt. Maj. William McBride (U.S. Army, ret.); Command Sgt. Maj. Kenneth J. Merritt (U.S. Army, ret.); Command Sgt. Maj. Tommy McKoy (U.S. Army, ret.); Command Sgt. Maj. Clayton Burtrum (U.S. Army, ret.); Ms. J. Kay Leonard, civilian protocol officer; Mr. Travis Bell; Mr. Fritz Healey; Mr. Wilbert C. Parker; Mrs. Marie C. Allen; the late Maj. Richard Meadows (U.S. Army, ret.); Sgt. Maj. Joe R. Garner (U.S. Army, ret.); Lt. Gen. James Johnson (U.S. Army, ret.); Brig. Gen. Herbert Lloyd (U.S. Army, ret.); Col. Charles W. Hendrix (U.S. Army, ret.); Command Sgt. Maj. George Vidrine (U.S. Army, ret.); Gen. John W. Foss (U.S. Army, ret.); Lt. Gen. James T. Scott (U.S. Army, ret.); Col. Stanley Olchovik (U.S. Army, ret.); Lt. Col. Richard Earle (U.S. Army, ret.); Command Sgt. Maj. Charles Cady (U.S. Army, ret.); Command Sgt. Maj. Lawrence D. McMillen (U.S. Army, ret.); Maj. Gen. Morris J. Brady (U.S. Army, ret.); Sgt. Maj. Ben C. Dennis (U.S. Army, ret.); General Volney Warner (U.S. Army, ret.); Sgt. Maj. David F. Ralston (U.S. Army, ret.); Lt. Gen. Michael Spigelmire (U.S. Army, ret.); Command Sgt. Maj. Harris L. Parker (U.S. Army, ret.); Col. Robert (Butch) Kendrick (U.S. Army, ret.); Command Sgt. Maj. Wilbert F. Brown (U.S. Army, ret.); Command Sgt. Maj. Royce D. Burkett (U.S. Army, ret.); Command Sgt. Maj. Lewis LePage (U.S. Army, ret.); Command Sgt. Maj. William T. Mixon (U.S. Army, ret.); Command Sgt. Maj. Stephen P. Holmstock (U.S. Army, ret.); Command Sgt. Maj. George W. Townsend (U.S. Army, ret.); Command Sgt. Maj. Joseph W. Lupyak (U.S. Army, ret.); Command Sgt. Maj. David Clark (U.S. Army, ret.); Maj. Gen. Bobby Porter (U.S. Army, ret.); Gen. Carl W. Stiner (U.S. Army, ret.); Capt. John Bell (U.S. Army, ret.); Maj. Gen. Don McNeil, U.S. Army; Maj. Gen. Thomas Needham, U.S. Army; Sgt. Maj. Lawrence L. Law (U.S. Army, ret.); Command Sgt. Maj. Michael J. Sinkovitz (U.S. Army, ret.); Lt. Col. William L. Wolf (U.S. Army, ret.); Lt. Col. Jake McFerren, U.S. Army; Command Sgt. Maj. Robert M. McLymore (U.S. Army, ret.); Sgt. Maj. Deiter U. Penner (U.S. Army, ret.); Col. Karl Johnson, U.S. Army; Command Sgt. Maj. George D. Rorabeck (U.S. Army, ret.); Command Sgt. Maj. Trivett Lloyd (U.S.

Army, ret.); Sgt. First Class William Newton (U.S. Army, ret.); Chief Warrant Officer Laverne G. Thompson (U.S. Army, ret.); Capt. Arnold Maher (U.S. Army, ret.); Maj. Gen. Claude Ivey (U.S. Army, ret.); Staff Sgt. Timothy Inch (U.S. Army, ret.); Brig. Gen. Alfred (Sandy) Sanderson (U.S. Army, ret.); Sgt. Maj. Johnny Kitchens, U.S. Army; Command Sgt. Maj. Simon Ramos (U.S. Army, ret.); Maj. Gen. Leon Childs (U.S. Army, ret.); Maj. Gen. Freddy F. McFarren, U.S. Army; Sgt. Maj. James H. Hall (U.S. Army, ret.); Sgt. Maj. Fred E. Dabney, U.S. Army; Command Sgt. Maj. Clayton Perkins (U.S. Army, ret.); Lt. Gen. Thomas H. Tackaberry (U.S. Army, ret.); Lt. Gen. Richard J. Seitz (U.S. Army, ret.); Col. Joseph F. Hunt, U.S. Army; Capt. Arthur N. Rogers (U.S. Army, ret.); Maj. Charles T. Clark (U.S. Army, ret.); Command Sgt. Maj. Carl Lopez, U.S. Army; Sgt. Maj. of the Army Leon Van Autreve (U.S. Army, ret.); Maj. Gen. Sidney Shachnow (U.S. Army, ret.); Lt. Gen. Daniel Schroeder (U.S. Army, ret.); and Command Sgt. Maj. James E. Hargraves (U.S. Army, ret.). First Sgt. John Gleason, U.S. Army; Col. Charles R. Johnson (U.S. Army, ret.); Sgt. Maj. Josigh Blue (U.S. Army, ret.); Master Sgt. Cecil-Malone (U.S. Army, ret.); Col. Bowman Olds (U.S. Army, ret.); Command Sgt. Maj. Franklin Fowler, U.S. Army; Command Sgt. Maj. Steven Slocum (U.S. Army, ret.); Lt. Col. Rick Spearman, U.S. Army; Lt. Col. Robert Girouard (U.S. Army, ret.); Lt. Gen. George A. Crocker, U.S. Army; Command Sgt. Maj. Steven England, U.S. Army; Brig. Gen. Richard Cody, U.S. Army; and Command Sgt. Maj. Kermit Short, (U.S. Army, ret.).

Tadeusz Gaweda
March 31, 1999
Fayetteville, North Carolina

Introduction

Moments after stepping off the airplane from Atlanta in April 1994, I saw a sandy-haired man of medium height holding a large homemade sign which read, *Mr. Charles Glover, Welcome to Fayetteville, NC.*

It was Tadeusz Gaweda. I was in Fayetteville to discuss a possible book about his extraordinary life. After greeting me with a firm handshake, he looked me up and down with his piercing blue eyes and asked me how old I was.

Holding in my stomach and pleased that I had put Grecian Formula on my hair that morning, I told him I was sixty-eight. "My God," he said in a lightly accented voice, "I can't believe your age. You are remarkably well preserved."

I had passed his first inspection.

On our way to the airport parking lot, I couldn't help but notice how he walked, ramrod straight and shoulders squared, almost as if he were on a parade ground. He was a presence. I soon found myself making sure I had a proper haircut and polished shoes before our subsequent meetings. He can do that to you.

Now, after three years with this strong and remarkable man, I can understand why scores of his comrades-in-arms—from his peers in the enlisted ranks to four-star generals—agreed, without equivocation, that

Tadeusz Gaweda simply was the best at what he did.

Colonels and generals, whom he knew as young lieutenants and captains, credit him with advancing their military careers. He "squared away" officers and enlisted men alike.

Summing up Tadeusz Gaweda, a colonel at Fort Bragg said, "The taxpayers of this country sure as hell got their money's worth when they paid the salary of Ted Gaweda, who was perhaps the finest soldier in the army."

English playwright and poet William Shakespeare once wrote, "What a piece of work is man! How noble in reason! How infinite in faculty, in form and moving! How express and admirable in action!"

Tadeusz Gaweda is an unusual man. His lifetime—from a Nazi labor camp to topkick of the Army's elite XVIII Airborne Corps—closely exemplifies Shakespeare's immortal words.

Charles E. Glover
Atlanta, Georgia

CHAPTER ONE

Darkness to Daylight

It was an All-American Day. Under a brilliant sun, the red, white, and blue colors of Old Glory were never more vivid. Battalion and regimental flags rippled in the fresh breeze.

Like a variegated garden, grandstands alongside the parade ground displayed a mixture of brightly colored women's dresses and United States Army green.

Parachutists swayed gently as they descended to the grass-covered field. However, the stars that day were not to be seen in the heavens, but on the reviewing stand at Fort Bragg, North Carolina.

They sparkled on the shoulders of a gaggle of Army generals there to honor and praise a most unusual soldier. As the 82nd Airborne Division band blared out military marches, formation after formation of paratroopers passed in review.

Standing in the back of an Army jeep, appearing for all the world like a Roman conqueror, the man of the hour inspected his fighting men and women. In the background, an artillery salute cracked and echoed with the sound of distant thunder.

It was Tadeusz Gaweda's last hurrah, his farewell to the Army he had served so well for thirty-five years, and with remarkable dedication and distinction.

In recognition of that service, Lt. Gen. John W. Foss, commander of the Army's elite 18th Airborne Corps, pinned a Distinguished Service Medal on Gaweda's chest, a chest so full of decorations, campaign ribbons, and badges, there was scarcely room to put another one.

This son of Poland and one-time Nazi prisoner had achieved his life's goal, and now he was leaving it. He was stepping down as the Command Sergeant Major of the XVIII Airborne Corps, the top noncommissioned officer of some 84,000 troops.

The road to this pinnacle of achievement had been long, tortuous, and hazardous. It wound its way through a number of countries—Germany, Korea, Russia, Vietnam, and many others.

Along the way Tadeusz became Ted, because his American comrades-in-arms found Tadeusz too hard to pronounce. And for most of the journey there has been Edith, his gentle and patient wife, and the mother of his two sons.

Her life began in pre–World War II Czechoslovakia. As young people Edith and Ted were frequently close in war-torn Europe, but only geographically.

Their lives would touch only after Ted followed a great circle route that took him from Germany to the United States, then Korea and, finally, back to Germany. And it seemed, Edith said, that all that time she was just around the corner waiting for him.

As Ted sat on the reviewing stand at Fort Bragg, North Carolina, listening to tributes from the Secretary of the Army, General Foss and other star-studded officers, he found his thoughts drifting back to the hard years in Poland, where he was born on October 20, 1933.

He did not pick the best of times to be born. Poland was in the depths of a deep economic depression that gripped the world. It had started in 1929 and would not cease for many until the end of World War II.

In the cities, bread lines were common and many of the unemployed roamed the streets aimlessly. Starvation was a worldwide problem. But Ted was raised on his parents' farm, where his family lived off the land.

"Our privileges and luxuries were not many," he said. "My father, Antoni, eked out what today would be considered a very simple living. For that time it was very satisfactory.

"He owned about one hundred acres of farmland. My father also was the local blacksmith. In exchange for his work, people would help him on the farm, plowing fields, planting seed, and harvesting crops.

"There were fruit trees of every variety. We had farm animals—geese, chickens, pigs, three cows, and a horse. We always had plenty to eat.

"All of the kids—me and my four brothers, Eddie, Henry, Walter, and Jan, and my two sisters, Pelagia and Wanda—helped with the farm work. There were lots of wolves and snakes in the forest. On harsh winter nights the wolves would come close to the farmhouse and howl.

"I remember that on Sundays, the entire family walked a mile or so to church, the older children holding the hands of the younger ones. I had the usual fights with boys at school. They called me "Shivek," which means "white horse," because of my white-blond hair.

"My mother was the main force in our religious upbringing. With 90 percent of Poland's population Roman Catholic, it was every mother's dream to have one son become a priest. I was the chosen one, but war and fate had different plans for me."

This pastoral peace was shattered on September 1, 1939, when German dictator Adolph Hitler unleashed a merciless Nazi blitzkrieg against Poland. Hundreds of German armored columns rolled across the Polish border as Stuka dive bombers wrought death and destruction below.

Two days later, Great Britain, France, Australia, and New Zealand declared war on Germany, thus starting the Second World War, which would become the bloodiest conflict in human history.

Adding to Poland's misery, Russia's Red Army invaded Eastern Poland on September 17. Only eight days before the Nazi onslaught, wily Joseph Stalin, self-proclaimed premier of the Soviet Union, signed a nonaggression pact with Hitler, assuring him a share of the spoils in what would become the rape of Poland.

Even though Poland was at war, little Tadeusz, not quite six years old, started school that autumn. "The teacher was very strict," he recalled. "The first thing she did every day was to examine your hands, fingernails, and ears to see if they were clean. If you failed the test, you were slapped with a paddle.

"My first memories of the war were of airplanes flying back and forth over our nearby town of Kamien-Koszyrski, 20 miles west of the family farm. Before long I started seeing German tanks and other motorized armored units moving across our land.

"The Germans began rounding up all of the Jews in the town, capturing many from hiding places. The Jews were carrying suitcases and other belongings.

"Many of the Jews were executed and buried alongside a road. My mother told me not to go there, but I did, with two of my older brothers. There was fresh blood oozing through the sand that had been pushed over the bodies by a bulldozer. The smell almost made me sick.

"Other Jews were put on trains and taken away. Rumors were everywhere. We heard later that the people taken from our area had died in gas chambers, that the gas came out of shower heads.

"I was told later that some Polish Jews in Kamien-Koszyrski took on the identity of Roman Catholics, went to worship services at the Catholic church, and survived the war."

The Polish Army surrendered to the Germans on September 28, 1939. Eleven days later, Hitler and Stalin partitioned the country, and Russian troops occupied Kamien-Koszyrski along with the rest of Eastern Poland.

For the Gaweda family, there was a period of relative quiet. Antoni was kept busy at his blacksmith's forge, repairing machines of war for the invaders.

But that all changed after June 22, 1941, when Hitler tore up his non-aggression pact with Stalin and launched a three-million-man attack against the Soviet Union.

As the Nazi hordes advanced toward Moscow, there was an uprising of Ukrainian partisans who wanted their own independence. "They wanted to kill everybody—Germans, Russians, and Poles," recalled Eddie, Ted's oldest brother.

Ukrainians and Poles had engaged in ancient land feuds for as long as anyone could remember. At the end of the First World War, land that had previously belonged to the Ukraine became part of Eastern Poland.

The Gaweda family farm had once been Ukrainian soil. The Poles and Ukrainians had existed together in an uneasy truce since 1919, but with a war raging, it was now payback time for the Ukrainians. They went on a rampage.

"They murdered my aunt and her daughter," Eddie said. "They were killing for land. Sometimes they would shoot people, but most of the time they knifed them.

"They would say, 'Are you Polish? Well, we have to get rid of you. We don't want any problems with you.' That's it."

Trapped between the marauding armies of Nazi Germany and the Soviet Union and the Ukrainian partisans, Ted's parents and Pelagia, his older sister, left the farm to live with his mother's parents in Kamien-Koszyrski. Antoni went underground with the Polish Resistance.

"Eddie became 'the man of the family,'" Ted said. "He was our protector and our spokesman. Although Eddie was only 15 years old, he cooked the meals and watched over us."

Eddie warned his brothers and sister not to say anything to anyone, Ted recalled.

"One time," Ted said, "Ukrainian partisans stopped him and started asking questions. I was a little fellow, standing there holding the hand of my baby sister, Wanda.

"'Where's your father?' they asked Eddie.

"'He went to town to pay taxes,' Eddie answered.

"'Where's your mother?'

"'She went with him.'

"'When are they coming back?'

"'Probably tomorrow.'

"And so on."

"We had some close calls," Eddie said, "but when I talked to Ukrainians, it was in their own language. I did not speak one word of Polish. It could have gotten us killed."

Sometimes there were scavengers in the area. When this happened Eddie would hide his wards in haystacks or take them to the nearby woods. It was the summer of 1943.

"When I said, 'Go to the woods and be quiet,' it was like a suspense movie," Eddie said. "Everyone was hiding in the weeds, not moving, not talking, just listening for any sound.

"Wanda, who was the baby of the family, was only five years old, but she never cried or screamed. No one made any kind of noise. When we were hiding in the woods, my mother would send us messages with a neighbor kid, telling us where to meet her and so on."

"When we would come out of the woods and go back to the house, the meals that Eddie had prepared frequently would be gone," Ted said.

As fighting between the German soldiers and Ukrainian partisans became more intense, Eddie decided it was too dangerous to stay on the farm.

"People were getting killed all around us," he said. "You know, the

Ukrainians killed a bunch of Germans. I was afraid we would be cut down in the crossfire."

Ted recalled hearing gunfire day and night. The German occupation forces pulled back to Kamien-Koszyrski, driving herds of cows, horses, and hogs before them.

Led by Eddie, the Gaweda children abandoned the farm and followed the Germans on the road to town. They walked to their grandparents' house in Kamien-Koszyrski, where they were reunited with their parents and oldest sister.

In the late autumn of 1943, the lives of the Gaweda family would take yet another turn as they were again caught up in a swirl of world-shaking events.

On November 6, 1943, the key Nazi stronghold of Kiev fell to the advancing Red Army. Masses of German soldiers were on the run, retreating to the south and west.

Hitler's legions came flooding through Kamien-Koszyrski near the end of November. "It was early in the morning," Ted said. "They awakened everyone. 'You will leave your homes and come with us,' they announced.

"We were allowed to take only blankets, the clothes on our back, and a few personal items that we could carry. Everything else was left behind."

The Germans loaded the town's able-bodied residents, including the entire nine-member Gaweda family, onto horse-drawn buggies and wagons. The old and infirm were left to take care of themselves.

At that point, Ted and his family, along with their friends and neighbors became German prisoners. The long line of wagons, escorted by German cavalrymen, rolled south toward the rail center of Kovel.

"It was bitter cold with snow on the ground," Ted recalled. "We covered ourselves with blankets. Dry bread crusts were our only food."

Ukrainian partisans twice ambushed the two-mile-long convoy and killed both Poles and Germans indiscriminately.

"From our wagon in the center of the convoy I could see fire and smoke at the back of the line," Ted said. "The Ukrainians were shooting everybody. The rear wagons were cut off, and Eddie told me that many of our people were slaughtered."

It took almost three days for the battered convoy to reach Kovel. Once there, the prisoners were jammed into the boxcars of three trains bound for Germany. Fortunately, the Gaweda family ended up in the same car.

"Many people were cold, tired, and sick," Ted said. "There was continuous coughing. There was just enough room to squat down. Men, women and children used a hole in the floor of the car to relieve themselves.

"The trains rattled west toward Germany. That was how I left my homeland. We had no idea where we were being taken. Many feared our destination was a Nazi death camp. We had heard the terrible rumors about concentration camp atrocities."

The four-day train ride was a nightmare. Children cried, the sick moaned, men cursed, and everyone shivered in the winter cold. The train was so long that when Ted looked out a tiny window on a sweeping curve, he could not see the locomotive.

On the third day, the trains stopped and the prisoners were unloaded. "Everybody has to take a shower," the German guards told them.

"Oh my God, there was absolute panic!" Ted remembered. "We had heard rumors of Jews and others being gassed to death in shower rooms, where not water but gas came out of the shower heads. People were sobbing and praying.

"In our case, there was no gas. After showering we were put on a different train. The next day we arrived at the Nazi labor camp at Eschwege, Germany, 230 miles southwest of Berlin. It was bitter cold, and there was snow everywhere."

The Gaweda family may have escaped being gassed by the Nazis, but Ted and his little sister almost lost their lives in the "poison pill" incident.

Because of freezing weather, flimsy shelters, and malnutrition, many prisoners caught colds. Among them were some 100 children.

"Everyone was coughing," Eddie said. "One day the German guards ordered all the children assembled so they could be given 'medicine' for their colds.

"The poor kids were lined up and the Germans came down the row handing out little red pills. 'These will make you well,' they said. Several Polish translators were there.

"When the guards came to the place in line where Ted and Wanda were standing, a voice whispered in Polish, 'Don't swallow the pills. They're poison.' Those dispensing the pills wore red crosses."

Eddie told Ted, "Put it in your mouth and then spit it out."

"I didn't put the pill in my mouth," Ted said. "I pretended to, but kept it in my hand. After the guards passed, I threw it to the ground."

Ted's mother, Helena, warned little Wanda not to swallow the poison pill.

"I spit it into my hand," Wanda remembered, "and my mother took it away from me. Then she washed out my mouth with water. Those people were the Gestapo (Nazi secret police), the real Gestapo.

"The next day, all of the kids that took the pills were dead. A German guard came around and pointed to us and said, 'See, these are the children who took the pills, and they are alive. The ones who didn't take them are dead.' He made it just the opposite."

"I remember seeing the small bodies covered with blankets," Ted sighed. "They were loaded like so much cordwood onto a horse-drawn flatbed wagon and hauled away. After that, I don't recall very many children being brought into camp.

"They made soap out of the bodies, some people said. There were all kinds of crazy rumors."

But why were they killed?

"The Germans didn't want to waste food on little kids who weren't productive workers," Eddie answered.

"The camp years were years of sheer survival," Ted said, and only the fittest survived. "My family came from hardy stock. Many others who were not so blessed perished."

Eddie and his father were put to work in a leather factory, making shoe soles. "Whew, what a stinking job," Eddie recalled. His mother and older sister became housekeepers at several Eschwege hotels.

Ted, by now eleven years old, worked in farm fields along with his brother Walter.

"There was always something growing on the farms," Eddie said, "something that could be eaten. Teddy's job was to peel potatoes. He used to steal raw potatoes. We would put them in a heating stove, and 'bingo,' we had baked potatoes."

"Peeling potatoes was a good detail," Ted said. "We would hide the stolen potatoes in our pockets and under our armpits. Of course, you had to keep your arms down to your sides. In the summer, the little kids like myself picked apples and pears. We ate as much as we picked."

No wonder the prisoners stole potatoes. Their staple diet was boiled kohlrabi, a kind of turnip, which the Germans also fed to the cows.

"The Germans had a machine that pulled the kohlrabi out of the ground, chopped it, and ground it up," Eddie said. "It was a like a meat grinder. At first, we couldn't eat the stuff. It had sand and dirt in it.

"The first time I ate kohlrabi turnips, they made me sick. I had an upset stomach and diarrhea. Then an old man told me, 'You don't eat it like that. You take the bowl and spoon it from the top. Don't chew, just swallow. And when you get to the sand and mud at the bottom, throw it away. Otherwise, it will make you sick and give you diarrhea.'

"There was a big kettle in the middle of the camp. The cooks would throw five hundred pounds of turnips in the pot and maybe one bag of potatoes and boil the contents over a big fire.

"That's about all we had to eat, one bowl of kohlrabi turnips a day. We were given a loaf of bread that was supposed to last us for seven days. But we ate the bread right away, because if you tried to make it last, someone would steal it from you. Then it was nothing but boiled kohlrabi for another seven days.

"Because most of the men were off fighting the war, German women ran everything—the trains, civilian airplanes, farm equipment, and the farms themselves. The German girls liked Teddy. They would tease him and put their arms around him.

"One pretty girl told him she would like to keep him, but added she could not."

"I wish you could keep me too," Ted had answered brightly. "She was very nice to me."

"Why wouldn't they want to keep him?" Eddie laughed. "With his blond hair and blue eyes, he looked like a pure German, a real Aryan."

Ted said, "There were good people among the Germans. The camp guards would sometimes share food with me. Some were compassionate about our plight."

After two million Allied troops landed on the Normandy coast of France in June and July 1944, American and British bombers and fighter planes stepped up their attacks on the Eschwege rail center.

"My father and I were in the middle of that, having been transferred from our jobs at the leather factory to work on the railroad," Eddie said. "There must have been more than thirty tracks over there. My father worked as a technician, repairing signals, things like that. I was in a work gang fixing tracks. When the warplanes would fly over, everyone scattered.

"We were never hit, although some explosions were only 50 yards away.

We would cheer for the airplanes. It was the greatest thing you could see, you know."

"I remember that sixteen American fighter planes would fly over every day at about four o'clock in the afternoon," Ted said. "Sometimes they would catch military trains loaded with soldiers, guns, and tanks. The Americans would just strafe the hell out of those trains. There were fires and explosions.

"I was watching from the camp one time when one of the fighter planes made an emergency landing in a nearby hayfield. The pilot climbed out with a gun in his hand to defend himself. But suddenly the Germans, many with pitchforks, were all over him. He dropped his gun, threw his hands in the air, and let himself be led away."

In late 1944 and early 1945, it was evident that the Germans were losing the war. Hitler's soldiers were fleeing west to avoid capture by the advancing Red Army.

"'The Americans are coming to save us,' the prisoners whispered to each other," Ted said. "'The Americans are coming.'

"It was never the British, the French, or the Russians who were coming; it was always the Americans. That was our dream, our hope to be rescued by the Americans from a terrible life that we had not chosen.

"By the end of March 1945, our Nazi masters had fled the camp. You couldn't see a German anywhere. I could hear what sounded like tanks rumbling in the distance. There was a lot of shooting—most of it small arms fire.

"Rumors kept everyone in a state of agitation. One rumor said that Nazi SS troops were on the way to our camp to burn it and kill all of the prisoners. I don't know what they would have done, but at the end they only had time to save themselves.

"The highlight of my young life came on Easter Sunday 1945, when two rugged-looking American soldiers rolled into Camp Eschwege in a U.S. Army jeep and liberated us.

"I remember their helmets, M-1 rifles, and bandoleers of ammunition draped around their shoulders. One soldier lifted his rifle and shot the wires from a utility pole, attempting to cut off German communications, I guess.

"He turned to us and said, in effect, 'All of you are free. You have been liberated by the U.S. Army.'

"It was like going from darkness to daylight. Right then and there, my future life seemed to be determined. My youthful admiration for those GIs was boundless, and I wanted to be like them. Someday, I told myself, I would be an American soldier.

"From that moment on, I stayed at their heels. Every waking moment I volunteered to run errands, wash their jeeps, whatever, in exchange for a candy bar, an orange, or a pat on the back."

"Truckloads of food arrived at the camp, and we were given white bread by the GIs and Red Cross workers. Our daily ration improved dramatically, going from kohlrabi turnips to bread and stew three times a day."

A week after liberation, the nine members of the Gaweda family were loaded on camouflaged two-and-a-half-ton Army trucks and transported to Gotha, forty miles southeast of Eschwege.

"Once there, we learned that the Russians would control East Germany," Ted said. "The Polish refugees were told they could stay in Gotha, which the Soviets soon would occupy, and be repatriated to Poland or wait for transportation to the west.

"Some people couldn't wait. They just started walking west. It seemed they would do anything to escape the Russians. My father, who had seen Poland's borders change several times, was determined not to return to a place now ruled by Communist Russia.

"We said good-bye to Gotha in June 1945, leaving on the same trucks that brought us there. Our destination was Wildflecken in West Germany, the largest displaced persons camp in Europe and home to some 125,000 Polish refugees.

"I didn't know it at the time, but this was the beginning of a difficult four-year journey, a journey that would lead toward fulfilling my family's dream—living in the United States of America, the greatest country in the world.

"I remember getting deloused. We were filthy with lice. They sprayed us with something like DDT, in the hair, the armpits, and the crotch.

"I had a bicycle in the camp, but it didn't have tires, so I cut up a hose and tied the pieces around the rims. I became a master at riding that bike.

"I went back to school and constantly tried to join the Polish National Guard. They would say, 'You're just a kid. Get out of here.'

"Besides having a police force, the Poles also had their own cooks and other functionaries. As a blacksmith, my father was in great demand. Eddie joined the Polish guards and wounded a German prisoner who was intent on getting Eddie's gun.

"'I shot him in the seat of his pants with my German Lugar,' he later boasted.

"After a year at Wildflecken, my entire family, for reasons unknown to us, was moved to another camp at Aschaffenburg. Then, twelve months later, we came back to Wildflecken. We were beginning to feel like gypsies.

"In the meantime, my parents applied for emigration, choosing the United States, Canada, and Australia, in that order. They were given a number, which came up in late 1947.

"Full of hope and anticipation, we were transported to Schweinfurt, where we filled out the necessary papers and took physical exams in preparation for emigration.

"Suddenly, our dreams came crashing down around us. My parents were told that Walter's chest X-ray showed tuberculosis.

"Going without him was out of the question. Our sad group was returned to Wildflecken. It was a very low point in our lives. I remember my mother crying.

"My parents were convinced that Walter did not have tuberculosis. They believed that his perfectly normal X-ray had been switched with that of someone who had the disease.

"That would not have been unusual at that time. The black market was thriving and bribery was common. There were people who would kill to get to America. As a displaced person or DP, without a country, one could not demand much.

"After another year passed at Wildflecken, Walter had another chest X-ray. His lungs showed no sign of tuberculosis. My parents' position was vindicated. Finally, in August 1949, our family was cleared for emigration.

"The last piece fell into place when a North Carolina farmer named George Kennedy volunteered to sponsor the Gaweda family's trip to the United States. In exchange, we would work on his farm for one year.

"We boarded the U.S. Navy transport *Muir* on October 1, 1949, at the German port of Bremerhaven. It was a wonderful day, and I was so excited I could hardly sleep. We slept below deck on canvas that was lashed to metal frames. The bunks were five high, climbing from just above the deck to the overhead.

"But the passage was not an easy one. Six days into the crossing and four days from New York City, the *Muir* was caught in a monster hurricane. It was one of the worst Atlantic storms in years.

"The ship was stationary for two days. To the passengers, it felt like the ship's crew had dropped the anchor to the ocean floor. Every hatch was battened down and no passenger was allowed to go topside. Giant waves crashed down and gale force winds battered the transport, which was rolling from the punches delivered by the storm.

"I am sure that a lot of people were praying, 'Please God, after all of this hardship, don't let me be drowned at sea.' But nothing, absolutely nothing, could diminish my spirit.

"The storm abated and the *Muir*'s decks were crowded with refugees, many of them Polish, when the vessel steamed into New York Harbor on October 11, 1949.

"It is almost impossible to give a full description of my emotions that glorious day. As the Statue of Liberty and the Manhattan skyline loomed before us, people cried and cheered at the same time.

"The panorama of the Manhattan skyscrapers was breathtaking. I could see multicolored automobiles rushing across the bridges and the highways.

"We had arrived on that golden shore! It was my birthday month. In nine days I would be sixteen years old. The years of war and deprivation had fallen from me. I was filled with enthusiasm and a willingness to work, and to work hard, to make a new life."

CHAPTER TWO

Through the Iron Curtain

EDITH's heart filled with pride and joy as her husband stepped forward on the Fort Bragg reviewing stand to deliver his farewell address to his beloved XVIII Airborne Corps.

It was all she could do to keep from crying when he told the assemblage of elite warriors:

"I have been most fortunate to have been married to a lady who has supported me throughout the years, during good times and bad times, who has unselfishly survived seven unaccompanied overseas tours, countless field problems, late night suppers, unexpected dinner guests and telephone calls.

"In addition, she raised two children, worked as a real estate agent, cut the grass, raked the yard, washed the car, and gave selflessly of her time to enrich and enlighten the lives of the entire family. Edith, thank you for being what you are."

Despite the honors, the pomp, and the exhilaration of the moment, she knew that Ted was going through one of the most difficult days of his life.

For him, it was the end of a thirty-five-year love affair with the Army. She knew how distraught he was. But for her it was a new beginning.

There would be no more lonely, empty nights without him; no more marking off the days of a calendar until his return; no more fears of the knock on the door, the telegram, or the telephone call with news of his death on some foreign battlefield.

Now he would be hers.

"Forever," she said.

Edith's trip to that reviewing stand, to that point in time, had not been a walk in the sun, as the soldiers used to say. In many ways, it was just as arduous as her husband's journey.

In October 1938, Nazi Fuehrer Adolf Hitler sent his storm troopers into Czechoslovakia's Sudetenland, annexing it and its three million German residents to the Third Reich. Prior to the First World War, the region had been part of Germany.

The German leader had browbeaten British Prime Minister Neville Chamberlain and French Premier Edouard Daladier into selling out Czechoslovakia for what Chamberlain called "peace in our time."

Hitler told the world that the annexation of the Sudetenland would be the last of his territorial claims in Europe. Eleven months later he attacked Poland and started World War II.

Little Edith Hubner was only four years old when she looked out an upstairs window of her home in Antoniwald, Czechoslovakia, and watched German troops march by in formation on the street below.

"I pulled a curtain aside and watched the soldiers," Edith said. "My grandmother watched with me for a moment, then closed the curtain and pulled me away from the window. She didn't want the marchers to see us looking down upon them.

"Antoniwald was only about ten miles east of the German border, so I guess we saw some of the first troops. Later, I remember the townspeople whispering 'krieg,' which is the German word for war. I had never heard that word before and did not know what it meant.

"Beginning in 1944, we began to see more and more airplanes. The adults called them 'silver birds.' 'The silver birds are coming,' they would say.

"We were never bombed because our little town was rural, with the houses far apart. When the air raid alarm sounded during school we would take cover in the cellar.

"One night in early 1945 I was in my grandmother's room, sick with a fever, when the sky turned fiery red. It seemed that the whole world was on fire. Dark, dirty clouds rose over Gorlitz, Germany, which was being bombed by Allied planes. Even though we were probably twenty miles away, I could see the fires clearly.

"Our town was governed by Hitler's Brown Shirts. One day they mysteriously disappeared. The Germans were retreating. My aunt told us that one soldier had been beheaded by his own people for deserting his unit. His head was found in a potato sack."

In the four days before the end of the war, some 1.5 million Nazi soldiers, who panicked at the thought of becoming Russian prisoners, rushed toward American, British, and French lines.

The course of post-war Europe turned in an unfortunate direction in April 1945, when Gen. George S. Patton's powerful U.S. Third Army was denied the capture of Prague, the Czechoslovakian capital, for political reasons.

The Americans, British and Russians had signed a secret agreement at the Black Sea port of Yalta in February 1945, putting Prague in the Russian occupation zone after the war. However, it was understood that the city could be taken by whoever got there first.

Despite Czech patriots rising up against their German masters and calling on the United States and Great Britain for help, Gen. Dwight D. Eisenhower, supreme commander of Allied Expeditionary Forces, ordered Patton to halt his advance at Pilsen, fifty miles southwest of the Czech capital.

Soviet Dictator Joseph Stalin had outbluffed his allies. On May 9, 1945, the Red Army seized Prague, which soon became part of the Russian Communist Empire.

It would not be the first time that Stalin betrayed the Americans and the British. It also happened in Poland. As his legions were sweeping across that country, Stalin solemnly assured a concerned President Franklin Roosevelt and Prime Minister Winston Churchill that free elections would be held in Poland as soon as hostilities ceased.

He did not keep his word, of course. Poland, like other Soviet-dominated nations in Eastern Europe, became a puppet state behind what Churchill called the "Iron Curtain."

"The Russians were the first foreign soldiers to come to our town," Edith said. "We were very frightened of them. We had been taught in school that they were 'untermenschen,' or subhumans, who would burn our houses and rape the women.

"There were rumors about acts of violence committed by Russian soldiers. One report said a gang of them tied a grandmother, a mother, and her thirteen-year-old daughter to a tree and raped them, and then killed them.

"I was shocked one day when two young Russian soldiers walked into our kitchen. I was there with my grandmother, mother, and younger sister. My father was not at the house, but my grandmother and mother pretended he was in the next room.

"It turned out to be harmless. The soldiers wanted something to eat, but they could not make themselves understood. Finally, one of them said the Russian word for egg, which has a similar sound in the Czech language. They left after my mother fed them eggs.

"Speaking of words, the first two English words I learned were 'breakfast' and 'supper.' They appeared on meal packages which were distributed by the United States Relief Agency after the war. I tasted peanut butter for the first time, and it was wonderful."

With the Red Army in firm control of Czechoslovakia, the Czech Communists began a campaign of oppression against German-speaking families living in the Sudetenland. It was payback time for Hitler's seizure of the region in 1938.

"All the German schools were closed the minute the war ended," Edith said. "I attended a Czech school, where everyone spoke the Czech language. Of course, we continued to speak German at home."

The Sudetenland, annexed to Germany in 1938, was returned to Czechoslovakia. Early in 1946, the Communist government in Prague declared that all those of German heritage living in the Sudetenland would be sent to Germany.

"I was eleven years old," Edith remembered. "The reason we stayed put for awhile was because my father, who was a glassmaker, did not have political ties. If that were the case, we would have had to flee as soon as the new government took over. Many people—Nazi party members, industrialists, and politicians—were arrested and taken away.

"When I was twelve years old, I applied for a ration card," Edith said, "but the Communists said I couldn't receive one until I went to a local movie theater and watched a documentary film about Nazi concentration camp atrocities.

"My mother took me. I remember seeing mountains of false teeth, twenty feet high or higher. There were piles of human bones. The announcer in the film said the Nazis made lampshades out of human skin. After it was over, I was given a certificate showing that I had attended the movie. Only then was I able to receive my ration card.

"We knew we were going to have to leave Czechoslovakia sooner or later. The dreaded knock on our door came on the night of November 19, 1946. 'You have thirty minutes to get your personal belongings together and leave,' we were told.

"We could only take what we could carry in our hands. We had a few suitcases and my teddy bear, whose belly had been slit open to hide coins and rings inside.

"It was time for me, my mother, father, grandmother, younger sister, Helfriede, and little brother, Klaus to say good-bye to our family home and the lovely little woods out back. We were trucked to the railroad station and loaded on boxcars bound for East Germany.

"My older sister, Hedi, was already married and lived in a nearby city. Her husband was on the Russian front and she was not permitted to go with our family. Once the Communists closed the Czechoslovakian border, no one was allowed in or out. I did not see her again until 1972.

"She had married her high school sweetheart and they had a brief honeymoon before he went back to the Eastern front. They were so young and so handsome. We all adored them. I remember their wedding was like a fairy tale. It was a crisp New Year's Day in 1944. A light snow was falling and all of us, riding in several horse-drawn sleighs, proceeded to the church. Such a scene now is viewed only in old movies, but it was real. She never saw her husband again.

"He later became an American prisoner of war in Bimini, Italy. After his release, the Communists would not let him into Czechoslovakia, nor let her out. He attempted to swim across the Elbe River but was apprehended. Later on, a 'long-distance divorce' was forced upon them. Her suffering cannot be described, but those were the effects of a war which the people had not wanted.

"My family lived in that one place all their lives. In fact, both of my parents were born under the flag of Austria. Czechoslovakia was created after the Austro-Hungarian Empire was dismantled at the end of the First World War.

"Like Ted's train ride to Eschwege, there were no sanitary facilities in the boxcar, only a hole in the floor. Like him, all I had to eat was dry bread.

There were about forty people in the car—the young, the old, the sick, and the dying.

"We were cold, hungry, and frightened. There were rumors that certain trains had been sent to Siberia because East Germany did not want any more refugees.

"After two days, the train stopped at Pirna, near bombed-out Dresden. It was very eerie. Bands of people roamed the streets at night. They were hungry scavengers, searching for food.

"We were taken to a former German Army camp. Each family was assigned a small space in a gymnasium, which was divided into small sections by hanging sheets for privacy. There were hundreds of raw wooden bunks covered with straw.

"Everyone had to take a shower. The men and women went separately. Our heads were sprayed for lice. Once a day we received a ration of mostly potato soup and a little bread.

"We spent Christmas 1946 there. Home seemed far away, but I do remember the love that bound my family together.

"We arrived at our final destination—Ilmenau, East Germany—on January 3, 1947. I recall that it was bitterly cold. With many others, my family was put in an old schoolhouse.

"After a certain time, I can't tell you how many weeks or months, we were able to move into a small apartment. We had four rooms and a kitchen. We set up a household practically from scratch. The locals were resentful of us at first, even though we spoke the same language.

"But, you know, anyone hates the intrusion of 'foreigners,' who might take your food and your job. There was so much immigration that after a while it didn't make any difference where you were from.

"My father, who was a real artisan, went to work making crystal, and I went back to school. Unfortunately, my father only was able to work for about a year. The ravages of war had caught up with him. He had stomach ulcers and became very thin and weak. It was from being malnourished for so many years, eating nothing but bread and potato soup.

"As a young girl, my mother, whose name is Elizabeth, had gone to a school for training in the household arts. She was taught, among other things, to sew. She became a dressmaker, maintaining a standard of living for our family, albeit a minimal one.

"There was little exchange of paper money. Much of her handiwork was traded for food. I remember that on Saturday mornings many of the townspeople would take trains to the country, where they would barter their valuables for whatever food they could get.

"Those trains were jammed with people. My father was usually aboard. I remember watching for him to come home on Saturday nights, so I could see what he had for us. He would bring eggs, lard, butter, flour, vegetables, and sometimes milk for my little brother, who was eight years younger than me. It was amazing what my father could get with a ring or a coin taken from my teddy bear's belly.

"To me, what he brought home was more important than a candy bar. A local joke said the farmers were doing so well that their pigpens had wall to wall carpet.

"I remember the first day that many foods were taken off the ration list. An ice cream parlor opened. You had to stand in a long line to get a concoction that tasted like frozen Kool-Aid, but I thought it was delicious.

"On one of my birthdays, my mother baked a cake made of flour, sugar, and chicory coffee. The coffee substituted for the chocolate color. It had an interesting flavor, but it was a wonderful birthday cake.

"I will never forget the day we received a package from my aunt in Vienna. She sent us wonderful things she had acquired from the United Nations CARE program. It was like Christmas. In the package was a pair of American-made girl's leather shoes. As the eldest, I had first choice. I immediately put them on and pretended they fit. They were so tight that one of my heels was bleeding. Despite the blisters on my feet, I continued to wear them. I must have broken them in.

"There also was a woman's heavy winter coat, which my mother could wear. The coat seemed to have a lump in it. When my father carefully opened part of the lining, six American cigarettes fell out. As a smoker, he was delighted. Cigarettes were expensive on the black market. You could trade anything for a cigarette.

"As time passed, life for us gradually became more endurable. Much of the debris of war had been cleared, and I became more attuned to my surroundings.

"Ilmenau is in mountain country, so there were lots of winter sports—ski jumping, ice skating, bobsledding. The town was famous for one of its towering ski jumps. The scenery could be breathtaking.

"Ilmenau and Eisenach, thirty-three miles to the northwest, are cultural centers. I had a passion for literature, theater, and history. One of the places my young friends and I would visit was a famous cottage in the woods, which was only a mile from where I lived.

"The cottage often had been used by Johann Wolfgang von Goethe, Germany's foremost author and poet. Goethe received international acclaim in the late eighteenth and early nineteenth centuries as the author of *Faust*, the story of a scholar who sells his soul to Satan for contentment and enjoyment on earth.

"As a student, I visited the University of Wittenberg, the cradle of the Protestant Reformation. I was thrilled by the sense of history around me."

After all, it was at Wittenberg that Martin Luther's determination culminated in one of the most significant events in civilized human history. An Augustinian monk, Luther came to disagree with certain policies of the Roman Catholic church.

In 1517, he nailed on the Wittenberg chapel door a list of ninety-five theses or arguments against the policies he found offensive. After refusing to recant his beliefs, he was excommunicated by Pope Leo X in 1521, touching off the Protestant movement that quickly spread worldwide.

The Wartburg Castle in Eisenach was Edith's favorite place to visit. It was there that Luther translated the Bible's New Testament from Latin to German in what is now known as the "Luther Room."

Despite these pleasant historical diversions, it became more difficult by the day for a young person such as Edith to live in the regimented society of East Germany.

"The East German Communist government controlled everything, absolutely everything," she declared. "You could not make a move without them knowing it.

"For instance, one day after school, I was talking with four or five of my girlfriends on a street corner. We were just young people having fun, but a policeman gave us a citation and ordered us to report to the police station.

"I was shocked! What had I done? Nothing! I was told that I had to learn the regulations governing the country. The rule was that no more than three people at a time could congregate on the street.

"During my last two years of high school, I took a business curriculum. It was similar to a junior college business program. Among the things I studied was business English.

"Mine was the last class to be offered business English. Later on, it was replaced with Russian. My sister, who is three years younger than me, had to take Russian language courses.

"After I was graduated from high school, I went to nearby Weimar to take a six-week course in business and economics. It was a fraud. All the instructors talked about was the Communist system and Marx, Lenin, and Stalin.

"I applied to take a college-level language program at a school at Leipzig. I wish I had kept the letter they sent me. It said that if I was accepted by the school, I must agree to take up arms to defend East Germany if called upon to do so. The letter also talked about a loyalty oath and joining an organization that would lead to membership in the Communist Party.

"I had had enough. It was time to go. From relatives and friends I had heard about the prosperity and freedom in the West. I had been living in a regimented society. Naturally, I wanted to go to a place where I would have freedom and opportunity.

"In the early summer of 1955, I began planning my escape through the Iron Curtain. I was not alone. A number of my friends were making the same plans or had already left. Many young people in East Germany felt they had nothing to lose. They would not be leaving behind spouses or children. They were only responsible for themselves.

"I worked in an office with a woman whose daughter had fled to the West. She supplied me with newspapers and magazines that had been smuggled from West Berlin. If you were caught with that kind of material, it would be confiscated.

"Some people crawled through barbed wire in open country, hoping to find freedom. Many were apprehended and some were shot. I decided to make my crossing in Berlin.

"I sent resumes in response to several classified ads in West Berlin newspapers for office work. Quickly I had a job offer and just as quickly, I accepted it. Now it was a matter of getting there. I had some knowledge of the German capital, having attended a Communist-sponsored World Youth Festival there when I was fifteen years old. I prepared a small map.

"Berlin at that time actually was in East Germany, but the city itself, following a post–World War II agreement by the victorious Allies, was divided into four zones—American, British, French, and Russian.

"My plan was to enter the Berlin subway system in the Russian sector and leave the train at a specific stop in the American zone. I had been told to make the crossing either in the morning or evening rush hours. During those years, Berliners were allowed to travel between East and West on day passes.

"There would be a crowd at rush hour, and I kept nervously telling myself that they couldn't check everyone.

"As this planning was going on, a new person entered my life. His name was Manfred, and he was a student at Ilmenau's Technical University. I met him on a train coming to Ilmenau from Eisenach, where he lived. We became friends, and I told him of my plans to leave East Germany. I don't think he believed I would do it.

"In mid-August 1955, I was ready to go. I had saved twelve hundred East German marks and packed a small suitcase. If the border guards had opened it, they would have known that I was trying to escape.

"I had packed an iron and a sewing kit. No girl leaves her mom without an iron and sewing kit. By now I had an apartment waiting for me in Berlin's American zone. I left with my parents' blessing. My mother spoke heart-wrenching words. 'Will we ever see each other again in our lifetimes?' she asked. Everyone cried.

"I left Ilmenau on a night train. At Manfred's insistence, I stopped over at his parents' home in Eisenach. His mother asked me not to go, saying Manfred cared for me. He also asked me to stay, but stay I would not. I took a train to Berlin the next day.

"It was dark, about 8:00 P.M., I would guess, when I entered the Berlin subway. Almost immediately, I encountered seven border policemen with two dogs.

"They questioned me where I was going. I told them I was on my way to visit a sick aunt in West Berlin. I lied, of course. If they had asked for a pass, which I didn't have, I would have been quickly arrested. There were other passengers milling about, and the policemen suddenly turned their attention to someone else.

"The train started to roll. I jumped on the last car—the guards didn't see me—and I was on my way. There were two stations to go before the Western Sector border. A bundle of nerves, I cowered in a corner of the speeding subway car.

"I got off at Gedachtniskisrche in the American zone and walked for several hours down Kurfurstendamn, which is Berlin's Broadway, before finding my apartment. My new landlady was a physical therapist who took care of patients at her house.

"My tiny room was about as big as my present laundry room. It had a Murphy bed that folded into a wall. The bed hit me on the head when I first pulled it down. But none of that mattered.

"The little apartment was my sanctuary, my haven. Best of all, I was free and in control of my own destiny. I was one of the lucky six million East Germans who had successfully made it to the West.

"However, my budget in Berlin was extremely tight. I exchanged my twelve hundred East German marks for about two hundred fifty West German ones. I remember existing on one Kaiser roll and two tea bags for several days.

"I wrote my parents and told them I was fine, but I did not write to Manfred. He asked my sister Helfriede for my address and we corresponded briefly.

"He began dating Helfriede, and before long they were married. They still are happily married, and my family and I share a wonderful relationship with them. As for me, I was waiting for the love of my life. I was sure he would come along."

CHAPTER THREE

Working in America

"Following a path taken by hundreds of thousands before them, my family entered the United States through Ellis Island in New York harbor," Ted said.

"Fortunately, there were no hitches. Eddie says each family member was given six dollars by U.S. immigration officials as we cleared Ellis Island. 'It was the first dollar I had in my pocket,' he says.

"All of us took a bus to the Pennsylvania Station, where we boarded a train for Wallace, North Carolina, a hamlet near our sponsor's farm.

"I opened my eyes on a sunny morning and looked out the window. We were at a crossing and several black children were waving at us. To me, it was an amazing sight because I had never seen black children before.

"We arrived at Wallace after a two-day train ride. There was no one there to meet us. Our sponsor, George Kennedy, did not know when we were arriving. Several American soldiers at the train station spoke a little German, and they told us where to catch a Greyhound bus that would take us to the farm at Harrells, fifteen miles west of Wallace.

"Mr. Kennedy turned out to be an elderly and friendly man. Our assigned housing was no more than a three-room shack, but we made the best of it. The agreement was that in return for the cost of our passage from

Germany, the entire family would work on the Kennedy farm for a minimum of one year.

"However, my stay on the farm was brief. My father had made the acquaintance of a fellow Pole at the displaced persons' camp at Wildflecken. We saw him again when we went through Ellis Island. He promised my parents that he would take me under his wing in New York City and pay for my education at proper schools.

"My parents told Mr. Kennedy about the opportunity, and he agreed to let me leave the farm after three months.

"On a cold February day in 1950, my parents gave me a twelve dollar bus ticket to New York City and eight dollars in cash for my trip. With all my earthly belongings in a small suitcase, I boarded a Greyhound in front of Mr. Kennedy's farmhouse. I was on my way to New York for a new life in a new land.

"It did not take me long to discover the true intentions of my so-called benefactor. He had no thought of sending me to the 'proper schools,' as he had promised. He wanted a young boy as his companion. He was gay!

"For the first time in my life, I was completely on my own and solely responsible for my survival. I got a job as an elevator operator at a Catholic school for fifty cents an hour.

"The job started at 7:00 A.M., but at 6:00 A.M. I was already at work. I spent my free time reading help-wanted ads in a Polish language newspaper. I constantly searched for any job that would pay me more money.

"Luck was on my side. The Knickerbocker Bakery in Brooklyn, owned by a family of Polish heritage, offered me eighty-five cents an hour. I quickly took the job, and for a time I had two jobs, because I continued to operate the school elevator.

"The bakery wanted me to come to work at 6:00 P.M., but I reported an hour earlier. I would leave the elevator job at 3:00 P.M. and get on the subway with my alarm clock set. By doing that, I could sleep for two hours on the way to the bakery."

In June 1950, Communist North Korean troops crossed the thirty-eighth parallel and attacked their neighbors to the south. The United Nations instituted a "police action" against the invaders, which developed into the bloody Korean War.

The largest commitment to the United Nations action came from the United States. President Harry S. Truman named World War II hero

Gen. Douglas MacArthur to command America's warriors.

"Radio stations were encouraging young men to join the Army and volunteer for Korea," Ted said. "I thought, 'Now is my chance.' There was a small problem, however, I was not quite seventeen years old, but I told an Army recruiter that I had already reached that age.

"He said the Army would take me at seventeen, provided my father would come to the recruiting office and sign a permission paper. There was no way that was going to happen.

"At that time, I shared an apartment with three other Polish immigrants. They were older than me, but not old enough to be my father. I needed someone about forty years of age.

I went to nearby Sunset Park, located between 40th and 44th streets and Fifth and Seventh avenues, and sat on a bench bemoaning my predicament and shedding a few tears.

"A stranger sat down next to me and asked me for 50 cents. I told him that I had no money to give away. He asked why I was so upset with the world.

"When I told him why, he said, 'I can fix that. I'll tell them I'm your father and sign the paper.' Since nothing is for nothing, we agreed on a down payment of one dollar, with four dollars more after he signed the authorization. Before going to the recruiting station, he asked me for my name and birthdate, and told me not to worry.

"My high hopes came tumbling down when the sergeant at the recruiting center quickly told me, 'You tried to pull a fast one on me. That guy could not even remember your full name. Come back and see me when you turn eighteen.'

"Not only had I lost a chance to fulfill my dream of being in the Army, but I was out one very precious dollar.

"I went back to searching for a better job and saved every dime I could. Stanislav Mazur, my boss at the bakery, told me about a Polish friend of his who ran the Goldcup Baking Company in Chicago.

"This time I bought my own bus ticket. The Goldcup Bakery was willing to pay me a handsome sum—$1 an hour—and my new boss, Mickey Michalowski, let me work all the hours I wanted. I established my first savings account and put away every cent I could. My budget was so tight it squeaked.

"There was a restaurant near the bakery, called Tony's. I would go there sometimes and ask for a cup of hot water. There were crackers and ketchup on the table. I would pour ketchup in the hot water, and presto, I had a free lunch of tomato soup and crackers.

"Of course, one of the nice things about working in a bakery was that you could help yourself to the merchandise. I filled up on bread, doughnuts, pies, cookies, and cake.

"About half of the people at the bakery were first generation Poles, and the rest were second generation. They spoke both Polish and English because they had to deal with English-speaking customers and suppliers, but when they wanted me to clearly understand what they were saying, they spoke Polish. We also told jokes in Polish.

"Reading comic books and watching television helped me to improve my proficiency in conversational English.

"My brother Walter, who was eighteen months older than me, came to Chicago in September 1950. He remained there until he died in 1990. We shared a room with Joseph Pupa, another Polish displaced person.

"On my eighteenth birthday, October 20, 1951, I became a capitalist. I bought my first automobile—a 1950 Ford Customline—from Mr. Michalowski for $850 cash. It was a beauty—Navy blue with only twelve thousand miles on the odometer. I polished that car until it sparkled like a diamond. It was my pride and joy.

"I drove the car to New York and to Boston for my brother Henry's wedding. Now that I had wheels, I could date. For a while, I went with a girl whose name I can longer remember. The world looked rosy, and I was on top of it.

CHAPTER FOUR

In the Army Now

"Besides buying a car on my eighteenth birthday, I also registered with the draft board," Ted said. "After eighteen months, I received a notice saying I had passed all requirements.

"I did not wait for my number to be called but volunteered for immediate service. One of my toughest partings was with my car. I sold it to a dealer for eight hundred dollars, only fifty dollars less than I had paid for it. It looked better than the day I bought it.

"Even though I still was a Polish national, I proudly raised my right hand on April 16, 1953, in Chicago and was sworn into the U.S. Army. My dream, which was kindled on that long-ago Liberation Day in Eschwege, Germany, had come true. With an uneasy truce in the Korean War, I felt I too was a liberator.

"I went to Fort Riley, Kansas, for basic training. Despite my language difficulties, I had a jump on my fellow buck privates. Tagging along after American GIs in Europe, I already knew the manual of arms. I also had learned how to assemble and disassemble an M-1 rifle, the Army's standard infantry weapon at that time.

"My uniform was always clean and pressed and my shoes shined like mirrors. Hell, I thought I was the sharpest soldier in the outfit.

"Not long after basic training, I was on the Navy transport, USS *Pope*, sailing west across the Pacific Ocean. Our destination was Sasebo, Japan, and ultimately, Korea.

"The ship held soldiers of many nations—Britain, Greece, Turkey, the Philippines, and many others. That was a proud moment in my life. I was wearing the uniform of an American soldier, and I felt I was in the best army in the world.

"I'll be honest about it. When I was in Korea that first time with Company E, Seventh Regiment, Third Infantry Division, I did all I could to make people notice me. 'Never volunteer for anything' is an old line in the Army, but I did the opposite. I volunteered for everything.

"If they needed someone to cook in the mess hall because there was a shortage of cooks, I would volunteer to cook. My friends said, 'Poor guy, he's going to be a cook.' If there was a need for someone in the motor pool, I would go.

"Although the war had ended on July 27, 1953, and the truce agreement had been signed, the units deployed along the 38th parallel—the demilitarized zone (DMZ)—were in full combat readiness.

"The Seventh Regiment was the most-disciplined unit that I ever served with. There was an automatic reduction in rank for any soldier caught in the off-limits area, for not being clean shaven at first light, or not wearing the steel helmet while out of a foxhole or bunker.

"Many soldiers were unable to perform up to those standards and were punished. But a person who complied with these policies did not have a problem.

"I think it was because of this attitude that my promotions came rapidly. I was promoted to private first class in December 1953, to corporal in April 1954, to sergeant in August 1954.

"The same August, I was diagnosed with rheumatic fever and flown by helicopter to the 44th M.A.S.H. Unit, which was very similar to the outfit later featured in a movie and a television series. They pumped out my stomach and put me on a liquid diet. After two days, I was starving. There was a 'red alert' one night and all the lights went out.

"Luck was with me. It just so happened that the dining hall was across from my ward. I crawled out of bed, and with small candles lighting my way, I crept to the kitchen, where I helped myself to all the peanut butter, crackers, and jelly that I could carry.

"The next morning, my nurse almost went into shock, not believing what she saw. My bed was surrounded by crumbs and empty wrappers and jars. The doctors surrounded me in disbelief and made me sign a statement declaring that I had raided the kitchen at my own risk.

"Two days later, I was discharged from the hospital. The rheumatic fever was gone. I figured that the peanut butter, crackers, and jelly probably cured me.

"In October 1954, the Third Infantry Division was rotated back to the United States, but I didn't go with them. I said. 'No, I have no reason to go back. I'm not an American citizen; I would just as soon stay here or go to Japan.'

"The real reason I wanted to stay overseas was to save money. Everything was cheap. For example, cigarettes, which cost $1.50 a carton in the United States, were fifty cents a carton in Korea.

"I was transferred to the Headquarters Company of the U.S. Eighth Army at Seoul, Korea.

"One day a notice went up on the company bulletin board, inviting foreign nationals in the army to become United States citizens. It went on to say classes would be held to help non-citizens study the U.S. Constitution and other documents.

"I went to the library and read about the Constitution and Declaration of Independence, but no classes were ever held. About thirty-five days later, about two hundred of us were marched into a theater. We listened to a patriotic speech, raised our right hands, and swore allegiance to the United States. That's how I became an American citizen while on Korean soil.

"From that moment on, I noticed myself walking straighter, looking better, and feeling good about myself. I was enormously proud.

"One cold and windy Sunday morning in December 1954, I was walking across a large grassy area between the Eighth Army parade ground and company headquarters. There were papers blowing everywhere, so I gathered them up and put them in a waste can.

"A sergeant approached me and said, 'The company commander wants to see you.' I immediately reported to the company commander in his office, which overlooked the parade ground.

"He was a major. After I saluted smartly, he asked me where I was from and the name of my unit. He also wanted to know why I picked up the blowing papers. I told him I had been taught that trash did not belong on an army post.

"'Soldier,' he said, 'I've been sitting here looking out my window for an hour, watching those papers blow all over the place. At least 100 soldiers walked across that grass, and not one of them bothered to pick up a single piece of paper. You are to be commended.'

"I was not in a promotion status at that time, but to my surprise I was promoted to sergeant first class on January 19, 1955. There was no explanation as to why. Obviously, the major had decided to reward me for my trash collecting skills.

"My brother Eddie, who also was in the U.S. Army at that time, couldn't believe how I had advanced so far in less than two years. 'Nobody gets promoted that fast,' he said. Actually, I had been promoted beyond my skills.

"When I first came to Korea, I encountered paratroopers from the 187th Airborne Regimental Combat team. They looked so smart with their fancy boots and obvious esprit de corps. I could tell they were elite troops. The Japanese called them 'Rakkasans,' which meant 'men with umbrellas.'

"I said to myself, 'My God, I want to be a paratrooper.' That became my goal.

"I left Korea in March 1955 and was assigned as a squad leader in the 74th Regimental Combat Team at Fort Devens, Massachusetts. In June, July, and August, I was at West Point, where I did patrol duty and taught cadets how to disassemble and assemble a tripod-mounted, .30-caliber machine gun in four minutes.

"But my eyes still were on the sky. My desire to become an airborne soldier was so strong that I took an honorable discharge from the army after my enlistment expired in April 1956.

"Twenty-nine days later, I reenlisted for duty in the 82nd Airborne Division. It was yet another dream come true. I was given orders to report to Fort Bragg, North Carolina, which is just outside Fayetteville.

"Wearing my khaki uniform, I arrived late at night in Fayetteville, needing a room. The desk clerk at the Prince Charles Hotel told me, 'Sorry soldier, we don't have a vacancy.'

"I went back to my car, changed into a navy blue suit and necktie, returned to the hotel, and was given a room without question. Obviously, the desk clerk was prejudiced against soldiers, looking only at the uniform and not the individual inside it."

At Fort Bragg, Ted was assigned to Company E, 505th Parachute

Infantry Regiment, one of the army's legendary units. On June 6, 1944—D-Day for the Normandy invasion in World War II—the regiment parachuted behind German lines at Utah Beach. Their exploits were featured in the book and motion picture *The Longest Day*.

"Although I was now an airborne soldier," Ted said, "I had never jumped out of an airplane in my life. But that would change quickly. Within a week, I was dispatched to jump school at Fort Benning, Georgia.

"There were roughly 450 soldiers in our group. However, that figure dropped dramatically when 120 failed the tough physical fitness test.

"Since I was a sergeant first class, I was the ranking trainee. Most of the other enlisted men were privates and corporals. I was given the job of filing a daily report on injuries, attendance, and so on for both officers and enlisted men.

"There was no class work. Everything was done in the field. In our month-long training, we jumped from platforms ranging from four to 250 feet. Finally, the great day arrived, the day we were going to take our final exam by jumping from an honest-to-God airplane flying at an altitude of twelve hundred feet.

"I was nervous and scared as hell when I hooked up to the static line, which opens the parachute automatically when you jump from the plane. I was the first man out the door.

"My chute burst open, and suddenly I was floating over what seemed to me the most wonderful scenery I had ever seen. The view was fantastic. 'Glory, glory, hallelujah!' I shouted.

"When you are free of the airplane and that big umbrella opens above you, well, you just can't believe the feeling. It is beyond description.

"Mine was a textbook jump. I could hardly wait for the second one. By the end of the week, I had made all five of the required jumps. It was yet another dream realized. I was a bona fide paratrooper.

"During the training program, sixty to seventy soldiers were hurt, with broken ankles and hips and other injuries. Four or five men refused to jump when they reached the door of the airplane. They were not punished but were simply sent back to what paratroopers call 'straightleg' units. In the end, 280 of us graduated and proudly received our paratrooper badges.

"When I returned to Fort Bragg I was painfully aware that other airborne noncommissioned officers of my grade possessed much more tactical and technical knowledge than I did. I realized that I couldn't compete with my peers. To complicate matters further, I was still trying to overcome my language handicap.

"But then a person entered my life who would set me on a course to confidence and success. His name was Henry L. Wooten, a black master sergeant with many years of experience in his profession.

"Wooten recognized my weaknesses and knew what had to be done to make me a better NCO. My duty assignment was assistant platoon sergeant, and Wooten was my direct supervisor.

"He was a good-looking soldier and everything I wanted to be. 'Please teach me,' I asked. 'Teach me everything you know, from your command voice to your knowledge of weapons.'

"'Okay, he said, 'because we're going to start working today.'

"In the evening we would go to a deserted parking lot, where he taught me how to give commands on the army's twelve basic exercises. They have to be done in sequence and on precise counts. One day, he said, 'You're ready,' and told the troops, 'Sergeant Gaweda is going to be your physical training instructor for tomorrow.'

"He taught me all about the weapons assigned to the platoon and squad and platoon combat formations. At the end of the day, he would give me an army manual to study, followed by a spot quiz the next morning.

"'G,' he would say (he called me 'G' because he found Gaweda difficult to pronounce), 'give me the five main groups of the 1919A6 machine gun,' and I would rattle off, 'the back plate, the bolt, the lock frame, the barrel extension, and the barrel.'

"We served together for a year. His training was like putting one brick on top of another. All at once, thanks to Sergeant Wooten, I had a substantial foundation. He put me on the path to greater things, and I always will be grateful to him.

"Sergeant Wooten's life ended tragically in 1963, when he was fatally injured during his retirement jump over Fort Bragg. His parachute deployment bag came out the jump door, which opened the chute prematurely, slamming Wooten's head against the side of the door. Unconscious, he floated to the ground with his chute open but died several days later of massive head injuries.

"During the summer of 1956, I decided to pay a visit to the home of George Kennedy, who was the Gaweda family benefactor. His farm, where we all had worked, was only 50 miles from Fort Bragg. Of course, I was six years older than I was when he had last seen me.

"I was dressed in my sharpest khaki uniform and wearing jump boots that were spit-shine polished. I knew I was a cool cat. His eyes widened when he saw my baby blue 1954 Cadillac convertible with red leather upholstery.

"Needless to say, he did not recognize the former immigrant boy who had knocked at his door. He was surprised and delighted that I had come to see him. He insisted I stay the night and asked about my family. He was impressed that everyone had done so well. My parents were already homeowners in Brooklyn, New York.

"In 1956, there was no allocation to promote anybody in the United States. All promotions were overseas. The only way to get promoted on American soil was to receive a stripe from a soldier who had lost one for misconduct or inefficiency.

"They were called 'bloodstripes.' The practice no longer exists, but it kept the army stable because instead of adding people, promotions were granted at the expense of those demoted.

"When I was sent to the XVIII Airborne Corps Artillery Academy as a full-time student in October 1956 to learn the basic skills of military leadership, I was terribly frightened that I would fail and be reduced in rank. Almost 40 percent of the soldiers in my class were college graduates.

"But, of course, I didn't fail. I studied hard and graduated. For the first time in my military career, I felt that I could compete with my peers academically.

"In April 1957, Sgt. First Class Arnold Maher was transferred from Ranger School to the 82nd Airborne Division and was assigned to a room with me."

"I reported to Fort Bragg as a 'straightleg,' which is kind of a dirty word in airborne units," Maher recalled. "The difference is that paratroopers are not straightlegs because of their jump boots.

"Later on, after I married, 'straightleg' was the first military word my wife learned. She would stick her head out the window, and if she saw someone who was not airborne, she would yell, 'Hey, straightleg.' She's kind of frantic.

"Ted was airborne all the way, while I was Mister Straightleg. We were working with recruits in basic training. There was a regular barracks and squad or platoon sergeant's room. Whatever, he and I were stuck in the same room.

"I had just come out of Ranger School, so I thought I was a pretty tough dude. I told Ted I was a better straightleg than he would ever be as an airborne soldier. He and I used to go at it, with a lot of loud arguing back and forth. I'm sure the people in the platoon thought we were fighting all the time.

"I went off to jump school and after that everything was fine. I had gone from Mister Straightleg to Mister Airborne.

"About that time, Ted and I came up with a bright idea on how to make some extra money. We went to a hock shop and bought a sewing machine. As soon as the recruits were ready to ship out, we volunteered to tailor their fatigues for a small fee. We took turns operating the machine.

"We could alter a set of fatigues in fifteen minutes. I mean we were quick. We also sewed on patches and buttons. I don't remember what we charged, but that little machine paid for itself many times over.

"Ted was always able to get things done. He always aimed to be the best soldier there ever was. He was hard core but fair and came across as a little gruff. When he called a company to attention, they popped. No one gave him any flack. They respected him. They were in awe of him is the best way to describe it.

"We used to run around together in his blue Cadillac convertible. He would portray himself as a big chicken farmer and would say that I was his bodyguard. Ted was never one for honky-tonking. I was a honky-tonker, but Ted, socially speaking, was quiet and laid back. He didn't chase the girls, but they chased him in his Cadillac.

"Ted and I went to summer camp at Fort Jackson in 1957 and shipped overseas together that August. Before we left, we sold our sewing machine for about the same price we paid for it.

"He and I both married German girls and, in fact, held each other's sons at their baptisms. In 1961, I went off to get a commission, and retired in 1971 as captain.

"It did not surprise me when he achieved the rank of command sergeant major of the XVIII Airborne Corps, but what did surprise me was his retirement ceremony speech. He had me staying in the VIP quarters and sitting in the stands beside all those generals.

"I was amazed by what I saw and heard. His demeanor was different. He was much more professional and knowledgeable, and his speech flabbergasted me. Back when I knew him, I never thought Ted would be capable of delivering that kind of address.

"I told him that I was overwhelmed by his standing up and delivering a terrific twenty-minute speech without even looking at a note.

"He told me, 'Well, maybe you don't realize just how much influence and knowledge that you must gain to be a command sergeant major.'

"He was right. After I became a commissioned officer, I kind of lost track of the importance of a command sergeant major and never gave enough significance as to how they got there."

CHAPTER FIVE

To Germany, With Love

"'What are my chances to get to Europe?' I asked a friend in the personnel office," Ted recalled. "'Hey, I want to go to Europe,' I said. 'How do I get a piece of that pie?'

"'Okay,' my friend answered, 'let me see what I can do.'

"He came through for me. I was assigned to escort seven hundred 11th Airborne Division paratroopers to Germany in August 1957. I was the provost marshal, responsible for discipline.

"It was a hell of a trip. Every time the train stopped between Fort Bragg and the Brooklyn Army Terminal, a bunch of the soldiers would jump off the train and buy beer. Since that was a no-no, they hid beer all over the train.

"We boarded the Navy transport USS *Upsher* for the trip to Germany. I was excited and proud about returning to Europe in my new status as an American paratrooper. I couldn't help thinking what a remarkable difference the last eight years had made in my life."

Retired Command Sgt. Maj. William McBride, then a private, remembers the trip well.

"Ted was a funny guy," he said. "We used to call him the 'Mad Prussian' because of his bearing, his immaculate uniform, and his heel-clicking when he saluted.

"Four or five of us didn't think we were getting enough to eat, so we broke a padlock on one of the ship's giant, frozen food lockers. There was nothing in the freezer except pies. So we ate pies until it was coming out our ears.

"After our misdeeds were discovered, the ship's captain summoned Ted and told him he must find those responsible for the great pie theft. We hid down in the hold, where we slept on hammocks, for three days. Ted never did find out who broke in the locker and ate the pies."

Ted and McBride, who would go on to become command sergeant major of the 82nd Airborne Division, would serve together at many posts before their respective retirements.

Without further incident, Ted safely shepherded his seven hundred charges to the 11th Airborne's Sheridan Kaserne (post) at Augsburg, Germany.

Retired Sgt. Maj. Lawrence Law, who was a buck sergeant in the 11th Airborne Division's Recreation Office at that time said, "When we arrived in 1956, U.S. forces in Germany were still occupation troops. Shortly thereafter, the Status of Forces Agreement (SOFA) was enacted between the United States and Germany.

"The new mission was to improve German and American relations, and the responsibility for planning and executing the mission was given to the local commands. The 11th Airborne chose athletics as the catalyst. Rather than selecting typical American sports, such as football, baseball, and basketball, the command opted for boxing and soccer.

"Finding boxers was no problem because of the number of amateur boxing programs in the United States. But soccer was another matter. The sport was as natural to the Germans as baseball to the Americans. It was their game.

"It wasn't too long before someone identified a sergeant first class by the name of Ted Gaweda in the Second Airborne Battle Group, 505th Infantry, at Augsburg as an accomplished soccer player. He had played in Europe as a youngster and later in New York and Chicago.

"Ted was asked to organize an 11th Airborne Division soccer team to play local independent teams and teams from German athletic clubs. Not only did the relations between the local citizens and our soldiers improve, but soccer was introduced into army sports programs as an intramural activity."

"I was the captain, manager, and coach," Ted said. "We played teams all over Germany. I had GIs on my team that had learned to play the game in their native Scotland, France, Greece, Poland, Russia, Germany, and Italy. I also held the same three positions with 505th Infantry team, which won the division championship against the other battle groups. It was great fun."

"When I was reassigned to Germany twenty years later," Law said, "my travels took me back to Augsburg, where I visited some of my old haunts. The locals fondly remembered the American soldier soccer teams of the 1950s and how they did so much to establish friendships between themselves and their German neighbors. I guess you could call that just another Ted Gaweda success story."

After Edith fled across the Iron Curtain to West Berlin in August 1955, she found work in an office. She almost ran out of the money she had saved in East Germany before her first paycheck arrived.

"I almost starved," she said. "On some days, I would eat only a breakfast bun and use one of my two tea bags for the fourth or fifth time. Things were very tight. I think I went to just one movie while I was in Berlin.

"As an unmarried refugee, I only was allowed to stay in West Berlin one year. I had given up my East German I.D. card, so I was basically a nonperson. I went to this giant camp in West Berlin, where all refugees reported. I registered, underwent a physical examination, and received a temporary permit to stay in the West.

"In early 1956, I learned through a friend that there were job opportunities for German girls who could read and write English at a National Cash Register Company in Augsburg. Ohio-based NCR had been in Germany for years and they were a well respected company. They had two thousand workers at Augsburg.

"I had to get out of Berlin and start over. I took my paperwork to Stuttgart's city hall, where I received a West German I.D. card. At last I was somebody again.

"I moved to Augsburg in February 1956 and went to work for Herr Reiter, who owned a factory that manufactured spinning machines for the weaving of all kinds of cloth. The company did a lot of exporting, so I would write correspondence in both German and English.

"I was Herr Reiter's main office girl, but he was a difficult man to work for. He was a terrible man. He would yell at his employees and stand in his office door with a stopwatch in hand as his workers went to the restroom.

"I prayed every day that I would find a better job so I could get away from that man. I called him the 'Bavarian devil.' Many an evening I went home crying.

"Telling Herr Reiter I wasn't feeling well, I took a day off and applied for work at NCR. My prayers were answered when I was called in for an interview and given a job in the company's technical department. Herr Reiter offered me more money to stay with him, but it was too late.

"My job at NCR was translating patents which came in from the company's world headquarters at Dayton, Ohio. My boss was a nice person, completely different from Herr Reiter. I worked in an office with about five other people, several of whom had been in World War II and kind of lost out on their education. But because they had learned the English language, they were in demand.

"In fact, one of my German colleagues had been a prisoner of war in North Carolina. Later, just before I left for Fort Bragg with Ted, he said, 'Say hello to North Carolina. I helped build the highways there.'

"Translating patents wasn't exactly what I wanted to do, but NCR was the best company in southern Germany. We had good benefits, a nice dining hall, and friendly people. Things were looking up for me.

"Amateur theater was my hobby, going all the way back to grammar school. I always was the one to give a reading or recite a poem at family weddings.

"My Augsburg theater group did mostly drama. I didn't play in any musicals. I'm not talented in music. Our group staged some marvelous plays which received citywide recognition. We became well-known.

"I met a couple of guys there, and I gradually began going out on dates, but there was nothing serious until Ted came along."

Along with the seven hundred paratrooper replacements, Ted also brought to Germany his 1954 blue Cadillac. On September 20, 1957, he was cruising around Augsburg when he stopped at a cafe to get something to eat.

The place was crowded and he couldn't find a seat. Then he spotted a lovely blond girl sitting alone at a table. There was an empty chair next to her.

"I approached her table and, speaking German, asked if she would mind if I sat with her."

"No, I don't mind," she said.

"When our eyes locked," Ted said, "I knew we were meant for each other. My search was over. I had found the girl who would share the rest of my life. I never would have started a conversation with her if I had not felt that she was the one. I was too busy with things that were taking place in the army. Women were not on my agenda."

"Yes, I suppose that's true," Edith interjected. "You're stubborn enough."

"I was sitting there all by myself, when in comes this handsome guy with blond hair and blue eyes. He wasn't the least bit shy. He was wearing a very sporty, good-looking suit. It was brown and white with tiny hound's-tooth checks. It was to become my favorite suit, and I remember many years later how I cried when he gave it away.

"I will admit that something within me clicked when I saw him. Somehow, I knew that there would be no more men in my life other than him.

"I wasn't sure he was an American, because of his accent. I was stuttering badly in my little Augsburg English, and he tried to show me that he knew some German.

"Over the next two hours, we shared our backgrounds. We quickly felt a special kinship for each other because both of us were European and both had been displaced persons swept up in the conflict of the Second World War.

"When he asked me for a telephone number, I said I did not have a home number, but I told him where I worked. I knew for sure he was an American when he drove me home in his Cadillac convertible. Only GIs could afford a car like that in postwar Germany."

Despite the warm feelings generated at their first meeting, Ted and Edith did not see each other for several months. He was kept busy working sixteen to eighteen hours a day, going on field assignments, and traveling with the 11th Airborne soccer team.

On a free day, he jumped in his Cadillac and cruised around the NCR plant as the workers were leaving for the day. And there, as he had hoped, was Edith.

"My God, she's gorgeous in that blue knit dress!" he said to himself.

"'Where are you going miss?' he called to me," Edith remembered. "He called me 'miss.' 'Well, get in the car and I'll give you a ride,' he said.

"I offered him tea, and we exchanged telephone numbers. We began dating on a more frequent basis. Actually, he lived quite close to me. The army post was only about a mile from my apartment. It was all quite convenient.

"Our dating was not a situation where we would see each other two or three times a week. It was more like twice a month. He had to leave the post many times without having an opportunity to call me, or he couldn't call because the mission was secret. I waited anxiously on Saturdays, because that was the only time I could see him. Sometimes he would show up and sometimes he wouldn't."

"One of the reasons I couldn't see Edith," Ted said, "was because after I returned from a major field exercise in March 1958, I volunteered to attend the Seventh Army Non-Commissioned Officers Academy. It was the only NCO academy in the army at that time.

"The course was most demanding, both academically and mentally, and spit and polish all the way. It cost me over seven dollars to properly block my wall and foot locker displays. Those lockers and my bed were inspected every day. Your clothing—socks, underwear, and uniforms—had to be laid out in a prescribed fashion.

"To keep from going through the meticulous task of making my bed and arranging the wall and foot lockers each day, I slept on an air mattress on the floor and kept extra clothing in my automobile. The daily inspections and other spit-and-polish routines made it a chicken shit course in many ways.

"My classmates had an average of more than ten years in the army compared to my five years. I was very proud to have passed the course and graduated. It was one of my most satisfying career accomplishments."

"One time Ted called me from Munich," Edith said, "where he was behind barbed wire, after returning from Beirut. I went to Munich to see him. It was strange territory to me. However, he could not leave the post to pick me up. I had to go to him.

"We spent an afternoon going to the post movie theater, the Noncommissioned Officers Club, the cafeteria, and the bowling alley. That's about all we could do. We had no privacy."

"That was in July 1958," Ted remembered. "Khrushchev (Russian Premier Nikita Khrushchev) had announced that if American troops were sent to Lebanon to put down internal uprisings, they would be pushed back into the Mediterranean Sea by Communist forces."

Secretary of State John Foster Dulles told Congress that unless the United

States intervened, the free world would lose not only the Middle East and three-fourths of the world's oil reserves with it, but also Africa and non-Communist Asia. Prodded by Dulles, President Eisenhower dispatched to Lebanon the 1st Airborne Battle Group, 187th Infantry, from Germany and nine thousand Marines.

"I was called out of bed at two o'clock in the morning and told I was going to Lebanon," Ted said. "I arrived in Beirut as a member of an advance party for my unit, but it was never sent. Nothing happened, and fourteen days later I returned to Munich and was assigned to the 1st Airborne Battle Group, 503rd Infantry. I didn't get back to Augsburg until October 1958.

"Going and returning to Lebanon, I stopped at a U.S. Air Force base in Turkey. As soon as I got off the airplane on my return to Germany, two officers met me on the runway and asked what I had seen at the Turkish base. I told them I had seen a group of U-2 Blackbirds lined up at the field.

"They told me that I had seen nothing and had me sign a paper stating that was the case. I guess you could say I was debriefed on the runway. On May 1, 1960, a U-2 spy plane, piloted by Gary Powers for the U.S. Central Intelligence Agency, was shot down near Sverdlovsk, Russia, by a Soviet missile. It created an international incident and was used by Russian Premier Nikita Khrushchev to embarrass President Eisenhower at a summit meeting two weeks later."

Ted and Edith's romance wasn't helped by these prolonged absences. Despite what the poet said, absence did not "make the heart grow fonder." Edith was ambitious, and new opportunities were opening for her at NCR.

Shortly after she met Ted, she was selected by management from two hundred women to go to computer training school at Frankfurt. She became part of an NCR team that traveled to Eastern European international trade fairs to promote the company. Edith was one of two computer operators on the seven-person team.

"I still was uncertain as to Ted's intentions," Edith said. "He had not convinced me he was serious. Before going to school at Frankfurt, I told him that I had this fabulous opportunity and asked him if I should take advantage of it.

"He did not say, 'Honey, I love you, and I want to marry you. I would rather you stay here.'

"If he had said that, I would have stayed at home. Instead, he said, 'Well, it's your life. Do what you want.'

"To me, that meant he was not seriously interested in making a commitment, that he had no plans to make our relationship permanent. To make matters worse, I was hearing all sorts of nasty rumors from other women who were dating or were married to American GIs. They were saying that Ted was married and had a wife and children in the United States. At first I was in shock, but then I wrote it off as gossip and jealousy.

"Ted's response to my question hurt a lot. I was an unhappy girl, but I didn't show it. I was going to keep trying. I could have cut him off and said, 'I never want to see you again.' But I didn't do that. I didn't want to do that.

"It's not all roses every day. You have to work things out. I didn't talk with him for several weeks. It was quite a while before everything fell in place.

"I also was terribly hurt by my mother's reaction, when I wrote to her about Ted. I told her that I had met an American soldier, who was a native of Poland, and that we were dating.

"The letter I received back from her was, to me, very brutal. It took me almost thirty years to forgive her and get over it. She said in no uncertain terms that in spite of war and hardship, she and my father had raised me to be decent and honest, and had given me an education so I would be intelligent enough to make the right choices.

"She wrote that it was absolutely unbelievable that I had sunk so low as to date an American serviceman, because 'where we came from, decent girls did not date occupation forces.'

"She expected me to break up with Ted immediately and said the biggest favor I could do for my parents was to abandon everything and come home.

"You know, despite all the hardships I had gone through to get to where I was, I never complained to my mom and dad in my letters because I didn't want them worrying. Even when I was half-starving in Berlin, I would always write, 'I'm fine, I'm fine.'

"My response to my mom was to be almost silent. I was punishing both of us, I guess. I wrote a very limited amount of letters home until it was over.

"After finishing computer school at Frankfurt, I made three trips with an NCR team to international fairs in Hungary, Czechoslovakia, and

Poland. Each trip lasted about three weeks, so I was gone a good bit of the time.

"When I came back from Poland with souvenirs for Ted and his father, he picked me up in his Cadillac. He said he had something for me. 'It is time for me to make a commitment,' he said. He gave me a gold wedding band and asked me to marry him.

"I was crying and laughing at the same time, when he produced two bottles of Coca-Cola and said, 'Let's celebrate.'

"In Germany," Edith explained, "there were no engagement rings as such. Exactly opposite of American custom, the wedding band was worn on the left hand during the engagement period and switched to the right hand at the wedding."

Ted was a determined suitor. Once, when Edith was at school in Frankfurt, she sent him a postcard with a picture of her hotel on the front. Ted told her he would come to visit on the upcoming Saturday.

"NCR had rented out hotel rooms for thirty-two of their students," Edith said. "There were no telephones in the room, so I had no idea what time he was coming. Saturday was a night out for the trainees. The whole group would go to the center of Frankfurt, where there was a lot of night life.

"We would eat in the restaurants and go dancing, and some of the older men would stand around and watch the prostitutes. It was really harmless.

"But on the Saturday night Ted was supposed to visit, I stayed at the hotel. And he didn't come, and he didn't come. It was getting late, and I said to myself, 'Oh, my Saturday's ruined.'

"I was talking to the desk clerk in the lobby when he answered the telephone and said, 'Fraulein Hubner? Yes. She's here.' He told me it was the police.

"I was so flustered, I didn't know what to think. Then, a police car pulled up outside the hotel, with its siren going, 'hee ha, hee ha, hee ha,' and behind the police car was Ted in his Cadillac."

"I had forgotten the postcard," Ted said, "and I couldn't remember the name of the hotel, so I went to the police station. All I could remember was that the name of the hotel began with the letters 'PF.' A policeman started calling around, and, sure enough, he found Edith.

"He started to give me directions to the hotel, but they were so complicated that I told him there was no way I could find the place. 'All right,' he said, 'follow me,' and that's how I got a police escort."

Ted and Edith were married October 14 at Augsburg in a civil ceremony.

"We lived in sin for four days," she laughed, "and then we repeated our vows in a Roman Catholic ceremony at the army chapel on Ted's post.

"There were eighty guests at our wedding, but not one relative from either side. Ted's family was in New York and mine was stuck behind the Iron Curtain. My husband would not meet his mother-in-law for another thirty-one years.

"After I married, all the condemnations of me by my mother were forgiven and forgotten, but still it was very sad. I still cry when I re-read the letter she sent me after the wedding, in which she wondered if we would ever see each other again in this life."

"I had an occasion to visit East Berlin several times in the four years I served in Germany," Ted added. "It always made me sad to see those people living in a regimented society. At the same time, I thanked my God that my parents had chosen freedom over life on the wrong side of the Iron Curtain.

"Our first son, George, was born in 1960 in Augsburg, and I was an extremely proud father. My life-changing tour in Germany ended in August 1961. I had gone there alone. Now it was time for me to return to the United States with my little family."

CHAPTER SIX

Field Soldier

THE Boeing 707 jetliner was on final approach to New York's Idlewild Airport. Leaning her head against a window of the plane, Edith strained to catch her first view of America. Suddenly, in almost disbelief, she blinked at what she saw. Spread before her was New York's awesome, skyscraper-studded skyline.

"For me, it was an earth-shattering experience," she said. "I was stunned and amazed. But my amazement turned to shock when Ted's youngest brother, Jan, and his fiancee drove us to his parent's house in Brooklyn. We went through the Bowery District, one of the worst slums in the world. There were people lying on the sidewalks, sleeping on newspapers. I didn't know what to think, and I didn't ask. I was too tired.

"Everyone in Ted's family was hospitable to me. I hugged his mom as if I had known her all my life. Still, I had some feeling in the back of my mind that I might be resented because I was German, and it was the Germans who drove them out of Poland. I didn't feel guilty, but I knew that many of the older generation still resented what the Germans had done in the war.

"But they were wonderful to me. We conversed in three languages to understand each other—a little English, a little German, and some Polish.

There also was quite a party when Jan and his fiancee were married in a Polish wedding.

"One day Ted and I went to the Statue of Liberty in New York harbor with his younger sister and her husband. It must have been one hundred degrees that August afternoon. The elevator was broken, so we decided to walk to the top.

"I was in good physical condition, and I couldn't understand why I became terribly sick climbing the stairs. Oddly, my sister-in-law also became ill. Ted's mom said, 'It's just a little stomach upset' and kept feeding me 7-Up.

"But it turned out to be more than an upset stomach. A month later, at Fort Bragg, I found out that I was pregnant with my second child, who we named Gregory when he was born in March 1962. Actually, he accompanied his family across the Atlantic.

"Why was my sister-in-law sick? Although she didn't know it at the time, she was also with child. Her son was born within weeks of Gregory's birth.

"Ted and I drove into Fayetteville on another hot August day. It was late in the afternoon and we didn't have a place to stay. After Berlin, Augsburg, and New York, I was not impressed. We stayed in an old boarding house downtown.

"The time came, however, when I would change my opinion. Ted and I would frequently visit his family in Brooklyn. I loved every minute of New York until the mid-sixties, when the city became dirty and full of hippies and drugs. It was no longer the same. By then, I looked forward to coming home to Fayetteville. It was clean and green.

"We were in the boardinghouse for only several days. Ted applied for post housing at Fort Bragg, but as usual there was a long waiting list. We looked at rental units and I will never forget what one rental agent told us. 'We don't allow children or dogs,' he said, all in one sentence. I guess he viewed them as equal nuisances.

"After we lived in a small rental house for several months, Ted's name finally came up for post housing. We lived on Fort Bragg until we bought our first house in Fayetteville in 1965."

Ted was assigned as platoon sergeant with Delta Company, First Airborne Battle Group, 325th Infantry. His performance in a training exercise would make his name known to the top brass of the XVIII Airborne Corps.

"I spent many days in a field training environment, working to make my platoon the best in the corps," Ted said. "In February 1962, Lt. Gen. Hamilton Howze, corps commander, wanted to review small unit leadership. Out of the blue, he initiated a twenty-four-hour field inspection of a select number of platoons in the 82nd Airborne Division.

"My company commander, Capt. Francis H. Quist, called me at night and said, 'Gaweda, your platoon has been selected for tactical inspection by General Howze. Be prepared to launch a twenty-four-hour training exercise at 0800 tomorrow.'

"I asked, 'Who is going to be my platoon leader? I don't have a permanent platoon leader.'

"'No you don't,' he answered. 'Therefore, you are the platoon leader.' Normally, platoon leaders are second lieutenants. Meanwhile, all the other platoons had failed the inspection. General Howze was an exacting man.

"The mission of our forty-seven-man platoon was to find and clear a minefield, build a bridge that would hold two-and-a-half-ton trucks, blow up another bridge to keep enemy trucks and artillery from passing over it, and do all this while camouflaged to look like part of the natural surroundings.

"General Howze came over in a helicopter. All my soldiers were hidden. The only person he could see on the ground was me and a smoke grenade that was pumping out green smoke. I gave a hand signal, so the chopper could land against the wind.

"The general got out of the chopper and asked, 'Where are your soldiers?'

"'Clockwise, the first squad is between 12 and 4, the second between 4 and 8 and the third from 8 and 12,' I told him. 'The fourth or weapons squad is dispersed among the other three squads.'

"He still couldn't see the soldiers, so I took him to their positions. He was impressed, and kept saying, 'Well done' and 'Good job.'

"With two axes and two saws supplied by Army engineers, the platoon felled pine trees and built a bridge across a twenty-foot creek. It was against post rules to cut down trees at Fort Bragg, but we cut them down as fast as we could. The time limit on building the bridge was ninety minutes, but we built that structure in an hour. I watched with great pleasure as the first two-and-a-half-ton truck rolled across.

"Other soldiers cleared the dummy mines from the minefield and estimated the mount of dynamite needed to blow up the existing bridge. Of course, we didn't really blow up the bridge. One lieutenant colonel told the general that he hadn't come up with enough charges to destroy the bridge.

"One of my squad leaders, Sgt. Michael Dacyszyn, told the general, 'Sir, that's a lie.'

"General Howze was a stickler for realism. He ordered his engineers to build a duplicate bridge and detonate the same number of charges that we had estimated would do the job. I must say that I felt great when that damn bridge blew sky high. I heard nothing more from the lieutenant colonel.

"The next part of the training exercise came that night. I was told that a fictitious Russian spy plane had been shot down in a thousand-square-yard area and that two men had ejected.

"Our mission was to find the make-believe Russians and take them prisoner. Even though they were U.S. Army soldiers, they were of Russian descent, fluent in the language, and wore Russian uniforms. We captured the two 'Russians' in less than two hours.

"Our final mission was to conduct a night attack and prepare our defensive position. Ours was the first platoon ever to pass General Howze's field inspection. After that, everyone at the First Airborne Battle Group, 325th Infantry, knew who Gaweda was. In June 1962, I was moved up a grade to platoon sergeant.

"During my first year with D Company we had four different commanders. Before Capt. Charles R. Johnson arrived, none of the three earlier company commanders stayed more than six months. Fortunately, Captain Johnson stayed almost a year.

"He was West Point, Class of 1955, so he had seven years of service when he took command. Tall, neat, trim, and physically fit, he was a good-looking officer. In my judgment, he also was very competent. I did not have a platoon leader, so my contact with him was on a daily basis.

"He was a great company commander and a superb coach. I learned a lot from him. He was very demanding, so I worked my butt off just to keep my head above water.

"On September 30, 1962, the 82nd Airborne Division was alerted and deployed to Columbus, Mississippi, because of civil unrest in Oxford, the site of the University of Mississippi. Rioting had occurred as James H. Meredith, a black, had attempted to enroll at the all-white school. Local and state authorities could not control the situation.

"Things worsened when a Mississippi National Guard unit and a host of U.S. federal marshals were deployed. In the ensuing riots that happened on the evening and night of September 30 and the morning of October 1, two civilians were killed and 245 persons were injured, including forty-eight military personnel, three Mississippi state troopers, seventy federal marshals, and fifteen Bureau of Prisons guards.

"We were joined by the 101st Airborne Division, plus several other army units stationed in the southeastern United States. We landed at Columbus Air Force Base in the midst of a driving rainstorm the night of September 30. With no shelter available, we stood in the rain until daylight. Finally we were moved to an area where we struck our tents and the drying-out process got underway.

"The university had a home football game scheduled at Oxford the upcoming Saturday, but the game was moved to the state capital at Jackson because of the racial unrest. The Friday before the game, army helicopters were flown to Columbus Air Force Base. Late that evening, all company commanders were summoned to Battle Group headquarters and briefed on a mission to move their troops to Jackson by the choppers. Once there, they were to provide security before, during and after the football game.

"What followed was something that always has been emblazoned on my mind. During the briefing of company commanders, Colonel John Lekson told them they were to segregate their companies and leave the black soldiers behind. Captain Johnson, our company commander, made a passionate argument against the order, pointing out that a number of soldiers in the rifle companies were black, as were many of the key NCOs.

"After debating the issue almost to the point of insubordination, Colonel Lekson told the company commanders to 'get on with the mission.'

"I was told to march my platoon's black soldiers to an assembly area, where Captain Johnson spoke to them. I couldn't believe what was happening. Retired Sgt. Maj. Josigh Blue, who was one of the squad leaders in the company, later said: 'Captain Johnson delivered a very emotional speech. I could tell he was upset and disappointed that we were not allowed to deploy with the unit.'

"Also listening to the speech was Sgt. First Class Cecil Malone, who later retired as a master sergeant. 'I recall,' he said, 'that we were all speechless after the briefing. We were very disciplined in those days, so we understood that directives and orders discharged by the chain of command must be obeyed and followed, no matter the circumstances. Sure, I was upset and humiliated and felt rejected, but that was not a time to put up a protest.'

"Ten years later, in 1972, Johnson, then a lieutenant colonel, told me that while reminiscing with then Major General Lekson, the general revealed that prior to the briefing that evening, he had been on the telephone with Attorney General Bobby Kennedy, who transmitted the order to segregate the troops.

"Lekson said that when he objected to the order, Kennedy told him it was from the commander-in-chief and added that if Lekson could not follow the order, he should get off the telephone and put somebody on who could do it.

"It was one of the worst things that happened in the history of the 82nd Airborne Division. The effect on morale was devastating, considering that so many of the key noncommissioned officers and many soldiers in the lower ranks were black. It was more than a year before the units fully recovered from that decision.

"After returning from Mississippi on October 20, the entire division was alerted for action because of the developing Cuban crisis. Training and material were brought to the highest state of readiness.

"In January 1963, Maj. Gen. John L. Throckmorton, commander of the 82nd Airborne Division, organized the counterinsurgency/raider course for platoon sergeants and staff sergeants who performed the duties of a platoon sergeant. Four weeks long, the course was physically demanding. More than 30 percent of the students were dropped from the program due to injuries sustained in hand-to-hand combat and other training activities.

"My company commander called me to his office in mid-April and told me that I would start the course in the first week of May. He asked me to select another NCO from my platoon who I felt could complete the course. Our unit previously sent four NCOs, but only one of them had made it all the way through.

"I chose Sgt. Robert Somerholder, one of the squad leaders in my platoon. The program developed the student soldiers by requiring them to perform effectively as small unit leaders in a realistic tactical environment under the sort of physical and mental stress found in combat.

"A goal was to instill confidence and competence in these small unit leaders, and create a climate of relatively high stress and deprivation in which the students, hopefully, would learn how they and their comrades act and react under pressure—the challenges of leading and following while overcoming obstacles.

"Each NCO had to prepare his own combat orders for squad and platoon tactical operations, from the planning to the execution stage. In addition, we were required to have a working knowledge of explosives and demolition. This involved computing and placing charges for the destruction of common military targets, utilizing electric and non-electric blasting caps. Each student had to survive on his own for a twenty-four-hour period, traveling and living off the land without being detected.

"The last seventy-two hours of the course were devoted to combat patrolling, without any sleep. The only food you had to eat was cooked over an open fire in twenty-gallon pots. The ingredients consisted of fish, snakes, frogs, lizards, squirrels, possums, potatoes, carrots, salt, and pepper.

"Each student had to consume a half of a canteen cup of this mixture in order to pass the course. One hundred and twelve NCOs started the course, and fifty-eight completed it. I am proud to say that Sergeant Somerholder and I led the way."

Retired Lt. Col. Ted Danielson, who served with Gaweda in the First Airborne Battle Group, 325th Infantry, remembers Ted as a man who refused to be brought down emotionally, no matter the circumstances.

"I was a young second lieutenant fresh out of West Point, and I didn't know anything," Danielson said. "It was sergeants like Gaweda that taught me to be a soldier. You could not get him down. You might work at it, but he would always persevere.

"He had a good sense of humor and the same smile he has today, but by the same token, he could be as hard as they come. If you didn't clean your radio, he might just pick it up and throw it at you.

"Sergeant Gaweda taught me that you always push problem-solving down to the lowest level. That helped me immensely when I became a company commander in the First Cavalry Division in Vietnam.

"You know, Prussia's Frederick the Great never had a discipline problem in his army, not for two minutes. You didn't have to say too much to get shot in his army.

"To my knowledge, Ted Gaweda, who had a bit of the Prussian in him, never had any discipline problems in his units either, and he didn't have to shoot anybody."

"In June 1964, our unit was redesignated as Company B, Second Battalion, 325th Airborne Infantry Regiment," Ted recalled. "At the same time, the strength of our unit dropped from 240 to 187 soldiers. The army decided to do away with the Fourth Rifle Platoon."

"There were a lot of hardships in the 1960s," Ted said, "times of extreme lows and extreme highs. The lows were when I had to leave my family and the highs were when I came home. I was sent far, far from home many times in the sixties."

CHAPTER SEVEN

"This is the 82nd Airborne, All is Well"

"In April 1965, I had plans to take my wife to dinner for her birthday," Ted recalled, "and I had told her to go out and buy a new dress.

"Instead, I was called to duty in the Dominican Republic and didn't see her for three months."

A civil war had been raging in the republic since April 25, when insurgents overthrew the established government in an armed coup and established a three-man military junta to run the country.

Fearing another Communist-inspired, Castro-type takeover of yet another nation close to America's doorstep, President Lyndon Johnson on April 28 dispatched 405 U.S. Marines to Santo Domingo, the Dominican capital, to protect and evacuate American civilians, whose lives were endangered by the civil strife.

When a truce between the warring parties broke down and fighting intensified, Johnson ordered another six thousand Marines and the entire 82nd Airborne Division to the Dominican Republic. Rebel forces numbered forty-seven thousand, including twenty thousand armed military reserves, twenty thousand newly armed civilians and seven thousand regular troops. Some seventeen hundred troops from Brazil, Costa Rica, Honduras, and Nicaragua were serving with the inter-American peacekeeping force.

In a television broadcast from the White House, the president announced, "Our goal is to save the lives of our citizens and the lives of all people, and in keeping with the principles of the American system, to help prevent another communist state in this hemisphere."

Ted landed April 29 (Edith's birthday) with the 82nd's Second Brigade at San Isidro Air Force Base and advanced with the brigade toward the Ozama River on a mission to secure the Duarte Bridge in Santo Domingo.

"I was immensely proud," Ted said, "when my platoon from Company B, Second Battalion, 325th Airborne Infantry Regiment, was chosen to lead the advance, where we were to seize the bridge, fight our way through Santo Domingo, and link up with Marines coming from the east.

"As we passed through the lines of the 17th Cavalry Unit to get to the front, we were told that a machine-gun position and a barricade were about a block ahead of where we would begin our advance.

"My new platoon leader, Second Lt. Herbert Lloyd, who had come from the enlisted ranks and had been in combat early on in Vietnam, put me with the lead squad. Also in the lead element were the lieutenant, Staff Sergeant Michael Dacyszyn, another native Pole, who was in charge of our 3.5 rocket launchers, and three riflemen.

Lloyd, who would retire as a brigadier general, recalled: "We began our advance through Santo Domingo about 2:00 A.M., and had several fire fights along the way. The no-man's land extended for fifteen blocks. It was a dark and moonless night, and the entire city was blacked out.

"All you could see were tracers sailing through the air and the flash of explosions. We were receiving sniper fire from the side of the street where San Pedro University was located. There was hardly anything to hide behind.

"We fanned out and fired our rifles in the direction of the university. We could hear people scrambling around and voices yelling. We stopped briefly, but could not afford to get bogged down. The Marines expected us.

"A few minutes after we returned fire, the noises faded away, and we began moving again. I was walking into a four-way intersection when three or four shots were fired at us. A sniper bullet hit a wall just above my right shoulder.

"Sergeant Gaweda was on the other side of the street, and saw where the rebel shots were coming from.

"'Look out Lieutenant Lloyd,' he shouted. 'He's on the roof.' I stepped back behind a building. Ted opened fire and yelled, 'By the water drum, by the water drum on the roof, by the water drum.'

"He was talking about a roof-mounted, fifty-five-gallon water drum that was used for showering. I peeked around the corner and could faintly see the drum on the skyline. Ted got off another shot, and by this time, I started firing my rifle."

"I saw a figure emerge from behind the drum," Ted said. "The person took two steps and tumbled from the roof of the building. We found his body later in a rubbish bin, into which he had apparently fallen."

"I think it was Ted's shots that hit him," Lloyd said. "I never really saw the man. Oh, Lord, Ted was absolutely fearless. Civil War historians say that when Confederate General Stonewall Jackson went into battle, he was transformed into another personality.

"I've only seen a few people do that in my long military career, and I spent almost four years in Vietnam. Ted was like that. He took on a certain look. Maybe this is not a good example, but it was almost like an actor going onstage and becoming another person."

"Our lead element crossed over the Duarte Bridge in the faint light of dawn," Ted remembered. "The platoon hunkered down along the street and was perfectly still. I heard the rumble of heavy vehicles on the cobblestone street, and then I saw the outline of a tank emerging from the grayness. I didn't know if it was one of ours or one of theirs.

"The agreed-upon method of identification involved flashlights with colored lenses. Lieutenant Lloyd and I made a circular motion with green-lensed flashlights. For what seemed like minutes, but in reality was only seconds, I saw a red light moving back and forth horizontally. It was the Marines.

"I stepped in front of the tank, spread my arms, and cried out, 'This is the 82nd Airborne Division. All is well!'"

"I was surprised when Ted moved so swiftly to where he could be seen," Lloyd said. "After all, those Marines had heard the rifle fire between our guys and the snipers. They must have been somewhat unsure as to what was going on. My God, those tanks carried a 90-millimeter cannon. I was afraid they might shoot first and ask questions later.

"It was an incredible act of bravery on Ted's part. When I walked forward, he was shaking hands with a Marine lieutenant. Ted was the man! He was the first 82nd Airborne soldier to literally link up with the Marines."

The significance of the link-up was recognized in an Associated Press story of May 3, 1965, which reported:

"U.S. forces today cut Santo Domingo in two, when 82nd Airborne Division paratroopers broke through a perimeter around the Duarte Bridge and linked up with a Marine unit that had driven out from the International Zone.

"The establishment of the one-street, three-mile long corridor opened a direct communication and supply link between the zone and the San Isidro air base to the east. As the paratroopers and Marines converged, rebel forces opened fire and two insurgents were killed."

The following day, the Russians introduced a resolution in the United Nations, condemning the U.S. "armed intervention" in the Dominican Republic as a "gross violation" of the UN charter and ordering the "immediate withdrawal" of U.S. forces..

Johnson responded by telling American labor leaders meeting in Washington that if U.S. troops had not been rushed to the Dominican Republic, the streets would have "run red with human blood."

"Our next mission," Lloyd said, "was to attack south and pin the rebel forces against the ocean. We had to clear out a corridor about five blocks wide so the streets would be safe from snipers in high buildings.

"Again, because of our combat veterans, we were chosen as the lead platoon. I had to go to the company commander's office to get my orders. The company commander was Capt. Charles W. Hendrix, a great guy who's now retired as a colonel.

"It was about four o'clock in the morning. We were going to kick off at daylight. He had a little candle burning in his office and was on the telephone with Lt. Col. Hugh MacDonald, the battalion commander.

"I couldn't help but overhear his part of the conversation. After some talk about coordinating the attack with other units, he said, 'Yes, yes, Lloyd will be leading. Yes, Gaweda will be up front. No, I don't think so. They can handle it. No, they're not tired.'

"At that point, Captain Hendrix looked up at me and winked. He hung up the phone, grinned, and asked, 'Gaweda is all right, isn't he?'

"'Oh, yes sir,' I answered, 'he's ready to go.' At the risk of sounding immodest, I thought that was a hell of a tribute to Ted and myself.

"We moved out at dawn and had advanced about five buildings down the street when we were confronted by a head-high concrete wall surrounding a five-story schoolhouse, which was painted green. Ted was up front and a sergeant named Williams was behind him. I followed with a radio operator. We worked our way along the wall and turned right into a small alleyway.

"We were trying to figure out a way to get in this place when five or six rifle shots rang out. A lug slammed into the wall right in front of Sergeant Williams. He jumped back and right into me, sending us both to the ground.

"Ted turned around and gave us a look that said, 'Okay children, let's get up and keep going.'

"'Are you guys okay,' he asked.

"'Yeah, yeah, we're all right,' we said.

"'Just follow me,' he said. 'Everything is going to be okay.'

"There was a building to the right that was about sixty yards from the schoolhouse. Humped over behind a cinder block ledge, we crept up the steps to see if we could get a better view of the schoolhouse.

"I know that it sounds like this whole story revolves around water drums, but it really doesn't. I brought up a machine gunner named MacFarland. He was a corporal, a tough guy, a real good guy.

"'Mac,' I said, 'you climb up there and see if you can see where the sniper fire is coming from.'

"He wasn't too happy about that, because he thought it would expose him to rebel gunfire. He reached a higher floor and hid behind, of all things, a water drum.

"Suddenly, there were more gunshots, and sniper bullets sent pieces of cinder block flying everywhere, just like shrapnel. Old MacFarland yelled out a bunch of obscenities that I won't even repeat.

"'There's a guy in the third window who's trying to kill me,' he shouted.

"He came down from the ledge and said, 'The guy's in the third window from the left on the top floor.'

"Another soldier came up with a grenade launcher, and MacFarland pointed to the window and yelled, 'He's in there; he's in there.'

"The soldier fired his first round too far to the right. When his second round was short, Sergeant Gaweda said, 'Give me that thing.'

"Ted's first shot was a little high, but his second went right through the top half of the window. The sniper position was silenced.

"'That's it, that's it,' Ted said.

"About thirty of our guys came forward and poured round after round of ammo into that window. Three GIs ran across the schoolyard and entered the building. There were blood trails everywhere. It looked like the sniper, who had to be badly wounded, went out the back door.

"We were in a building that had been a physician's home and office when a sniper fired at us from a building only fifteen feet away. I was in the kitchen when the slug came through the window. We were hunkered down, so no one was hit.

"'Ted, I yelled, 'get a machine gun on the balcony.'

"I heard Ted's boots go 'wham, wham, wham,' as he ran up the stairs. 'My God,' I thought, 'Ted has no idea what's going to be up there when he reaches the top. It could be nobody or fifty rebels.'

"But he goes storming to the top. I heard a door fly open, followed by Ted shouting, 'Get the machine gun up here; get the machine gun up here.'

"Meanwhile, sniper bullets continued to slam into the kitchen. Then I heard the wonderful sound of an M-60 machine gun chattering away, and Ted yelling, 'You got him, you got him, you got him.'

"I was so proud. We had come through these fire fights without losing a man. We felt good about ourselves. We knew what we had accomplished, and everyone else knew it too. Guys from other companies in the battalion would come around and speak to us with great respect. They knew who led the fighting.

"Ted's heroic support of me in combat turned out to be a crossroad in my military career. Not too long after the actions I have described, I was made a company commander, even though I had only been a second lieutenant for eight months.

"I replaced a captain whose performance fell short of expectations. After the captain was dismissed, Battalion Commander Colonel MacDonald said, 'Lieutenant Lloyd, you are now the commander of Company C. You take this company and shake it like a wet puppy. These people need some combat leadership. You get this thing straightened out until I can get a captain down here to take command.'

"Several nights later, one of our positions was attacked by thirteen half-drunk rebels, and our guys killed all of them. Sergeant Gaweda was at another position when the attack was repelled, but he ambled over to see what was going on.

"Here was Colonel MacDonald talking over the situation with the big man himself, Lt. Gen. Bruce Palmer Jr., commander of the XVIII Airborne Corps.

"'Well Mac,' the general said to Colonel MacDonald, 'your boy did a good job last night. You keep this thing level until I can send you a captain to take over this company.'

"'General,' Colonel MacDonald said, 'as long as I command this battalion, Lloyd's going to command this company.'

"I almost fainted. General Palmer looked over to Second Brigade Commander Robert 'Butch' Kendrick, with whom I had served as a sergeant, and asked, 'Butch, what do you think about that?'

"'Oh, he'll be all right,' Butch answered.

"Ted, who had been standing there looking stoic, walked over, gave me a friendly punch in the ribs, and said, 'Good stuff.'

"And so I became a general. It was far beyond my wildest expectations.

"If it wasn't for Ted Gaweda, I never would have reached general officer rank. He made me look good. There are a hell of a lot of other officers who would never have progressed in their careers had it not been for Ted Gaweda telling them how, showing the way and not letting them make mistakes that would reflect badly on their efficiency reports. I always give him full credit for what happened to me. Together, I always felt that Ted and I could do anything.

"Was I surprised when he became command sergeant major of the XVIII Airborne Corps? Absolutely not. To me, he always was the ultimate fighter-leader of the airborne-warrior class."

The Dominican crisis was resolved in July 1965, when a provisional government was established with the help of a special committee from the Organization of American States.

President Johnson said at a White House new conference on July 13, "I am encouraged by indications that leaders on both sides are prepared to stand aside in favor of a new government."

"After three months in the Dominican Republic," Ted said, "I was sent home in July, where I finally was able to celebrate Edith's birthday.

"On the day of my departure from the Dominican Republic, Lieutenant Colonel MacDonald presented me with the Army Commendation Medal with the 'V' (valor) device. This was my first of four such awards. It came after twelve years of service."

CHAPTER EIGHT

Christmas Good-byes

"After a three-month absence, I was delighted to be home with my family in Fayetteville," Ted said, "but my time there was to be brief. For Edith that was particularly distressing.

"Here she was with a part-time husband and father with two frisky sons, one five years old and the other three. It was very difficult for her. I tried to explain that I was a soldier who had to obey his orders, but I'm not sure it helped much.

"It was obvious I was going to Vietnam. I received orders to attend the six-week Special Warfare MATA (Military Assistance Training Advisor) Course at Fort Bragg, and in October 1965, I was sent to the Army's Language School at Monterey, California, where I learned Vietnamese."

"I was shocked to hear that Ted would not be given any leave after completing his language course," Edith said. "Instead, he was to be sent directly to Vietnam. I could not let him go without saying good-bye.

"I was housebound with my two babies, but fortunately I found Mrs. Gertrude Tucker, a German woman who offered to take care of them. I had never been away from my children before, but I knew I had to see Ted.

"I flew to Monterey on December 17, 1965, where I was able to spend five emotion-filled days with my husband. I left for Fayetteville on

December 22, after Ted's graduation from language school. Our parting was very sad, with lots of tears on my part.

"Dear God, it was three days before Christmas, and he was being sent to the other side of the world where people were killing each other. I prayed he would return safely to his family.

"It was nighttime when my airplane landed at Fayetteville. Nevertheless, I hurried to pick up my children. I didn't want to spend another night without them. I needed them.

"I hugged them hard, put them to bed, and turned on the television to watch the late news. There were pictures of dead Americans in body bags being loaded on a truck, and Walter Cronkite was narrating. I cried almost all night. I couldn't sleep anyway, knowing that Ted was getting ready to fly to Vietnam.

"It was a gloomy Christmas, but the kids and I managed. I had no relatives nearby and hardly knew a soul in our new neighborhood. Before Ted went to Monterey, we suddenly had to find a new place to live because the army would not permit wives to stay in post housing while their husbands were overseas.

"A realtor took us around and showed us a bunch of little old houses with holes in the ceilings and walls. We also couldn't find anything decent to rent. We ended up buying a new sixteen-thousand-dollar house on a GI loan.

"There was no air conditioning, but the house did have hardwood floors, three bedrooms, two baths, and a single-car garage. Most importantly, all 1,125 square feet of it was ours. It was our first real home. Before he left, Ted poured concrete for a fifteen-by-twenty-foot patio.

"I could have stayed with Ted's family in Brooklyn, but I wanted to be near the army at Fort Bragg. Fayetteville was now home base. Gradually, I met my neighbors, and they were very nice. Many wives were in the same situation as me. They had young children and their husbands were overseas. We used to go to church together and visit in each other's homes on holidays.

"I marked an X on my calendar for each day that Ted was in Vietnam. I was like a prisoner marking off the days of his sentence or a pregnant woman counting the days to delivery."

"When Edith left, I felt empty and alone," Ted said. "Not being able to see my boys before departing for Vietnam was heartbreaking for me. That Christmas was the saddest in my army career.

"The morning after Edith flew home, I left the United States on an airplane bound for Saigon, arriving there on Christmas Eve. I was in for an eventful twelve months."

CHAPTER NINE

Vietnam

Capt. Maurice "Moe" Winter, U.S. Army advisor at Dien Ban, was taking a break near a South Vietnamese village on a steamy afternoon in late December 1965, when he heard the sound of a vehicle crashing through the brush.

"Out of the woods came a jeep, which stopped in front of me," he recalled. "A soldier literally leaped from the jeep, stood at rigid attention, saluted smartly, and said, 'Captain Winter, Sergeant Gaweda reporting for duty, sir!'

"I started laughing and said, 'What in the hell are you doing out here? We were going back to our command post in a few minutes.'

"'I know, I know,' the sergeant said, 'but I wanted to come out and meet you, and see what was going on.'

"That's how I met Ted Gaweda, the finest soldier I would ever know. He was assigned to my team as senior advisor on light weapons, where he would teach South Vietnamese popular force troops the finer points of the M-1 rifle, Thompson submachine gun, mounted machine guns, and the Browning automatic rifle.

"Ted was the fifth man on our little team, which would be augmented later by two Australian Army warrant officers and a U.S. Marine gunnery sergeant. My assignment was to act as the senior American advisor to the district chief in our subsector.

"The Aussies were tough guys. All they wanted to do was break things and kill people, which was the opposite of our mission in December 1965.

"I dealt with a small South Vietnamese Army officer, who was not only district chief, but mayor of the region as well. His name was Ngui Trong, a wonderful guy who had been fighting the Communists for twenty years. He was the leader of what was known as the Regional Popular Forces. Technically, he was our boss.

"The large build-up of American troops had not yet happened. At that time, we truly were advisors. I had a dual role. If I heard that a truckload of rice or wheat was coming in from American taxpayers, I would arrange an acceptance ceremony and make a big deal out of it. Photographs would be taken of friendly American advisors handing out food to local Vietnamese as they made their heroic stand against Communist invaders from the North. However, many of the smiling locals became Viet Cong at night, obeying orders from Ho Chi Minh, the top honcho in North Vietnam.

"As for the military side, whenever the major's intelligence told him that the Viet Cong or local bad guys were getting ready to spring an attack on one of the villages in our area, we would march out with his troops, always making sure that Trong's people were up front. Otherwise, it would have been a loss of face.

"Sergeant Gaweda, an all-around smart guy on weapons and infantry tactics acted as my team chief. I also had a radio operator and a brilliant medic who could do everything but heart surgery, and who probably could have done that if called upon.

"We owned the countryside in the daytime, but when the sun went down, the Viet Cong owned it. They roamed as they pleased, digging tunnels, placing mines, and attacking villages. The VC would cut off a village at night, rape the women, capture the men and burn everything to the ground.

"Ted, of course, was a can-do guy. For example, as the new guy, he asked, 'Where's my bunk?'

"'There it is,' I said.

"'Okay,' he answered, adding, 'Gee, this place looks terrible. I'm gonna clean it up.'

"We were staying in this hut, which was about twenty by forty feet in size, with a thatched roof. Ted got out a broom and a bucket of water and started scrubbing. He cleaned the place in about two hours.

"And then he asked, 'What do you guys eat?'

"I said, 'Well, we eat C-rations.'

"'That's terrible,' he said, 'I'm gonna' fix you guys a meal.'

"He lit our little stove, mixed our C-rations with water in pots and pans and served us a hot meal.

"I said to myself, 'I have died and gone to heaven. Ted Gaweda is the finest and most ingenious guy I have ever seen.'

"Oh my, he was perfect at everything he did. I mean, whether it was scrounging for food, cooking meals, bettering his team members, or worrying about me and making sure I did the right thing. We had rapport going in five minutes.

"Ted also got me going on a physical training program. We would do thirty-five push-ups twice a day and throw a football around for thirty minutes. He needed a way to release all of his energy. We had contests to see who could do the most sit-ups and other physical things of that nature. He always beat me because he was in ten times better shape than I was, even though I had been a college athlete.

"Sergeant Gaweda was constantly concerned about making a good appearance. He would say to me, 'Sir, you should put on a new shirt. We're going to the village today, and I want to make sure we're both lookin' good.'

"Hate him or love him, Ted was going to take charge, and I was the kind of guy who felt confident enough to say, 'Look, man, take over.' I need help. I came out of an armored unit. I didn't know that much about the infantry.

"Hell, Ted was in Korea when I was in high school, and he was fighting in the Dominican Republic while I was cutting my teeth in a cavalry division on the borders of Germany.

"If Ted charged into a room of civilians and did his number, some might think he was a fanatic, but he is not a fanatic. He is competent; he's so damned competent and dedicated. He lived and breathed his army life and enjoyed it as he went along.

"So many people piss and moan, complaining, 'Oh God, it's hot here. Do we have to go out today?' or 'Gosh, it's raining or blah, blah, blah.'

"I'm telling you, the worse it got, the more Sergeant Gaweda would stick his chest out and say, 'We've gotta go, sir, we've gotta go.'

"'Okay Ted,' I would say, 'we'll go. I'll do whatever you want to do.' And he was not reckless in any way. We all respected him for that. He set up a night watch schedule, and everybody pulled a shift, including me, because for most of the time there were only five of us.

"During the remainder of my army career (Winter retired in 1986 with the rank of lieutenant colonel), I would hear a fellow officer say from time to time that one of his men was the perfect soldier. I would always laugh and reply, 'Obviously, you never met Ted Gaweda.'

"Many nights when I was on watch or couldn't sleep because of the tropical heat, Ted and I would sit on our little stoop and talk about life, the world, and why we were in Vietnam. Both of us felt there was no way America could really win what was a civil war in Vietnam.

"We believed in 1966 that our mission to teach modern warfare to the South Vietnamese Army should be declared accomplished and then leave, which is what finally happened in 1975. Meanwhile, more than fifty thousand U.S. servicemen died defending South Vietnam.

"It was so difficult at the beginning. After I arrived at Saigon in August 1965, I was taken to U.S. Army headquarters with five other advisor-captains, where we were briefed by Gen. William Westmoreland. Wearing the starched fatigues of an airborne trooper, he was the most beautiful-looking man you would ever want to know.

"He pumped us full of smoke, saying, 'You're going to go up country and train the popular forces to fight the Communists. You're going to be out there by yourself, because help will not arrive for four months.'

"At that time, there were no killers there, just advisors and several Special Forces teams. Our job was to keep the peace. We tried to stay alive and serve the popular forces, rather than killing and maiming people.

"But when division after division of soldiers and Marines continued to pour into South Vietnam, the pacification effort was largely shunted aside. Suddenly, we were in a full-scale war. Despite that, Sergeant Gaweda and I continued our original mission with our little team, which was to protect the locals in our subsector, control the Viet Cong, and keep Highway One open between Dien Ban and Da Nang, some twenty kilometers away.

"The Marines came to Vietnam a short time after Ted arrived. They secured the naval base at Da Nang and kept moving further and further inland from their supply center. The Marines, who are shock troops, became a poor, bedeviled lot with no one to fight except the Viet Cong, and that was like grabbing smoke. They were like fish out of water.

"You know, I used to tell Gaweda stories to every officer and NCO who would listen. One of the great ones involved those poor, starving Marines.

"Ted and I drove to Da Nang one day with a quarter-ton trailer hooked to our jeep. We were driving around the navy yard when we spotted this huge supply depot. There were three gigantic warehouses, each the size of a football field and each filled with food.

"We drove up to the gate, and I tried to con the guard into giving us some food. 'We're from down the road,' I said, 'and all we have to eat are C-rations. We need a little chow; can you help us out?'

"'I am sorry, sir, but I cannot do that,' the navy guard replied.

"'Sir,' Ted said, 'why don't you go have a cup of coffee and let me talk to this guard for a minute.' Only moments later, he drove over to where I was drinking coffee and said, 'Come on, get in.'

"We turned around and, sure enough, the guard opened the gate. We went into the warehouse and our eyes were bulging. Every kind of food you could imagine was stacked to the ceiling. Sergeant Gaweda started throwing cases of tomatoes, peas and other canned goods in the trailer.

"'What are you doing?' I asked.

"'Just stick with me, sir' was all he said.

"And he filled the trailer and the jeep with everything he could get his hands on and we took off, saluting the guard as we left.

"I said, 'How in the hell did you get us in there?'

"'I promised the guard a bloodstained battle flag taken from a dead Viet Cong,' he answered.

"'We don't have any damned VC battle flags!' I said.

"'I know, sir,' he laughed, 'but I'll have our little tailor in the village make some and smear on some phony blood.'

"On one of his runs to the navy depot, Ted brought back a case of steaks. 'What are we going to do with a case of steaks?' I asked. 'You know we don't have any refrigeration.'

"'I'll tell you what I'm gonna do,' he said. 'I'm going to trade them to the Marines for 60-millimeter mortar ammunition.'

"And, sure enough, we drove out to where the Marines were sitting in a static position with no system of logistics. They were hungry as hell. Boy, the company commander almost kissed us on both cheeks when we drove in.

"'Where you guys from?' he inquired.

"'Oh, we're from down the highway,' I said. 'Come on down and have a cup of coffee with us someday, but now can we talk business?'

"'What do you need?' he asked.

"'We need 60-millimeter mortar rounds for our popular force troopers,' Sergeant Gaweda said.

"'Well, whatta ya got?' the company commander asked.

"'We've got a case of frozen steaks right here,' Ted answered.

"Wow! As soon as the word 'steak' left Ted's mouth, the Marine said, 'Done deal, done deal.'

"So we come home with two dozen mortar rounds, which we couldn't get from our own people because the poor Vietnamese popular forces always seemed to be at the end of the supply line."

In the spring of 1966, Winter's team was told to prepare for the arrival of a company of Marines, who would be landing on Dien Ban's helicopter pad.

"I used green smoke signals to guide the choppers in," Ted remembered, "and other Marines took over and directed their comrades to their positions. I felt sorry for those poor guys. They had been on troop ship for thirty days before disembarking at Da Nang. I could tell they were out of shape.

"It was hot. The temperature was over one hundred degrees and they were carrying heavy equipment. They had to walk three miles to reach their positions. I couldn't believe the size of the company. The commander said he had 240 Marines, which is nearly double the average size of an army infantry company.

"'My God, help these young Marines,' I said to myself. 'They're gonna' die because they are not physically fit to fight.'

"After the company marched away, we received word that another chopper was headed for our pad with a Marine general aboard. 'Someone needs to meet the general,' I told Captain Winter. 'Sir,' I said, 'this is protocol. Why don't you go over to the helicopter pad and tell him what's going on?'

"'What is going on?' the captain asked.

"'Sir,' I said, 'go out there and tell him who we are, what our popular forces are doing, where the town, the airfield, and Marine positions are located and so forth.'

"Captain Winter was at the pad when the general arrived, and I was right behind him. That Marine general was tough, and I mean TUFF. Everybody was afraid of him.

"'Who are you?' he asked.

"'We're army advisors.

"'What's goin' on?' he said.

"'We told him about our mission and all of the other things Captain Winter and I had discussed.

"'How are my Marines doin'?' the general inquired.

"'Great,' Captain Winter and I said in unison. 'But they're carrying too much equipment,' I added.

"'Don't worry about it, soldier,' the general said, 'They're Marines.'

"I was concerned because the Marine operation didn't end until about eight o'clock that night. We lived by a rule that said, Don't be away from your command post after 5:00 P.M. because the VC come out of the ground at sunset, just like the fireflies.

"I would only violate the rule in extreme conditions. If I couldn't make it back by at least 5:30 P.M., I would not depart from wherever I was. If I was in Da Nang, I would wait until eight the next morning, when the convoys began to roll from Hoi An. Some areas were under Viet Cong control day and night. I wouldn't go into those zones unless I had at least two hundred men with me.

"It wasn't long before the Marines' supply lines broke down. Their living conditions were lousy. Their enemies, the Viet Cong, were invisible. However, the VC were observing the Marines from their underground bunkers and sniper nests in the trees of the forest.

"If you developed a pattern of doing the same thing day after day— same patrol maneuvers, same security setup, same defensive positions—I guarantee that you're going to be attacked. And that happened to the Marines.

"The VC never did anything unless they believed they could win, while the Marines perceived all the ground, except that which they occupied, as enemy territory. However, I am sure that the VC had a network of tunnels and bunkers under the ground that the Marines occupied.

"One time, I was sitting on part of a fallen tree, eating lunch with a group that included one of the Marine regimental commanders, when a South Vietnamese lieutenant colonel named Lap walked up and said, 'What are you guys doin' here? You're sittin' in a dangerous spot. Are you supervising this VC complex?'

"Colonel Lap had eyes like an eagle. He walked to the base of the tree, where I was sitting, and pulled up some vegetation, revealing a small opening in the ground. It was what we called a spider hole. I was too large to go through it, and I'm not a big guy. Most of the VC were small people, weighing no more than ninety pounds.

"I was very impressed, saying to myself, 'My God, these guys are indestructible.'

"Before long we found another entrance, and by the time it was over we had flushed seven VCs out of that rabbit warren with tear gas. They were taken away for interrogation. I was really awed by the South Vietnamese colonel. He himself was unarmed, but he traveled with at least fifteen armed men in his personal security platoon.

"I was awakened at three o'clock one morning by a report of a fire fight between the Marines and the Viet Cong. About 20 VCs had ambushed a Marine unit at one of the villages in our sub-sector.

"We arrived with help at about 4:30 A.M., but it was too late. We found thirteen dead Marines and one machine gunner who was still alive. Also, there was one badly wounded VC, who was unconscious. He was dressed in black shorts and black pajama top, but had no identification on him. He died later on.

"I asked the wounded Marine to tell me what happened. 'I really don't know,' he said. 'It happened so fast.'

"That was typical of a VC attack. As raiders of the night, they struck quickly and vanished before you knew it, leaving behind the dead, the dying, and the wounded. They literally crawled back into their holes."

"Before Ted arrived," Winter recalled, "we didn't have much of a personal relationship with the district chief and his popular forces. Shortly after joining my team, Sergeant Gaweda asked me one evening, 'Where's the Dai Uy (captain) tonight?'

"'Oh,' I said, 'he's probably in his hut.'

"'Why don't we have him over for dinner?' Ted asked. 'In fact, why don't we have him over for dinner every night? We can get to know him better and do some joint planning with his people.'

"'That's a brilliant idea,' I said. And once we got on this gravy train with the food that Ted had scrounged from the Navy, it worked fine. Ted would prepare these fabulous meals and we would sit around and talk with the Dai Uy or district chief.

"His closeness to us may have caused Ngui Trong's death. Later, he was sitting in his little mayor's hut when a Viet Cong round came through and killed him. I'm sure that was not a random thing. I believe the VC targeted him."

Even though the mission of Ted's unit was pacification, there was little peace.

"We always had to worry about sniper fire and booby traps," Ted said. "I was awakened one night by explosions and fire caused by a Viet Cong attack on the nearby town. I grabbed a radio from a jeep and ran to a bunker.

"I called Hoi An and asked for help. In about three minutes, one of our planes came over and lit up the area like a Christmas tree. The VC disappeared into the night, after destroying a first-aid station, police headquarters, and a power plant, which was out of service for about a week.

"Another time, I witnessed a strange incident involving several Viet Cong at a bridge on Highway One. It was about 1:30 in the afternoon on a beautiful day when Captain Winter and I, riding down the highway in a jeep, saw a commotion on the bridge we were approaching. At that time, all the bridges on Highway One were under twenty-four-hour guard.

"There was a small, hand-pulled manure wagon in the middle of the bridge, surrounded by six South Vietnamese soldiers. It seems that several Viet Cong were hiding in a bamboo compartment under the manure. Once the wagon got on the bridge, the VC came out shooting.

"They killed two guards before one of them was killed by a grenade. The other VC was hit and was lying on the ground, still alive. As I approached, a South Vietnamese sergeant stood over the wounded man, cursed him in Vietnamese, put an M-1 rifle to the VC's head, and blew his brains everywhere. It was sickening.

"I said to Captain Winter, 'That man could have been taken prisoner and interrogated. I'll bet you the sergeant is a VC himself. He probably killed that guy to keep him from giving us valuable information.'

"Captain Winter and I didn't do or say anything. After all, we were alone in the middle of nowhere. It was best not to mess with that situation.

"In about that same time period, I had the closest call of my military career. It was at dawn. I was advancing with the popular force soldiers toward a village, which we heard had been overrun by Viet Cong. The senior American military advisor for our subsector, a major named Blough, was with us.

"After Major Blough kept marching up front, I told him, 'Sir, you cannot do that. You have to be behind Captain Trong, the district chief.'

"As we approached the village, I was behind the lead squad of South Vietnamese and Major Blough was behind me. One of the Vietnamese moved forward to open a bamboo gate at the entrance to the village. We had taught the popular force soldiers to be very careful about touching anything in the field because of possible booby traps.

"I guess the soldier didn't see anything because he opened the gate. There was a loud explosion, and shrapnel flew everywhere. The man who opened the gate was mortally wounded.

"Shrapnel shattered my rifle stock and put a hole in my canteen, draining the water. As I threw myself to the ground, I heard Major Blough cry, 'I'm hit.'

"I spun around and ran over to the major. He had been hit in the arm and neck, and was bleeding badly. I called for a medic, took Major Blough's first-aid bandage out of his kit, and wrapped it around his neck. Then I used my own bandage to wrap his shoulder and arm.

"I called Captain Winter on the radio and told him to send a helicopter. As a medic named Staff Sergeant James Poole came up and took over the care of Major Blough, I walked over to the wounded Vietnamese soldier, whom Poole had loaded with morphine. He was in a bad way. He had been hit in the groin, and there was nothing I could do for him.

"He asked me for a cigarette, so I gave him a Salem. The Vietnamese were very fond of Salems. We used to call them Vietnamese penicillin. The soldier took several puffs, passed out, and died a few minutes later.

"The Medivac chopper arrived in about fifteen minutes and carried away a very pale Major Blough. I was delighted that he survived to be sent home.

"The reason I say I had a close call was that I was holding my rifle at port arms, or in front of my left chest, when the booby trap exploded. Without the protection of the rifle stock, which splintered as I said, the shrapnel would have slammed into my chest, probably killing me.

"I think the most frightening thing I ever experienced was being subjected to heavy artillery fire. I was in the field with the popular force guys, looking for Viet Cong, when we spotted a concentration of about forty VC. I called the Marines, gave them the location of the VC, and requested an artillery bombardment.

"Instead of landing three hundred yards in front of me, the shells began exploding only seventy yards from my position. It was my fault. I had given the Marines the wrong grid. The 105-millimeter howitzer shells were going 'boom, boom, boom.' The sound was ear shattering. Tree limbs, rocks, and bamboo were flying like shrapnel. It was hard to see anything in the smoke and fire.

"My God, I thought the world was coming to an end. I fell to the ground, and then jumped up and ran away from the explosions. It was a terrifying experience. After that, my respect for artillerymen increased a hundred-fold. No wonder concentrated artillery fire in World War II demoralized entire armies. It kills, maims, and scares the hell out of people."

Retired Command Sgt. Maj. Harris Parker at the time was a sergeant first class, serving as senior enlisted advisor with the 39th Vietnamese Ranger Battalion. He remembered Ted as a person who went out of his way to provide support to those who operated in his district.

"I could always count on Ted to give me Rapid Indirect Fire Support and accurate information on the enemy situation. Ted also was a pretty good host. He would allow us to use his facility, share his food and medical supplies. He also was able to get our mail delivered to us out in the field.

"One night I called Ted for artillery support, and within minutes I could hear the rounds on the way to the target. This kind of support was almost impossible to get from Vietnamese channels."

Ted said, "I had established a good working relationship with the US Marines artillery fire base, located nine miles from us. The Marines really knew how to deliver timely and accurate artillery fire."

"Before I left Vietnam," Winter recalled, "Sergeant Gaweda was instrumental in getting this old armored guy a Combat Infantryman's Badge and a Bronze Star.

"We were at the adjutant's office in Hoi An one day, and Ted was doing his NCO stuff and I was doing officer business. He found out that my slot as an advisor called for an infantry officer. Also, there was some ridiculous rule that said to qualify for the badge, you had to be shot at ten times. Shit, I figured if you got shot at once, you ought to earn it.

"There was always sniper fire around, but I didn't know anyone was counting shots. Apparently Ted was. He kept his little log, where he recorded our team's actions. With the help of a major from New York, named Columbo, Ted submitted documents, recommending me for the infantryman's badge and the Bronze Star, with the V symbol for valor. The recommendations were approved and the awards were presented to me at a little ceremony that Ted had organized."

Ted was awarded a Bronze Star on November 14, 1966, for "meritorious achievement in ground operations against hostile forces in the Republic of Vietnam from December 1965 to November 1966."

"The last time I saw Sergeant Gaweda was on August 10, 1966," Winter recalled, "when he put me on a helicopter in Dien Ban district, delivered a snappy salute, and said good-bye.

"We had been together for seven months. I thanked him for his support and friendship, and told him I would never forget him.

"I didn't keep track of Ted as the years passed, but in 1986 I was looking over a personnel diagram of the headquarters staff of the XVIII Airborne Corps, and there was Command Sergeant Major Tadeusz Gaweda. I'll tell you, I had goose pimples. I thought of all the things that he had to do to get that far. Yes, he had proved that he was the 'perfect' soldier.

"I telephoned him at Fort Bragg and we had our wonderful talk about the old days and what had happened in our careers. I told him that I was not the least bit surprised that he had attained his high status."

"After Captain Winter left, I was a pretty sad guy," Ted confessed. "Suddenly, I had no one to talk to. My situation was made worse when Captain Winter's replacement was an officer with whom I could not relate.

"Right off, he told me, 'Sergeant Gaweda, we no longer need security watches here. We're in a secure area. We're going to count on the South Vietnamese for our security. Also, shut down the radio at night. We don't need it.'

"To make sure there would be no breakdown in our security, I stayed awake all that night, monitoring the radio. The next morning I went to Hoi An and reported the captain's orders. I told a colonel there, 'If I can't maintain security at Dien Ban, then I request reassignment.'

"I was having lunch in the mess hall at Hoi An when I was called back to the colonel's office. 'Gaweda,' he said, 'go back to Dien Ban and do what you've always done. I guarantee that you will have your security.'

"By the time I returned to our command post, the captain had received the word. Actually, he had disobeyed orders by cutting off security, and he knew it. He never said anything to me about it, but as you can imagine our relationship became very cold.

"By now, I was ready to go home. I felt Vietnam had become a no-win situation. In my personal judgment, the loss of one American soldier to sniper fire was more important than the dropping of 10,000 tons of bombs on the Ho Chi Minh Trail.

"I can't really say why the pacification program didn't work. Perhaps the South Vietnamese, who for the most part were peasant farmers, were so terrorized by the Viet Cong that they were afraid to resist. After the buildup of American forces and the incursions by the North Vietnamese Army, I believe many South Vietnamese simply tried to stay out of the crossfire and remain alive.

"If you were told that you had a choice—either cooperate with the VC or watch your wife and children shot to death before your very eyes, I believe I know what your decision would be. Also, think about this: In the daytime, you might feel relatively safe with the Americans and popular forces around, but at night the VC could very well put a knife to your throat.

"Try as we would, with five hundred thousand U.S. servicemen on the ground and scores of B-52 heavy bombers spreading death and destruction across the land, we could never eliminate the VC problem, despite the fact that we probably killed hundreds of thousands of Viet Cong and North Vietnamese infiltrators.

"The Communists didn't seem concerned about casualties. We had violated an old military maxim, which said: Never become engaged in a land war in Asia. Politicians had preached the domino theory, which held that if we didn't stop the Communists in Vietnam, then Laos, Cambodia, and Thailand soon would fall like dominoes. As we know, that didn't happen.

"Of course, the government of South Vietnam was corrupt, but strangely the people in the countryside didn't know it until they were told so by the VC media. The Communist propaganda machine, supported openly by China and somewhat clandestinely by the Soviet Union, never stopped running full blast. It was a no-win situation from the beginning, and that never changed.

"During our separation, Edith and I wrote to each other every single day. I was ready to go home to her and my two boys. My departure was set for December 13, 1966, but to my horror the date was delayed because my papers were lost by a promotion board in Saigon.

"I went to the same sergeant who had checked me in when I arrived in Vietnam in December 1965 and asked him if I could have my records. When he couldn't find them, he asked me how long I had been in grade.

"'Four years,' I told him.

"'Oh,' he said, 'your records are at the promotion board.'

"'When does the promotion board meet?' I asked.

"'On December 17,' he said.

"'My God,' I said, 'I am supposed to go home on the thirteenth. How can I go before the promotion board?'

"'Don't worry,' he said. 'I can make it happen.'

"He delayed my departure ten days and gave me a list of instructions covering the time I was supposed to report before the board and the type of uniform I was to wear, which was khaki. I didn't have any khakis, so I bought some on the Saigon black market and had them starched at the Victoria Hotel where I was staying.

"I appeared before the promotion board at 10 A.M. December 17 and answered all the questions directed to me. When I left the room, I knew I was going to be promoted to first sergeant.

"It became official on December 21. I had a tailor sew on my new stripes and flew out of Vietnam the next day."

CHAPTER TEN

Interlude

For Ted and Edith and their sons, Christmas 1966 was as joyous as Christmas 1965 had been dismal. Ted arrived in Fayetteville on December 23, a year to the day that he left California for Vietnam.

"For me, his homecoming was wonderful," Edith said. "I had my husband back, and the boys had their father, who I knew would make them obey his orders.

"Being kids, they would test me to see what they could get away with. When they had about worn me out, I would say, 'Just you wait until your daddy gets home! He'll make you mind.'

"Getting George and Gregory in bed on time had been a problem for me in Ted's absence. You know, every little kid hates going to bed. After I sent them to their room, I would hear them jumping around, and I had to keep calling out, 'Go to sleep!'

"It was such relief to have my husband back as the disciplinarian. He would say in his commanding voice of authority: 'Boys, go to bed, and don't let me see you in the hall anymore tonight.' Everything would be quiet. It was great."

"My happiness was short-lived," Ted said. "When I reported to Fort Bragg, I was handed orders assigning me to the 101st Airborne Division at

Fort Campbell, Kentucky. I was not a happy camper. Joining the 101st would have me back in Vietnam in six months. I knew the division was on alert for deployment to Vietnam.

"My family was now established in Fayetteville. Going to Fort Campbell would have meant either pulling up our roots or my not being with Edith and my boys for another prolonged period of time.

"Luckily, I crossed paths with Virgil West, command sergeant major of the 82nd Airborne Division. After I told Virgil my long, sad story, he asked me if I would like to have my assignment changed to Fort Bragg. 'Yes, yes, yes' was my answer.

"I ended up in the same unit that I had served with in the Dominican Republic—Bravo Company, Second Battalion, 325th Airborne Infantry Regiment. I was named the company's first sergeant.

"I wasn't long in that assignment before I realized that the massive troop build-up in Vietnam had turned the 82nd Airborne Division into a replacement depot. Personnel turnover was rapid and sometimes turbulent. Soldiers were constantly coming from and going to Vietnam.

"At one point, my company was asked to provide forty-six soldiers to the 101st Airborne Division, which was scheduled for immediate departure to South Vietnam. We lost all of our cooks within three weeks. When the 82nd Airborne's Third Brigade was deployed to Vietnam, we provided thirty-four paratroopers to go with them.

"We had numerous soldiers assigned to us, who actually were at Fort Bragg's Womack Army Hospital recovering from wounds received in Vietnam. My own company commander left for Southeast Asia within two months of my arrival, followed by all the platoon leaders.

"That prompted me to go to Lt. Col. E. T. Nance Jr., battalion commander, who asked me, 'How can I help you, first sergeant?'

"'Sir,' I said, 'I need a company commander.'

"He smiled and told me, 'I've been working on that for two weeks, but unfortunately there are no incoming captains.'

"Pointing to Second Lt. Robert N. Seigle, I said, 'I'll take him.'

"The next day, Lieutenant Seigle began his charge-of-command inventory. After assuming his new position, he sat down authoritatively behind his desk, smiled broadly and asked, 'Okay, Top, what do I do now?'

"We spent an hour discussing what was administratively important, such as command policies, property accountability, and the status of the personnel report, otherwise known as the 'morning report.' It was important for the company commander to be present to sign the morning report at 7:00 A.M., six days a week.

"Despite the problems created by the constant personnel turnovers, morale was remarkably high because of a superb command climate. In those years, infantrymen were called upon to do everything—from cooks to clerks at the company level.

"I was prepared to accept all of the help I could get in those turbulent times. One day, while visiting the sergeant major of the brigade, I saw an old acquaintance of mine sitting in the office, holding a pair of crutches.

"It was Sgt. First Class Micheal J. Sinkovitz, who had been recently released from Womack Army Hospital, where he had been treated for a severe leg wound received in Vietnam. After being hit, he was moved from hospital to hospital in South Vietnam, Guam, Japan, Hawaii, and finally Fort Bragg. In the process, his personnel and finance records had been lost.

"Broke and without a uniform, he had been bounced around to several jobs at Fort Bragg, but nobody wanted a soldier in his condition. It was a terrible situation. He told me that he had been sitting around the brigade sergeant major's office for the last five days.

"After he told me his tale of woe, I informed the brigade sergeant major that I would accept Sinkovitz in Bravo Company. I personally escorted him to the personnel office, where a new record was started and a tracer put on his old one.

"Next we went to the finance office, where after a number of questions, he was given four months' back pay. We drove him back to Bravo Company, where the supply sergeant gave him a full set of uniforms. I arranged for Sinkovitz to get a five-day administrative leave to get his personal and military affairs in order.

"When he reported for duty, I asked him what he thought he could do, given his physical condition. I had a list of projects for the company, one of them being the building of a day room.

"Sinkovitz told me he could supervise that project, and as he recovered the use of his leg, he could take part in the labor. I gave him the assignment, and what happened next was truly amazing. This guy had people showing up with two-by-fours, plywood, sheet rock, nails, heavy-duty power tools, and you name it.

"When I asked him where he was getting all of those things, he looked at me, smiled, and said, 'Oh, I have some connections.'

"He built the finest day room in the 82nd Airborne Division, and then went to work on remodeling the mess hall. After his wounds had healed, he became a platoon sergeant in Bravo Company. It just shows what can happen when you put a little faith in a person."

"As a platoon sergeant under First Sergeant G, which was what I always called him, I was able to witness his style of leadership," Sinkovitz said. "It was in sharp contrast to what I was accustomed. The only style with which I was accustomed had superior NCOs saying, 'Do what I say because I said so, or you will reap the punishment.'

"In contrast, First Sergeant G would say, 'Let me explain to you the right way to do such and such. If you still don't understand, I will explain it to you again and show you how to do it.'

"He seemed to have a legitimate concern for all of the young troopers in his company. His way of doing things has become one of the keystones of leadership in the modern American Army. I learned many administrative details from First Sergeant G, which I would use when I became a first sergeant and, later, a sergeant major.

"Because of improved medical techniques used in mending my broken femur (amputation was the old method), I recovered with my leg intact. Fourteen months after being wounded, I received orders to return to Vietnam, where I stayed for another six years."

"In one period, we didn't have a single trained cook in Bravo Company for twenty days," Ted said. "I solicited help from Chief Warrant Officer Laverne Thompson, brigade food service advisor. He spent many days in the company mess hall, teaching our infantrymen to be food handlers.

"In spite of Thompson's best efforts to get us cooks, experience had taught me not to accept non-airborne cooks. Thompson personally supervised food preparation in the mess hall until he secured a qualified airborne mess sergeant for the company.

"In the summer of 1967, Lt. Col. Alfred 'Sandy' Sanderson assumed command of the Second Battalion. One of the first things he asked about was the food service operation in Bravo Company. Even though I wasn't sure our food handlers were up to the task, I invited the colonel and his staff to breakfast.

"Thanks to Thompson's making sure that the pancakes and eggs were 'just like mom used to make,' everything went well.

"The positive command climate continued to flourish under Sanderson and his command sergeant major, Clayton Burtrum. They were a great command team.

"At the company level, Lieutenant Seigle turned out to be a superb leader. Although he was only a second lieutenant, he acted and performed like a seasoned captain. The two of us consistently took advantage of training opportunities off-post and conducted many field training exercises at Fort Bragg.

"Most of our training centered on small unit tactics, such as squad and platoon combat patrolling. Our soldiers were a mix of those who had been to Vietnam and those who were about to go. We simulated many situations that would be encountered there for the sake of those who soon would depart our ranks.

"Mistakes were considered a learning experience, and our soldiers took the lessons learned with them to Vietnam, where they were put to good use. Sure, we had a few bad apples, but they had no effect on the company's high esprit de corps and proficiency. They were a great bunch of soldiers whose morale was so high that they didn't mind working fifteen- to sixteen-hour days.

"I was not home much either. I was working from four in the morning to eight or nine at night. I only went home to sleep. I also worked Saturdays, so the only time I had off was Saturday night and Sunday."

"I felt sorry for him," Edith said, "but I also felt sorry for myself. We never had any personal adjustment problems, but there simply was no time to talk to each other. He would come home exhausted, and by the time I could say, 'Honey,' he would be sound asleep on the carpet in the den.

"There were no candlelight dinners, no romantic evenings. There was nothing but work, work, work and army, army, army. It was a bad time for us, but we adjusted as best we could."

"Shortly after assuming command of the 82nd Airborne Division in April 1967," Ted recalled, "Maj. Gen. Richard J. Seitz became troubled by the appearance, lack of military courtesy, and the poor discipline of the troops. He published a letter expressing his dissatisfaction in these areas and asking for assistance in upholding basic airborne standards. A copy was sent to every first sergeant in the division.

"One day I visited the division finance office to find out why some of my soldiers were not being paid properly. The first person who greeted me was a sergeant, non-airborne, who was wearing low-quarter shoes and needed a shave and a haircut.

"I asked the sergeant who his supervisor was and asked to talk to that person. The NCO in charge showed up, and I noticed that he too needed a haircut and his boots were not polished. I said to him, 'As of now, the finance section is closed. You and your clerks go to the barbershop right now and get haircuts.'

"The NCO in charge went to his immediate superior, who was a second lieutenant. When the young lieutenant questioned my authority, I shoved into his hand a copy of General Seitz's letter. He excused himself and brought back the division finance officer, who was a major.

"The major agreed with my position, but said his people were too busy to get their hair cut during duty hours. 'Major,' I told him, 'if these men are not marched over to the barbershop immediately, then I will talk to the division chief of staff about it.'

"Obviously angry, he said, 'Sergeant take yourself and these men to barbershop,' and turned away."

Ted's service in the 325th Regiment's Second Battalion left a lasting impression on his commanders.

His company commander, Robert N. Seigle, who was a lieutenant at the time, remembered: "He was my first sergeant when I was a brand new company commander back in 1967. Ted's the guy that sort of raised me up in the army way of doing things. He taught me how the system worked and how you could make it work for you.

"I was just bumbling around trying to find my way in the service. To me, Ted was this grizzled sergeant with a lot of years in the army, who was trying to hold things together in a very troubled time. He had a hard time stomaching some of the crap that was going on at Fort Bragg in those days.

"The draft had brought some really bad people into the Army. Bragg was nothing more than a replacement depot. Guys were either on their way to Vietnam or just coming back from Vietnam. It was hard to maintain any stability in your units.

"In those days, soldiers were paid in cash. The pay officers would go to the division, draw their bags of money, return to their units, and count out the dollars individually to every soldier. The lieutenants carrying the money bags were easy targets. It was not unusual for money carriers to be held up and robbed.

"Worse, some of the pay officers would pay the troops only part of the cash due them and pocket the rest. I don't know how they did their accounting between Fort Bragg and Fort Benjamin Harrison in Indiana, where the army's finance center is located. This went on for several months before the Army Criminal Investigation Division finally caught on and nailed the perpetrators.

"Despite all these problems, First Sergeant Gaweda knew how to run an operation. He always had the best orderly rooms and the best recreation rooms for his guys. He had the wonderful ability to select guys who could make magic happen, and once he picked them, he supported them fully.

"Someone told me one time that certain sergeants major felt that all of Ted's friends were colonels and generals. They believed he was trying to curry favor. Perhaps they said things like that because he was not a beer drinking, wild gambling sort of low-life soldier. He always operated at a higher standard.

"He was a true professional, and he was hard and tough. He never asked his men to do something he wouldn't do, and probably do it better. He loved being in the field, soldiering.

"He explained to me once that when an army is on the battlefield, you get to check a soldier's courage every single day, because he's either out there fighting or he is not. In peacetime, you need other ways to check a soldier's courage.

"'Every time you stand in the door of an airplane and feel that rush of air before you jump, you're checking your courage to see if you can still do it,' he told me. 'It isn't as good as a combat check, but there's nothing closer.'

"The only reason I stayed in the army was because of noncommissioned officers like Ted. Of course, I am glad I stayed, because I was able to watch it become a great army before I retired as a colonel in 1993."

Retired Brig. Gen. Alfred Sanderson, Ted's battalion commander in 1967, said, "It didn't take me long to find out that Ted Gaweda cared more for his troops than any soldier I have ever known. With his spit-and-polish appearance and his somewhat gruff manner, he was almost scary. So much so, in fact, that I was glad I was a lieutenant colonel and he was a first sergeant.

"He did not tell you what he thought you wanted to hear. He told you the way it was, and if something was screwed up, he would tell you it was screwed up. Even though he was the first sergeant of a company, I believe he gave me more valuable advice than anybody in the battalion, including my own staff.

"I'd drop down to Bravo Company to talk with him about various things and ask for his views. And I would usually take his advice. If I were a young soldier, Ted's the kind of guy I would worship. If he said, 'Jump over that cliff!' I would jump over that cliff. He is a very unique person, and there are not many around like him."

"After fifteen months with the 325th Airborne Infantry Regiment, I was ordered back to Vietnam," Ted said. "There was one hitch. My records did not clear the finance office. Supposedly, the office was unable to find my payroll records. Quickly, I made an 8:30 A.M. visit to the same major who had been of the haircut incident three months earlier.

"'If you don't come up with my records in the next twenty-four hours,' I told him, 'I will have to see the chief of staff. Less than fifteen hours later, I was told that my records had been 'located.' Edith was devastated at the news of my going back to Vietnam."

"I was resentful of the army for again taking my husband away to that awful place, where American soldiers were being killed," she said. "I was terribly worried that I would not get him back alive. Brought on by the stress of his leaving and dreading another long separation, I could hardly function. Harsh words were exchanged between us.

"It was our deep love for each other, and for our children, that kept us together. Many army families came apart in those times, but deep in our hearts we knew that wouldn't happen to us. It was tough, but we survived."

CHAPTER ELEVEN

Vietnam II, MACVSOG

"I flew to Saigon in early March 1968," Ted said, "and was assigned to a job I hated from Day One. I arrived just a month after the Tet offensive, in which the North Vietnamese Army proved they could launch a costly and coordinated attack against our forces. The action wiped a lot of smiles off the faces of the American commanders.

"Since I was never a city boy, Saigon was not exactly my cup of tea. Worse, I was given a routine desk job at the headquarters of the Military Assistance Command Vietnam, Studies and Observation Group, called by its people MAC-V-SOG. It was a hush-hush outfit that watched over a number of covert operations in North Vietnam, Cambodia, Laos, and Thailand.

"In conjunction with the U.S. Central Intelligence Agency, the army was using its elite Special Forces soldiers to insert intelligence-gathering teams into North Vietnam, all the while denying that such operations existed.

"About the only thing I did in Saigon was send and receive messages about casualties, transfers, supplies, and so on. To me, it was boring as hell. I wanted to be where the action was. A confrontation I had with an officer of the U.S. Navy made my wish come true.

"One of my responsibilities was to make sure that no classified material ended up in the wrong place. One day, I saw this officer with gold leaves on his uniform wad up a decoded classified message and toss it in the wastebasket. I thought he was an army major.

"'Hey, Major,' I said, 'take that classified message out of the wastebasket.'

"'I'm not a major,' he answered angrily, 'I am a lieutenant commander in the U.S. Navy.'

"'I don't care who you are,' I shot back. 'Take the message out of the goddamn wastebasket and put it where it belongs.'

"Well, he didn't like it. He didn't like the way I talked to him, but I could have cared less. I knew he couldn't do anything to hurt me. He issued a complaint a few days later, and the next thing I knew, I was moved to Long Thanh, where I was briefed for four days on covert operations in Thailand. I could have kissed that navy sonofabitch.

"From Long Thanh I went to Monkey Mountain Forward Operational Base (MMFOB) outside of Da Nang for additional briefings on my new top-secret mission. Four days later, I landed at Nakhon Phanom, Thailand. I had found my action. From April 28 to November 30, 1968, I was the Operations NCO at Nakhon Phanom. Initially, my boss was Maj. Charles Dugan.

"Nakhon Phanom was the launch site for teams being inserted into North Vietnam, even though, officially, North Vietnam was a 'Denied Area of Operations.' The Army called the operation Short-term Reconnaissance and Target Acquisition (STRATA). The ten-man teams were made up mostly of former North Vietnamese soldiers who had been recruited from our prison camps by the CIA. Some teams were made up of Cambodians or Laotians. I viewed them as mercenaries, who would do anything for money.

"We inserted the teams with CH-53 helicopters, which were better known as 'Jolly Green Giants.' The teams would normally stay on the ground twelve to fourteen days, radioing information on North Vietnamese Army (NVA) troop movements and pinpointing targets for our fighter-bombers.

"We always made sure that the people we took out were the same ones we put in. There was a case officer on each mission whose job it was to recognize the members of the team. Sadly, we lost a complete team one time. I don't know what happened. They disappeared after the insertion and we could not raise them on the radio. I assume they were killed or captured by the NVA.

"All of us in the MACVSOG operation wore 'sterile' uniforms, which meant that our fatigues or air force coveralls carried no names, insignia, or indication or rank. The air force guys, who thought we were CIA civilians, called us 'sir.' Many of them thought we were rated pilots.

"The teams would be briefed at the MMFOB and then flown to Nakhon Phanom in 'Blackbirds,' which were C-130 or C-123 transport planes painted black with no markings. After landing, the aircraft would taxi to a remote corner of the airfield, where an unmarked air force van with no windows backed up to the plane, so no one could see what was going on, and collect the team.

"They were then driven to a secure compound, which was guarded by MPs and attack dogs. We rebriefed the new arrivals, fed them, repacked them, and, when it was their time, loaded them on a Jolly Green and flew them the 110 miles from Nakhon Phanom to the North Vietnamese frontier, where they were inserted. Once they were on the ground, they were on their own. To my knowledge, no American ever accompanied them behind enemy lines in North Vietnam. I took part in approximately ten helicopter insertions and extractions, which were always done in the daylight. For safety's sake, the choppers would only be on the ground for a couple of seconds.

"We maintained four teams at a time in enemy territory. No team knew about the existence of the others. We tried to stay in daily contact with them by radio, and the only way you could do that was to get in an airplane and fly over the area. I flew fifty-six missions over North Vietnam in O-2 and OV-10 observation planes as an airborne advisor to the pilot.

"The O-2's were unarmed, except for white phosphorus rockets in twin pods. I carried a .38-caliber pistol and two hand grenades. I figured if I was ever shot down, I would use those grenades to take out anyone trying to capture me, even if I took myself out with them. There was no way I was going to be captured alive. That was how I felt at the time. Only God knows what I would have done.

"In June 1968, I was in an O-2 and doing my damnedest to control a helicopter rescue mission that was in trouble because of NVA troops approaching the extraction site. We were deep in hostile territory. I told the pilot he had to fly low so I could establish and maintain contact with the team on the ground, and also to divert the enemy away from them. We were flying through valleys in mountainous terrain.

"We swooped down to almost treetop level. At one point, I looked at the altimeter. I read two hundred feet, which made us particularly vulnerable to hostile ground fire. We were nicked a couple of times by AK-47 gunfire, but our maneuvers kept the bad guys from reaching the team, which was quickly extracted.

"For this action, I was awarded the Distinguished Flying Cross by the Seventh Air Force. The citation reads in part: 'The professional competence, aerial skill and devotion to duty displayed by Sergeant Gaweda reflect great credit upon himself and the United States Army.'"

By the time Ted left Vietnam the second time, he had a fist full of medals and decorations, including five Air Medals, a Joint Services Commendation Medal, a South Vietnamese Gallantry Cross with a silver star, Vietnamese Staff Medal, U.S. Navy–Marine Corps Parachute Badge and parachute badges awarded by Thailand and South Vietnam.

"The situation reports from the ground were delivered in code," Ted explained. "For example, the team leader might say, 'Line One, Six, Eleven, Fifteen.' Line One might mean 'Everything is fine.' Line Six could translate into: 'We have received gunfire.' Lines Eleven and Fifteen could give us the coordinates on an enemy position and so forth. They could not just talk on the radio anytime they wanted."

Retired Special Forces Col. Stanley Olchovik, a major when he replaced Maj. Dugan as Ted's commander at Nakhon Phanom in June 1968, recalled transmitting "Alpha Bravo" to a team on the ground, which meant, "We cannot pick you up. Stand by for supplies. We will pick you up later."

"The weather was bad and I was having trouble finding them," Olchovik said, "so I kept repeating, 'Alpha Bravo, Alpha Bravo.'

"Suddenly, I heard a voice say in accented English, 'Don't need no more Alpha Bravo, need doctor.' There was no code to cover that situation. We gave them medical assistance as soon as we could.

"Keeping the teams supplied with water was a constant problem. Much of the mountainous terrain of North Vietnam consisted of porous limestone that would not hold water. In the monsoon season, tons of water would pour down, and in a few minutes it would be gone.

"Ted and I worked hard at trying to design crash-proof water containers. About the best we could come up with was wrapping canteens in foam rubber. They were dropped out of O-2 observation planes a few at a time because of the limited space in that aircraft. It worked and no one died of thirst."

Russian-born Olchovik, who would retire in 1985 as a colonel, is a man with a fiery personality, who fought on several sides as a teenager in World War II. Ted remembers well the night this tough Special Forces commander tried to take out the air force in a bar fight at Nakhon Phanom.

Scratched and bruised and with a torn shirt, a raging Olchovik awakened Ted one night, demanding, "Get up and get some clothes on. We're going over to that air force club and get those guys. Let's go get some ax handles. Let's do something."

"What guys?" Ted asked. "Do what?"

"I'll tell you the major was really mad. He was so mad he was shaking. I tried to calm him down by saying, 'We'll take care of the problem in the morning. Tell me what happened.'"

Olchovik related the following:

"After a long day, I went over to this club to get a drink. I expected it to be quiet, but when I opened the door, the place was full of air force guys. I didn't know that weather had canceled their flights.

"They were drinking champagne and raising hell. They were a pretty wild bunch. Some of the guys who flew night fighters wore black uniforms with things on them like 'Yankee Air Pirate.' They looked like Darth Vader costumes.

"Finally I got to the bar, after maneuvering my way through the broken glass on the floor, and ordered a scotch and soda. I saw this guy smash a champagne bottle on the bar and then pick up another one and aim it at the clock on the wall behind the bartender.

"By now, I'm fighting with myself. 'Don't do it,' I tell myself. 'You shouldn't be drinking with this bunch. Should I leave? Hell no, I'm not gonna leave.'

"Two enlisted men go outside and come back with a fire extinguisher. One's got it strapped to his shoulder, and he squirts me in the face with that stale, cold water. And, boy, I just decked him with a right to the jaw. It wasn't like the movies, where a guy gets up after he's been hit. This kid went down for the count. His buddy was easy. He was holding part of the fire extinguisher when I sent him to the floor. Damn, that was good.

"By now, everybody was fighting. They were throwing bottles and hitting each other on the head with them. Guys were trying to tear up my new shirt. I finally got against a wall and made my way to the door.

"There were a couple of air force types trying to get out too. By now, vengeance was mine, you know. I grabbed those guys, threw them back into the brawl, and slammed the door.

"After Ted calmed me down and said, 'I know those guys. They'll replace your shirt; there won't be any problem,' I thought if this ever gets back to my boss, a Colonel Cavanaugh, my career is over. I was contemplating how great it would be to retire as a major.

"Anyway, the telephone rang about eleven o'clock the next morning, and it was the commander of the air force squadron. Gaweda had called and told him what had happened. He also asked him to replace my torn shirt. I was proud of that shirt. It was called a MacArthur shirt. It was blue with five white stars imprinted on it.

"'I called you to apologize,' the squadron commander said. 'Our guys didn't know you were military. They thought you were a civilian contractor. To show you there are no hard feelings, why don't you come over to our hooch and we'll have a drink?'

"I called Ted and asked him to marinate some steaks, because he really knew how to marinate a steak. We took a case of those steaks over to the commander's hooch and Ted cooked them. We had a few drinks and the incident was forgotten. And, oh yes, they did replace my shirt.

"Of course, the news got out, but no official report was ever written. Colonel Steve Cavanaugh, who was the chief SOG, never said a word. I'm glad there was no investigation because he might have found out that we were also stealing jeeps. I would send my people over to his supply depot, where scores of jeeps were parked. They would pick out a couple of jeeps and drive them over to our place, where we painted them black and put a number on them.

"One time, we attended a party at an air force base, and our guys drove five or six black jeeps over there. They all had the same number—NKP 1—but no one noticed."

"The teams we inserted were always glad when they finished their mission," Ted said. "Going in, the team members looked pretty miserable, as if they believed they were taking a one-way trip. One time, they were so hungry and exhausted that they couldn't wait to get out. I had some C-rations on the helicopter, and they were trying to tear open the cans with their hands.

"Enemy fire would put holes in the chopper sometimes, but no one with me ever got hit. I don't think the intelligence gathered on those missions was really that significant. On the bottom of the choppers was a three-eighths-inch steel plate, which slugs from a Russian AK-47 could not penetrate. Shots would hit the landing gear and the sides of the bird.

"We always went in with two helicopters, one flying high and the other low. If the 'low chopper,' as we called it, got shot down, the guys on the high chopper would come to their rescue. However, I never saw that happen.

"I remember one time when the helicopter in which I was riding was hit in the landing gear by an AK-47. We were descending in a Jolly Green to pick up a team, when I saw a guy standing in a river bed. He was only about 250 yards from our extraction point.

"He got off a couple of bursts before we opened fire with a .50-caliber machine gun. I never saw him after that, but it's hard to tell what's happening when a helicopter is moving at fifty to sixty knots. We completed the pickup and flew back to base with a bunch of bullet holes in our landing gear and tail.

"Another time, flying over North Vietnam in an O-2 observation plane, I spotted a yellow bulldozer. I can promise you that a yellow bulldozer really stands out in the midst of all that greenery. When we dropped down for a closer look, the ground lit up with flashes of light from scores of rifle muzzles.

"We climbed away, but not before firing two white phosphorus rockets to mark the location. We also radioed the location to base. With all of those muzzle flashes, there could have been an NVA battalion down there. Major Olchovik called for an air strike, and the area was pounded with more than one hundred 500-pound bombs. The yellow bulldozer disappeared.

"My personal belief at that time was that landing American helicopters on the soil of North Vietnam and inserting former NVA soldiers into the country to gather intelligence had more of a psychological effect on the enemy than anything else. It let them know we were there. It kept them looking over their shoulders.

"Can you imagine being a province or security chief in North Vietnam and seeing those helicopters coming down? You would have to say to yourself: 'What's going on? Why are those helicopters so active in my area?' And then you would send a thousand guys to look for them. It had to be like a Chinese fire drill.

"Much of the information we received was fed to the air force guys, who then used the reports to launch attacks on North Vietnamese positions and supply lines. Despite all of this, we never did shut down the Ho Chi Minh Trail, which operated almost exclusively at night.

"The NVA was well disciplined. There was a complete blackout: no smoking, no lights, no nothing. The NVA trucks were completely covered by canopies. They were impossible to spot. The camouflage and discipline were the best I have ever seen. Despite the B-52 carpet bombing, the NVA still managed to get through. In one mountain pass, the Mu-Gia Pass, that I used to fly over, there must have been twenty thousand bomb hits. It was crater after crater after crater, as close to each other that they looked like the depressions in an egg carton.

"There was a big difference between my first and second trips to Vietnam. On my second tour, I thought the morale of the troops was noticeably lower. The officer corps was not the same. Hell, men were being promoted to major after only six or seven years in the army. There were captains with only two years.

"Officers were being rotated out of command after six months. I was really surprised that the army let Gen. William Westmoreland, commander of all U.S. ground forces in Vietnam, get away with that, because the first six months was a learning period. Once these guys had some understanding of their jobs, they were taken away. And the men had to start over with new officers. It made absolutely no sense.

"There also were reports of draftees 'fragging' their company commanders, which meant shooting them in the back or rolling live hand grenades under their cots. To my knowledge, that never happened in an airborne unit.

"I never blamed the soldiers. I blamed the leadership, because they allowed it to happen. When you've got a top-notch leader, he will have complete control over his soldiers. You take care of your soldiers and they'll take care of you. Obviously, the people in those leadership positions did not take care of their troops. When that happens, the soldiers will do any damn thing they want.

"Regardless of your personal feelings, as a professional soldier you follow your orders to the best of your ability. If you are required to sleep for only three to four hours, that's what you do. In a combat zone, there is no time for political philosophy, even though deep inside of me I knew we could not win the Vietnam War.

"There was talk that the war might not last much longer because of the killing ratio between our side and the NVA, but the monstrous casualties did not stop Ho Chi Minh. It was like the old story about Chinese and Japanese casualties in World War II, where the losses from a battle were reported as one hundred Japanese and ten thousand Chinese. An observer pondered the figures for a moment and said, 'Pretty soon, no more Japanese.'

"By the end of 1968, Viet Cong activity had subsided. They had prepared the groundwork for the NVA and had totally infiltrated every hamlet, village and town. With the NVA now doing the fighting, many VC returned to their jobs as schoolteachers, police officers, and South Vietnamese government officials.

"But in August 1968, I put the Vietnam War out of my mind. I was going home on my reenlistment leave, home to Edith and my boys."

"It was time for me to get away from all those crying and complaining women," Edith said, explaining her need to break free from other army wives with husbands overseas. "I couldn't stand that kind of life. The children were about to enter school, and I felt it was time for me to do something worthwhile.

"So I decided to go into the real estate business. I studied, passed my test, received my license in 1968, and went to work. Within three months I had earned fifteen hundred dollars, which was a bunch of money during those years for a woman without any particular kind of degree.

"Nevertheless, the loneliness and fear remained. There was always the dread of someone coming to your door with a telegram, saying, 'We regret to inform you that your husband has been killed.'

"When I would hear a car rolling slowly down our street at night, I would get up and look through the curtains, praying it would not turn into my driveway.

"And then one day the postman rang my doorbell, and when I opened the door, I saw that he had a large yellow envelope in his hand. It was a telegram. I just stared at it. After he left, I carried it to the back bedroom. I was terrified.

"My mind was floating away from me. I sat on the bed and slowly opened the envelope, and, would you believe, I was unable to read. I couldn't comprehend what it said. Finally, I managed to get hold of myself and focus on the words.

"It was from my sister-in-law in New Jersey, inviting me to attend the baptism of her new baby. She had asked me to be the child's godmother. I telephoned her and said, 'Please, but please, don't ever send me a telegram when Ted is away.'

"It was great to have my husband home on leave. He was supposed to be with us for thirty days, but he was called back to Vietnam after twenty-three. There was again another dreaded day of departure, when your entire body tightens up. You have nerves that you didn't realize you had. As wonderful as it was to have him home, there was that awful thought of his going back to that messy war."

"I returned to Nakhon Phanom, Thailand," Ted said, "to learn that President Lyndon Johnson was prepared to declare North Vietnam a no-fly zone. The peace talks had started in Paris, and he wanted to announce that all B-52 bombings of the north would cease. It was not a coincidence that the U.S. presidential election was just a few weeks away.

"There was a problem, however. We still had intelligence teams to extract from North Vietnam, and the only way we could accomplish that was by air. Unfortunately, the weather had turned to garbage, and our aircraft could not get off the ground. The guys on the ground were afraid to use their radios for fear of alerting the NVA.

"I sent A-1 Skyraiders to search for them and to provide support for their removal. The people in Saigon were really applying the pressure, saying, 'The weather here is beautiful,' but that wasn't the case where I was.

"Thank God we didn't have to abandon the teams. After four or five days of fog and rain, we made contact with the teams and sent the Jolly Greens into the rugged mountain terrain to rescue them. We sent word to General Creighton W. Abrams, who had replaced General Westmoreland as Commander in Chief of US Forces Vietnam, in Saigon, who transmitted it to Washington. Because of the risks taken by the air crews, I recommended that all of them be awarded the Distinguished Flying Cross. To my delight, every last one of them was approved.

"President Johnson announced October 31, 'As of November 1, 1968, all air, naval and artillery bombardment of North Vietnam will be stopped.'

"Despite Johnson's announcement, Democratic candidate Hubert H. Humphrey lost the presidential election a few days later to Republican Richard Nixon, who promised to get America out of the Vietnam War.

"In the first week of November, I was ordered to MMFOB, just outside of Da Nang. I didn't want to go. I even said I was responsible for something like two million dollars worth of equipment at Nakhon Phanom, because I had signed for it.

"That didn't work. 'Proceed to Monkey Mountain Forward Operational Base, as directed, on first available flight,' they replied. I jumped on a plane to Bangkok and caught a C-130 transport to Monkey Mountain, where I became acting sergeant major.

"One of the first persons I ran into was Capt. Dick Meadows, who was operations officer. I had come to know Captain Meadows in Thailand. He flew over to Nakhon Phanom several times to check out our operation. I think we impressed him.

"I worked twenty hours a day, seven days a week at Monkey Mountain. Every area of the operation needed attention. Captain Meadows and I kept the same hours. We both knew the good and the bad things about the operation.

"On one occasion, Captain Meadows stopped by my office at 1:00 A.M. and said, 'Top, you and I must be the biggest fools in the Army.'

"'How's that?' I asked.

"'Because you and I are the only ones working here,' he answered.

"Captain Meadows was very dedicated to his work, but he preferred to be in the field with the troops. He came to my office one day and announced that he was going to accompany Sgt. First Class Joe Garner on a mission to rescue a bunch of embattled Marines from a mountain on the Laotian–South Vietnamese border. The Marines, who had almost run out of food, were pinned down by North Vietnamese Army soldiers. Nobody had been able to get in and out of the area, which was called Tam Boi.

"'You cannot do that,' I said. 'You know the policy as well as I do. What do you want me to say when the Special Operations Group commander wants to know where you are?'

"'You'll think of something,'" he said, as he walked out the door.

"The helicopter rescue mission was a huge success. Before departing Tam Boi, Sergeant First Class Garner said that the Marines blew up the remnants of the largest North Vietnamese weapons and material cache of the entire war.

"I considered Joe Garner the finest enlisted warrior at Monkey Mountain. Because of his dark complexion, he was called Indian Joe. He was one hell of a jungle fighter, highly courageous and honest, with a great heart.

"I organized a hero's welcome for Dick and Joe when they returned. I recommended that Captain Meadows be awarded the Distinguished Service Cross and Sergeant First Class Garner the Silver Star. The decorations were reduced to a Silver Star for Dick and a Bronze Star for Joe.

"Meadows was one of America's greatest soldiers. He was a master sergeant when General Westmoreland awarded him a battlefield commission to captain, the first of the Vietnam War. He wrote a letter on my behalf in February 1970, which said in part:

"'In combat and in training operations—in situations demanding independent and resourceful leadership—Sergeant Gaweda consistently and reliably displayed an extraordinary ability to plan and to organize for the mission, and to lead and execute the mission successfully.

"'His duties were of a classified nature and carried a degree of responsibility normally assigned to a commissioned officer. From a small volunteer group of officers and noncommissioned officers selected for similar sensitive assignments, Sergeant Gaweda was nominated invariably for the most difficult, arduous, and dangerous missions . . . I recommend that Sergeant Gaweda be promoted to the next highest grade as soon as possible. I would fight to obtain his services in any unit that I commanded or was part of.'

"When Dick Meadows died of leukemia in July 1995, I knew that someday I was going to die too. I always thought he was indestructible. I ran with him many times at Fort Bragg. He was a fantastic athlete, a great runner, and an outstanding volleyball, handball, and racquetball player. It was only after he died that I found out he had only one lung."

Meadows, who retired as a major, died only hours before he was to be awarded the Presidential Citizens Medal by U.S. Special Operations Command Chief Gen. Wayne Downing. The general later awarded the medal to Meadows' family. Meadows also was inducted posthumously into the Ranger Hall of Fame.

President Clinton marked his death with a statement, saying, "I mourn the passing of Maj. Richard J. Meadows, whose dedicated and exceptional service is cherished by everyone who knew of his extraordinary courage and selfless service . . . To Major Meadows' family and friends and to the Special Operations community, I extend my heartfelt condolences. We will all remember him as a soldier's soldier and one of America's finest unsung heroes."

"I attended his funeral with Colonel Olchovik," Ted said. "It was a sad day. He was an American hero in the finest sense of the word.

"Even though it would not end for another six years, the Vietnam War was stumbling down the road to defeat. I left the country that we had fought so hard to save for the last time in April 1969, and I did so with a heavy heart."

CHAPTER TWELVE

Troubleshooter

"Before Ted came home from his second tour in Vietnam," Edith recalled, "the sister-in-law who had scared me almost to death with her telegram came to Fayetteville with my new godson, Robert.

"He was about four months old, and my two sons were enchanted with their tiny cousin. I remember their trying to drag him around by the arms and giving him his bottle. One of them, I can't remember which one, asked me, 'Why can't we have a little Robert too? Or someone like little Robert?'

"'Wait until your daddy gets home,' I answered.

"A few weeks after my sister-in-law and little Robert left Fayetteville, Daddy was on his way home and the boys and I went to the airport to meet his flight.

"Ted greeted me and asked, 'Well babe, how are things at home?'

"'Fine, everything's fine,' I told him.

"Then Gregory opened his mouth and said, 'Guess what, Daddy? Mommy is going to have a baby, just like little Robert.'

"I was shocked and hoped the ground would open beneath me so I could sink into it.

"'Oh yeah, is that so?' was all that Ted said.

"I was so upset that I could have killed Gregory, but after hearing the story of little Robert, Ted thought the whole thing was funny. It took me a while to correct Gregory's thinking."

Gregory, who is Ted and Edith's younger son, remembers his father as being something of a "scary man" to his young friends.

"Our neighbors would tell their kids, 'I'm going to tell Sergeant Gaweda about this' or 'Just you wait until Sergeant Gaweda comes home,'" Gregory recalled. "That would scare the kids, and they would straighten up. My father had a very formidable appearance. I always thought of him as an authority figure.

"Dad's approach was not to strike terror in our hearts, but to shower us with responsibility. He would give us all the responsibility in the world and then counsel us when we failed to meet his expectations."

Gregory's older brother, George, said, "He was firm. You knew you couldn't push him around. As a youngster, I learned quickly that when he told me to do something, I had better do it without hesitating. I learned later that he was a pretty tough cookie in the army. Even though he wasn't a large man, he took care of business.

"His being away a lot didn't seem that strange to me, because it was part of a normal pattern. That was the way it was if your father was in the Army. Since we were in a military community, my playmates were in the same position.

"If it wasn't my father, there was always a 'dad' in the neighborhood, a soldier stationed at Fort Bragg, who was a kind of an 'acting dad' to all the kids. The soldiers rotated in and out, but we always had somebody. When my father was home, he was my dad, of course, but he also was an acting dad to other kids.

"I was grateful that Mom, Gregory, and I were not always being uprooted and dragged from post to post, like the so-called army brats. Fayetteville was our home base. We had continuity in our lives."

"I was scared to death of him" is how Gregory's wife, Amy, described her first meeting with her future father-in-law, when Gregory brought his college sweetheart home to meet the family. "Greg had told me that he was a big military man," she said, "and there was no military background of any kind in my family.

"I was somewhat intimidated because I couldn't understand a word he was saying in his Polish accent. We laugh about it now, but I remember telling him, 'Mr. Gaweda, you will have to talk slower so I can understand you.'

"Greg and I were married in February 1988. Now, of course, I don't even notice his accent. He has mellowed with age. He's like a teddy bear."

Peggy, who married George in December 1979, had a totally different reaction from Amy's upon meeting Ted Gaweda. "My father also was a command sergeant major at Fort Bragg, so I had been around army people all of my life. George and I were high school sweethearts when I met him. George played football and I was on the track team.

"I thought Sergeant Major Gaweda was really nice. He had just returned home from Korea, and it was a happy time for him. He was laughing and joking and cutting up. After George and I were married, I would help him with his speeches. He would rehearse them in front of me, and I would correct his grammar and tell him how certain words were pronounced.

"Amy used to tell me that she was nervous around him, and I told her not to worry about it because he really was just a sweet pussycat."

Ted wanted to return to his old outfit—B Company, Second Battalion, 325th Airborne Infantry Regiment—but, despite his resistance, was assigned as first sergeant to A Company in the same battalion.

"Lt. Col. Robert Prehn, the battalion commander, looked me in the eye, and said, 'First Sergeant, I know you want to go to B Company, but I want you to go to that screwed-up A Company and straighten it out.'

"One of the first things I did was to run twelve guys out of the company. I learned from the 82nd Airborne Division's G-2 (intelligence) unit that they were part of a secret, underground anti-war group. They called themselves the Braxton Breeds, which was a take-off on Braxton Bragg, the name of the general for whom Fort Bragg was named.

"They would hold anti-war meetings and spread anti-war leaflets across the post at night. They were draftees and, in my opinion, became anti-war only when they thought they might have to go to Vietnam and fight.

"When I came to the unit, the company commander never bothered to tell me about these guys. Everybody was afraid of them. They were allowed to do whatever they wanted to do.

"I said to myself, 'Well, shit, these guys have to perform their army duties before I'll even let them use the mess hall.' When they didn't show up for my first morning formation, I waited twenty-four hours and then declared them absent without leave.

"After I didn't see them for thirty days, I listed them as deserters. If picked up by the military police, they would have been punished and given dishonorable discharges. They disappeared and I never heard anything about them again. It was good riddance.

"Now I had the company's attention. From then on, we were rolling. I had ninety days to prepare the company for an inspection by the inspector general. My clerk and I stayed up many nights to get everything in order. We passed that inspection with flying colors, receiving a commendable rating."

A delighted Colonel Prehn sent Ted a letter of commendation, saying:

"Your unit has set enviable records within the brigade, largely through your industry, motivation, and deep dedication to duty. You have established personal standards of professionalism which I have rarely seen equaled and never surpassed."

"In January 1970, not too long after A Company passed the inspection," Ted said, "Battalion Sgt. Maj. Tom V. Fulton came to my office, sat down, and said, 'Top, they are talking about transferring you to the Third Battalion Headquarters Company.'

"'Who are they?' I asked.

"'Colonel Ringler,' he answered. Arthur Ringler was commander of the Second Brigade.

"'You tell whomever you have to tell that I am not the man for the job,' I said.

"'Hey, Top,' he answered, 'this is out of my hands. I cannot help you.'

"'I need a spokesman on my behalf,' I said, 'to talk to Colonel Prehn and ask him to tell Colonel Ringler that I am too hostile for that job, because there are too many politicians in headquarters companies.'

"'By the way,' he said, 'Colonel Prehn wants to see you at 1:00 P.M.'

"I went to his office and he said, 'Look, I would like to keep you in A Company, but Colonel Ringler wants you to be the first sergeant of the Headquarters Company of the Third Battalion.'

"'Sir,' I said, 'I would like to remain in A Company.'

"'First Sergeant,' he said, 'it is out of my hands.'

"The next day I went to see Colonel Ringler. He showed me a confidential letter from the commanding general of the 82nd Airborne Division, expressing concern and disappointment over the performance of the Third Battalion Headquarters Company.

"'Why don't you take three days to think about your decision,' he suggested.

"I said to myself, 'This guy needs help.'

"So, the next morning I went over to the headquarters company to see what the hell was going on. Only about forty-five of the 280 men in the company showed up for the morning formation. 'How could I go wrong with this sorry outfit?' I asked myself. It was my chance to show them what I could do.

"I visited Colonel Ringler that afternoon and told him, 'I'm ready to go to the headquarters company.'"

Retired Brig. Gen. Richard Potter, who as a major was the executive officer of the battalion, remembered, "First Sergeant Gaweda had the barracks cleaned and painted and built a new mess hall. He and other outstanding NCOs were the glue that held the battalion together in a very difficult time.

"We had a hollow army in those days. We were grossly understaffed in noncommissioned officers, and about a third of the battalion was waiting to be mustered out of the army after serving their two- or three-year hitches. So they were not the most receptive of soldiers. For the most part, the quality was abysmal.

"Drug use was beginning to show itself, and because we had not faced that problem before, many of us were a bit perplexed as to how to handle it. In that environment, we were a pretty good battalion.

"God, we worked our butts off, getting up at four o'clock in the morning and getting home at nine o'clock at night. Ted knew how to take care of his soldiers. As a result, they were always well turned out. They always looked good.

"One thing about First Sergeant Gaweda was that he gave his troops very broad left and right limits, but if anyone stepped one inch outside of those limits, he knew about it. In those days, it was not fashionable for officers and NCOs to stay with the soldiers.

"I was asked, 'Why do you guys get up at dawn and work twelve to fifteen hours a day when you're in garrison? What sense does that make?'

"'Well, somebody has to hold things together,' I replied.

"By the early 1980s, we had a superb army, and the quality has continued to improve every year. The leadership of today's army is made up of men who stayed with their soldiers. Those men are the legacies of First Sergeant Gaweda and myself, because we stayed the course with them. I believe we placed our stamp on today's army. We were a band of brothers.

"You know, the American people gave Ted and I, and others, the greatest gift they could give. They gave us their sons and daughters to mold and look after and, hopefully, to return them home safely.

"The unique thing about the American Army, and Ted knows this to be a fact, is that the unit will take on the personality of its commander. During my last tour of Vietnam, I knew a great officer who had held every rank from private to colonel.

"He truly loved his men and they truly loved him, but he personally absorbed all the grief of every casualty. So he became cautious, and by being cautious he took even more casualties. The division commander saw what was happening, and he relieved that colonel.

"There wasn't a dry eye at the fire base when the colonel departed. His replacement was a big prick, but he turned that battalion around in six weeks. If you were one of his company commanders and you broke contact with the enemy, you were relieved.

"His policy was that once you got your hands on the enemy, you stayed with him. His men hated him, but he was saving their lives. The casualties dropped dramatically. What the guy did was to infuse in those soldiers the spirit of the warrior, which had been lacking before.

"That's what First Sergeant Gaweda and I did during those long twelve- to fifteen-hour days. We stayed with our soldiers and trained them meticulously, so when the time came, they would be combat ready. We instilled in them the spirit of the airborne infantry warrior.

"You know, you're put on this earth for a brief period of time, and you have to make your pea patch green while you're here. Ted Gaweda certainly made his pea patch green."

General Potter, who was thrice wounded in Vietnam, retired from the army on December 1, 1994.

"Squaring away the headquarters company," Ted said, "was a demanding job. It was a huge company, with a medical platoon, an anti-tank platoon, a motor maintenance platoon, a mortar platoon, a communication platoon, and a reconnaissance platoon. And no one seemed in charge. One of my tasks was to make every man combat ready, no matter his area of expertise. Every soldier had to know how to fight.

"The hard work paid off. For the first time in years, the Third Battalion Headquarters Company of 325th Airborne Infantry Regiment passed the inspector general's command personnel management inspection, and we were the first unit in the 82nd Airborne Division to do so.

"Colonel Ringler was pleased. He sent me a letter of commendation, which said, in part:

"'You have made the standard of "First" a legend within this organization. You have been able to utilize that quality of leadership which enables you to understand the needs and problems of your men, while demanding exacting standard of performance . . . In utmost sincerity, I say, "Well done."'

"'Nice words,' I thought. I also was awarded my third Army Commendation Medal for 'meritorious service.' That was all well and good, but my greatest satisfaction came from seeing the unit transformed into a top-notch outfit. That was my real legacy.

"All of 1970 was not just a walk in the sun for me. I had an unlucky Friday the thirteenth in February. I remember there was a full moon that night, and I was preparing for a training jump with the headquarters company.

"Seconds after I exited the airplane, I became entangled with a fellow paratrooper, and my main chute didn't open. I had to fight to reach the ripcord on my reserve chute, which finally opened. The other jumper was unable to open his main or reserve chutes.

"As we plunged rapidly toward the landing zone, he held onto my legs. Both of us were knocked unconscious when we slammed into the ground. I regained consciousness within moments. I could not believe I was alive. I was flown to Womack Army Hospital and X-rayed.

"I had a hairline fracture in my back, and I could not stand up straight for several days. However, to the surprise of my friends, I was back jumping fourteen days later. If you make enough jumps, you are going to get hurt now and then. That was not the only time I would be injured in a landing.

"The other paratrooper, who was more seriously injured, was flown to Walter Reed Army Hospital in Washington. He did not return to the unit, and I never did find out what happened to him.

"My time at Fort Bragg was coming to an end. I had been there for nearly eighteen months, and in the regular army that meant it was time for another overseas assignment. I was given orders for yet another trip to Vietnam, but they were canceled because I had too much rank. They didn't need any more first sergeants over there.

"'How would you like to go to Korea?' I was asked.

"'Fine, I said, 'I'll go back to Korea.'

"I began negotiating to take my family with me. 'Yes, we can do that,' I was told, but then, without warning, my request was denied. The United Nations command had gone on full alert with the seizure of the U.S. Navy gunboat *Pueblo* and its crew by the North Koreans.

"It was going to be another lonesome tour. I left the United States in November 1970 to become the first sergeant of the U.S. Eighth Army Honor Guard Company, United Nations Command at Yongsan Garrison in Seoul.

"It was a multi-national company of 260 soldiers, sailors, marines and airmen from six nations—Americans, Brits, Thais, Filipinos, Koreans and Turks. My job was to train the entire honor guard and select the members of the color guard.

"It was not as difficult as one might think. Every soldier had to qualify for the guard, and each one was hand-picked. They were in great physical condition, and the minimum height was six feet.

"For the American color guard, each man was at least six feet, four inches tall and had a waist of thirty-four inches or less. All the GIs marched in dress blues. We marched about 150 men at a time in the full, multinational honor guard, and I marched out front with a saber. We moved along smartly at 120 steps a minute.

"Always accompanied by the U.S. Eighth Army band, we performed at various functions at least three times a week. It was a great show, and we received more accolades than we could count."

In May 1971, Capt. James D. Johnson wrote in an efficiency report, "First Sergeant Gaweda represents the epitome of the senior noncommissioned officer. He is aggressive, ambitious, and soldierly in bearing and appearance . . . First Sergeant Gaweda is the most knowledgeable and thorough NCO I have yet known or worked with in the army."

"Meanwhile," Ted said, "I continued working to bring my family overseas. Then, two months before I was to be rotated back to Fort Bragg, I managed to get the army to lift the ban on bringing families to South Korea. For me, it was too late, but it opened the door for those who followed.

"I left Korea after thirteen months and returned to Fayetteville for another warm and wonderful Christmas homecoming."

CHAPTER THIRTEEN

Return to Fort Bragg

"I was only home a few days," Ted said, "when I received devastating news. I was given orders to Baumholder, Germany, and because of an army budget crunch, I would not be able to take my family with me.

"Edith and my sons were as upset as I was. The thought of going off alone again for at least a year was almost more than I could bear, but I had no choice.

"I went down to the Fort Bragg transportation office to pick up my airline ticket to Germany, when I ran into an old friend—Col. Robert 'Butch' Kendrick, whom I had served with in the Dominican Republic when he was commander of the 82nd Airborne's Second Brigade.

"'Hey, old soldier, where are you going?' he asked.

"After I told him my long, sad story, he said, 'Go home, get out of those civilian clothes, put on your Class A uniform, and meet me at the corps commander's office.'

"By the time I arrived at corps headquarters, Colonel Kendrick was coming out of the office of Lt. Gen. John Hay, the corps commander. He told me, 'First Sergeant, go to your house and stay by the telephone.'

"I went home and Edith and I sat next to the phone, where we said a little prayer. Hours passed, but about midnight the phone rang. I quickly answered it and heard the voice on the other end of the line tell me that I had been reassigned to the 82nd Airborne Division at Fort Bragg.

"Edith wept with joy and I thanked my God. To my delight, I found out the next day that I was being reassigned as first sergeant of Company B, First Battalion, 505th Parachute Infantry Regiment. I was pleased to be back with this legendary regiment, where I had first served in 1956."

Kendrick, whose likeness is the leading figure in the new Korean War Memorial in Washington, later would say of Ted Gaweda, "He is a great man. He just kind of glows with his efficiency and his enthusiasm. He is firm and he is fair. He could be just as much at ease talking to the president of the United States as he would talking to the lowest private in the army."

"Once I reported for duty," Ted said, "I didn't go directly to Company B. Instead, I was made acting sergeant major of the parent First Battalion, reporting to Lt. Col. Clarence Cummings, the battalion commander. Sixty days later, the replacement sergeant major, Tom Twomey, showed up and I went to Company B as first sergeant.

"I had seventy days to prepare for the annual general inspection by the staff of the 82nd Airborne inspector general. A group from the IG's office began the inspection on a May morning in 1972.

"One of the items I had put on the company bulletin board was a notice of the last punishment of the unit, which involved a staff sergeant who had been absent from one of the company's morning formations. He had been fined fifty dollars.

"The lieutenant colonel in charge of the inspection saw the notice and told me to take it down, saying that noncommissioned officers were not supposed to be posted for punishment.

"I refused to remove the notice, saying that I had followed proper procedure and that the colonel's position was wrong.

"'I am the ranking person here, First Sergeant, and I am ordering you to take down the notice,' he snapped.

"'No, sir, you're not the ranking man here,' I replied. 'I am the ranking man and you're the ranking visitor, and right now you are not welcome.'

"His face turned red, and he said, 'Okay, the inspection is over,' and he told the team to go to lunch. Colonel Cummings came to me and said, 'You have just put my military career in jeopardy.'

"'Sir,' I told him, 'you have twenty-two years in the Army and I've only got eighteen. If anyone is in jeopardy, it's me. Besides, I know army regulations, and believe me, sir, I am right and the inspector is wrong.'

"The inspecting colonel had only twelve years in the army, and, as far as I was concerned, he was a real asshole. He returned with his inspection team after lunch, and not another word was said about the notice on the bulletin board.

"My guess was that he checked the regulations and found out that I was right. The team completed its inspection, and we passed with flying colors. Colonel Cummings just shook his head and laughed.

"In January 1973, I went with the battalion to Washington, where we participated in President Richard Nixon's inaugural parade. The same month, my name appeared on a list of men selected for promotion to sergeant major."

Ted heard this news in a bizarre fashion. Retired Brigadier General Sanderson, Ted's battalion commander in 1967, was commander of the 82nd Airborne Third Brigade when the word came through. He saw the list and decided to have some fun.

"The entire division was on maneuvers somewhere in the swamps of the Eastern Carolinas when I received a message one evening, saying that Ted was on the promotion list. I guess I was about five miles from where his battalion was located.

"I thought so much of this guy that I jumped in my jeep and drove at night over those five miles to his battalion headquarters to find out where his company was operating.

"I went into the company command post and said loudly, 'Where is Gaweda?'

"I'll tell you, when the brigade commander comes into a company command post, everybody jumps through their skins. The company commander was about ready to shit a brick. He may have, but I didn't notice it.

"'I want to see Gaweda, and I want to see him immediately,' I demanded.

"He was right next door, and when he came in, he looked like he was scared to death. He didn't know what the hell was going on. I started chewing his ass out about being out of uniform. I was reaming him up one side and down the other.

"'What is your excuse?' I said. 'You know you're wrong and blah, blah, blah.'

"'Sir,' he said, 'I don't know what you're talking about.'

"I thrust the promotion list into his hands, and said, 'You are out of uniform because you should be wearing the stripes of a sergeant major, not those of a first sergeant.'

"He looked bewildered for a moment, and then said, 'I am not out of uniform because I am not a sergeant major yet. This is only a list.'

"About that time, I burst out laughing, brought forth the bottle I was carrying and said, 'Let's have a drink to celebrate your promotion.'

"With his promotion in the offing, I named Ted acting sergeant major of the Third Brigade's First Battalion, 508th Parachute Infantry Regiment. When it comes to having a sense about the troops and their needs, Ted is one of the smartest guys I've ever known. He was a role model for thousands of young soldiers."

Lt. Col. Carl Stiner, the Third Brigade's executive officer, worked in the field a number of times with Ted Gaweda in those days.

"I was with him one time, when he said something I will never forget," Stiner remarked. "We were putting the troops through some pretty stringent training. It was just like we were ready for battle. This particular unit had dug a humongous anti-tank ditch with bulldozers.

"It ran for more than a mile and was from twelve to fourteen feet deep. Ted Gaweda and I were walking along looking at it, when he said, casually, 'This brings back terrible memories for me. When I was a young boy in Eastern Poland, I saw a ditch like this, which the German Army filled with their captives and then shot them.

"'The bodies were covered with dirt, and if you walked on top of it, blood would ooze up between your feet. We just don't know how fortunate we are to be in this great country. These young men here do not understand the true value of their freedom, or the price that was paid for it.'

"Several NCOs and soldiers overheard what he said, and they just looked at him in awe.

"Of course, I think airborne people are the elite folks in the army. They are twice volunteers, you know. They volunteer for the army, and they volunteer again to be airborne soldiers. In my view, they are the best of the best.

"As for Sergeant Major Gaweda, he was a man that was motivated and dedicated for all the right reasons, and not one was for personal gain."

Stiner went on to command the 82nd Airborne Division and the XVIII Airborne Corps. In 1990 he retired as a four-star general from his position as commander-in-chief of the U.S. Special Operations Command.

CHAPTER FOURTEEN

Command Sergeant Major

"In January 1973, the army sent its first class to the new Sergeants Major Academy at Fort Bliss, Texas," Ted said. "To my delight, I was selected as a member of the second class, which assembled in July.

"It meant that I would be away from Edith and the boys for six months, spending most of my time in intensive study. Nevertheless, I was proud to have been chosen.

"Actually, at that time, I felt my retirement from the army was not too far off. On April 16, 1973, I completed twenty years of service. Edith and I decided it was our time to build a retirement home. With the boys growing up in Fayetteville, we had put down deep roots in the town, and there was where we decided to remain."

"All four of us, Ted, George, Gregory, and I, piled into our Ford Pinto for the trip to Fort Bliss," Edith said. "We detoured along the way to visit the Grand Canyon and watch a bullfight in Juarez, Mexico. I never want to see another one. After we arrived at the post, we left the Pinto with Ted, and the boys and I flew home to Fayetteville.

"When we left for Fort Bliss, there was a pile of sand in the backyard and almost no grass on the ground. I put in grass that summer, but there wasn't too much I could do in the way of landscaping because of my real estate business. I also had two active sons who kept me busy. George was thirteen and Gregory was eleven."

"There were 205 of us in the second Sergeants Major Academy class at Fort Bliss," Ted recalled. "I was pleased that I had three close friends from Fort Bragg with me. They were Lewis LePage, George Townsend, and Ernest Smitka. We all stuck together; we were a tight, buddy-buddy group."

Townsend remembers Ted as a serious student who stayed close to his billet. "He didn't party," Townsend said. "Actually, none of our foursome did, because our assignments kept our noses close to the grindstone. We stayed close to our billets, studying most of the time and occasionally visiting the bowling alley."

"I'll never forget when Leon L. Van Autreve, sergeant major of the army, spoke to the class at Fort Bliss," Ted said. "He was informative and inspirational. I said to myself, 'Hey, I can make a speech like that.' I took my first step in public speaking, a discipline that would give me great pleasure the rest of my military career."

Smitka remembers Ted asking him for help on his speeches. "Initially, he had me write some of his presentations," he said. "It wasn't that I just sat down and did it. He would give me the information, and I would put it in better English.

"At that time, he had some real problems with the language. He could speak it fairly well, but had trouble putting it on paper. Later, at Fort Bragg, he would come to my office, give me a piece of paper and say, 'Hey, look at this. I've got to make this speech. Do you think it's all right?'

"I would go over it and tailor it just a bit, and a couple of days later, he would come back and make the speech to me. He became very good at it. You don't mind helping if someone really is trying. You have to give Ted credit. I have never seen him give up. He always strove to be the best he could be.

"He had to study a lot harder than the rest of us, because his command of the English language wasn't that great, but he buckled down and worked to improve himself constantly. Ted made a career out of being correct. I was not surprised when he became command sergeant major of the XVIII Airborne Corps. I expected him to go even higher, but I don't think he wanted to because that would have meant leaving Fort Bragg and his family."

Van Autreve, who retired in 1975, would later say of Ted Gaweda, "What

Ted exemplified to the army was that he obtained the ultimate position in the airborne, command sergeant major of the XVIII Airborne Corps. Being born in another country is by no way and by no means an indication that you cannot be all that you can be.

"He was all soldier—integrity, honesty, and dedication. Dedication just flows from the guy. If I were a company commander or a battalion commander and I had to go to war, there's no one I would rather take with me as my sergeant major than Ted Gaweda."

"On October 1, 1973, a list of new command sergeants major was posted," Ted said, "but because I was a student, it would not be official until I graduated from the academy.

"The word 'command' is added to the title of sergeant major for those who actually led troops as a platoon sergeant, first sergeant, and so on. The decision was made by the Army's Command Sergeant Major Selection Board at Fort Benjamin Harrison, Indiana.

"There was bad news with the good. I was told that after graduation, I would be assigned to 101st Airborne Division at Fort Campbell, Kentucky. Edith and I were in a state of confusion, having barely moved into our new home.

"I wanted to remain in a fully active airborne unit, but the 101st was no longer on jump status. When General Creighton Abrams, former commander-in-chief of all U.S. forces in Vietnam, visited the Academy, I expressed my dissatisfaction with Army assignment policies.

"One of his aides took down my Social Security number, and in December, I received new orders, assigning me to the 82nd Airborne Division at Fort Bragg. This was a happy day for me. I immediately telephoned Edith and gave her the good news.

"A few days later, I graduated in the upper third of my academy class and put on the insignia of a command sergeant major. I was ready to go home."

"He arrived on December 19," Edith recalled, "and, like so many times before, he showed up after a long absence to celebrate Christmas, just like Santa Claus."

Gaweda family in 1948, Wildflecken DP Camp. Top row from left to right: Walter, Ted, Henrick, Jan, Edward. Bottom row: Mother Helena, Wanda, Antoni.

Chicago, 1951, Ted's eighteenth birthday.

April 1953, at Fort Riley Kansas. First four days in the Army.

September 1954, while stationed in Korea, Ted's first RR in Kobe, Japan.

Augsburg, Germany, 1959, Ted and Edith getting married.
On the left: our best man Richard J. Bradley.

Dien Ban, Vietnam, May 1966. Top left to right: Capt. Maurice Winter,
Maj. Colombo. Bottom: PFC Shukoski and Ted.

February 1968, Fayetteville, North Carolina. Ted, Edith and our sons George and Gregory.

1978, Fort Bragg, North Carolina. Ted marching with Army and Air Force Color Guard.

1985, Ted with Lt. General James J. Lindsey and Sergeant Major of the Army (Retired) Leon Van Autreve.

1986, Ted with Governor of North Carolina James Martin and Fritz Healy, President of Braxston Bragg Chapter Association of the U.S. Army.

October 1983, Ted on the Island of Granada with Colonel James T. Scott.

October 1984, Ted and Secretary of Defense Casper Weinberger, on first anniversary of Granada invasion at Andrews AFB, Virginia.

1985, Ted visiting with troopers of First Battalion 508th PIR in Sinai desert.

1987, Ted and Lt. General John W. Foss, Commanding General XVIII Airborne Corps and Fort Bragg.

1988, Ted's farewell speech to the soldiers and guests during retirement ceremony on Main Post Parade Field, Fort Bragg, North Carolina.

1997, Ted and Edith with President George W. Bush during the 25th Golden Knight Reunion of The U.S. Army Parachute Team.

CHAPTER FIFTEEN

The Legend Grows

"I came back to Fort Bragg as command sergeant major of the Second Battalion, 325th Airborne Infantry Regiment," Ted said, "but I was only there for thirty-five days.

"Lt. Col. Heath Twitchell, the new commander of the First Battalion of the 508th Parachute Infantry Regiment, apparently had heard good things about me when I served with the battalion prior to attending the Sergeant Major Academy. He requested that I be reassigned to his unit. He had made some sort of deal at the 82nd Airborne Division headquarters, and, all of a sudden, I was told, 'You are going to the 508th.'

"When I first came to the battalion, it was in bad shape in a number of ways. Colonel Twitchell had been cracking the whip and demanding perfection. There was a real morale problem, and many of his officers were afraid of him.

"They would go to great lengths to avoid seeing him. Some would come by my office and ask, 'What do you think the old man would do if I did such and such?'

"I confronted Colonel Twitchell about his treatment of his staff officers, and, basically, he told me to mind my own business. He also reminded me that he was the one who rated my performance.

"I replied that I never worried about my own report card and that I was not going to start worrying about it now. However, his threatening remark made me extremely angry. I had a long talk with Edith, and we both agreed that I should put in for my retirement. I told Hugh Davis, command sergeant major of the Third Brigade, of my decision, and he convinced me to put my retirement plans on the back burner.

"In my judgment, Colonel Twitchell was under tremendous pressure. Unbeknownst to his officers, he had made a contract with himself to publish a biography he was writing about Maj. Gen. Henry T. Allen, who, among other exploits, had commanded the 90th Infantry Division in the First World War.

"On weekends, he would be in his office working on the book, while everyone thought he was handling battalion business. When the other officers saw his car parked in the battalion lot, they felt obligated to work weekends too. It was a bad situation. After about six months with the battalion, I discovered that he was working on his book and not on battalion issues.

"Then-captain Joe Young, who retired as a major, came to the battalion June 1974 as the battalion motor officer. He later told me, 'My initial impression of Lieutenant Colonel Twitchell was that he was a man who would, if allowed, intimidate people to obtain his desired level of performance from his subordinates. As an officer with combat experience, which included a background as a senior noncommissioned officer, I was well prepared to either confront or perform as required under Colonel Twitchell.

"'The equalizer in the battalion was Sgt. Maj. Ted Gaweda. He was as concerned about the performance of an officer as he was about an NCO. I found him capable, professional, and fair in every situation. In his position, he could have played the role of a cutthroat, but he did not.

"'The battalion was a high-speed, kick-butt unit. Also, I must add that as the only minority officer in the entire brigade, I was never exposed to any form of racism.'"

"A turn-around began shortly after Maj. Roy Ray became the executive officer of the battalion," Ted said. "He had a doctorate in communications, and right away he saw the principal problem. The only communication in the battalion was from the top down.

"Major Young agreed, saying, 'The arrival of Major Ray was a new page in the development of a highly trained, deployable unit. He was an old country boy with a high level of education and expertise. Through the efforts of people like Roy Ray and Ted Gaweda, we passed all the major readiness inspections. The battalion was designated combat ready in all areas—personnel, administration, and equipment.'

"Major Ray," Ted said, "received permission from Colonel Twitchell to conduct an experimental organization and development workshop that he had developed. I heard about the program at the Sergeants Major Academy. With the help of a university professor, Major Ray put together four groups of four men each.

"As command sergeant major of the battalion, I was invited to participate in the program. The others were all officers. We gathered at a hotel in downtown Fayetteville, where we were sequestered for three days, just like a jury.

"We were not permitted to use the telephone or receive calls, except in the case of a dire emergency. All sixteen of us met together in the first meeting, where the drill was explained. Then we broke up into our four groups.

"Each person was asked to relate his problems with Colonel Twitchell. Several spoke of the personal humiliation he had inflicted upon them, saying that he had not only chewed them out, but called them unprintable names as well.

"After two days, Major Ray brought the four groups together, and we compared notes. The complaints were all about the same. He asked us to put together a list of ideas as to what we could do to help Colonel Twitchell improve his relationship with his subordinates in order to operate a more effective battalion.

"When Colonel Twitchell came to the hotel and heard a summary of the complaints against him, he broke down and wept. He said he was going to the division commander and ask that he be replaced. We unanimously disagreed with that.

"'No, that's not the answer,' we said. 'The answer is that you learn from the past, and now go forward with a positive attitude.' He did just that and became a great battalion commander. We became good friends, and he later recommended me for the position of sergeant major of the army.

"His book, *Allen*, was published, and he went on to write another on the Alaskan Highway. An article about the organization and development workshop, written by Colonel Twitchell, appeared in the September 1977 issue of Army Magazine. It was entitled 'First Battalion, 508th, Shapes Up.'"

Twitchell would later say of Gaweda, "He was a crutch, a rock, a source of energy and always calm. I never saw him lose his temper, although I'm sure he had one. He was just unflappable, and a very good source for advice and a great sounding board.

"Whether we were in the field, baking under the hot sun at Fort Bliss, Texas, or freezing at Fort Drumm, New York, he would come up with the damnedest stuff—a delicacy or two at the command post, a candy bar when no one else had one. When a jeep needed a new motor, he managed to come up with one. I soon learned not to ask him where those things came from. I sort of assumed that if we needed something, Ted would find it."

Asked about his memories of Ted Gaweda, Major Charles Clark, operations officer of the First Battalion and a key player in the organization and development workshop, responded, "He was the best sergeant major I ever served with.

"I'm not a real fan of sergeants major," he said, "because, by and large, I think most of them have egos that keep expanding, which keeps them from doing what they are supposed to do, and that's looking after the troops. Ted Gaweda never reached that point. He never forgot what he was supposed to be doing.

"Some sergeants major think they are greater than God and end up with offices larger than those of the generals. They get to be in very powerful positions and have the ears of the senior commanders. They can do a lot of damage and some do.

"I had a really bad experience with a sergeant major when I was a second lieutenant. I went to see a major, who had been one of my mentors. He was talking to someone else, so I waited. There was only one chair in the outer office, and the clerk told me I could sit in it.

"Well, anyhow, this yahoo comes out of the major's office, sees me in his chair. I start to get up, when he walks over, sticks his finger in my face, and bellows, 'You, get out of my chair!' I won't tell you what I said to him, but I am sure he has never forgotten it.

"Unhappily, the guy I talked to was not one of a kind. There were a bunch of them around. They were dinosaurs, who got where they were by cussing and being tough. That does not work in today's army.

"Ted, on the other hand, was a real soldier, and he was such a great model for the kids to look up to. He would get out there in the field and get grubby with the rest of the troops. I knew some sergeants major that were afraid to get their hands dirty. Sergeant Major Gaweda was superb in the field. He was absolutely untiring when it came to looking out for his troops.

"Sergeant Major Gaweda was a soldier's soldier, with total honesty and integrity. He would give it to you straight each and every time. I was not surprised when he became the command sergeant major of the XVIII Airborne Corps. I thought he should have been sergeant major of the army.

"When I first met him, he had some problems with the English language, but instead of staying at one level, he just continued to grow and grow."

Retired General Volney F. Warner, former commander of the XVIII Airborne Corps, remembers meeting Ted Gaweda in 1972, "when he was running up and down Ardenness Street with several hundred troops. I was chief of staff of the 82nd Airborne Division at the time, and I would tag along on those early morning runs.

"Later, after I was assistant division commander, I served with Sergeant Major Gaweda on a promotion board. He worked closely on the selection process and determining criteria for the promotion of noncommissioned officers. In a way, it was sort of a post-Vietnam analysis.

"We shared views on the future structure of the NCO Corps and how to make sure that command sergeants major would not just be puppies or tag-a-longs to the senior commanders. Sergeant Major Gaweda, who had great military bearing, always was outspoken in a good sense of the word, being able to articulate his views.

"He had a sufficient amount of service to back up his positions with examples and to tell us what reactions we could expect if we shifted more of soldier orientation and training responsibilities to the NCOs.

"Because of Sergeant Major Gaweda's performance, I would put him right at the top of command sergeants major I have known. No matter where he went, no matter what command he was in, he was always a contender to be the top command sergeant major. By virtue of his appearance, character, and ability, he was always destined for higher command, and that came to him when he was named command sergeant major of the XVIII Airborne Corps.

"He was a tremendous combat leader, a soldier who never whined or asked for a special break, just a great person."

Retired Command Sgt. Maj. Robert D. O'Brien, who served as first sergeant of Company A when Ted was battalion sergeant major, said, "Ted was a super-demanding guy. He sure as hell would never ask anyone to do anything that he personally would not do himself.

"In that type of environment, you could not ask much more than that of a leader. Wherever his troops or unit went, he was always there. He had a lot of influence on a lot of guys. I run into people all the time that go out of their way to tell me that."

"I was particularly honored in August 1974," Ted said, "when Major General Frederick J. Krosen, 82nd Airborne Division commander, appeared in my office and told me that I had been chosen by the Department of the Army to serve on the Command Sergeant Major Selection Board at Fort Benjamin Harrison, Indiana. This kind of recognition made all my hard work worthwhile.

"Colonel Twitchell left the battalion in February 1975 and was replaced by Lt. Col. Douglas M. Craver, who was one of the first officers chosen to command a battalion by a Department of the Army Selection Board. Prior to that time, battalion commanders were chosen by division commanding generals. Colonel Craver was a great commander who demonstrated a genuine interest in every soldier and officer in the unit. He was a fine motivator.

"In May 1975, I was chosen to become command sergeant major of the 82nd Division's Third Brigade by its commander, Col. James J. Lindsay, where I would have the responsibility for three thousand troops. Colonel Lindsay had been my hero from the day I met him.

"He was the most physically fit brigade commander in the entire U.S. Army. Despite my conditioning, he could run me into the ground. He was a real horse. He could run four miles in twenty-one minutes, whereas it would take me twenty-five to twenty-seven minutes. When he ran in organized events, whether it be six, ten, or fifteen miles, he was always in the front of the pack. To me, he was the American Airborne Caesar.

"He always was concerned with the welfare of his soldiers, showing up at all sorts of places to check things out. The mess sergeants called him 'gray fox' because of the color of his hair. He frequently would show up at mess halls at first light or just after physical training to see what his soldiers were eating. The mess sergeants would tell me, 'Hey, Sergeant Major, the gray fox was here.'

"Just before my departure from the First Battalion, 508th Parachute Infantry Regiment, to the Third Brigade, Colonel Craver came to my office and asked me not to go to the brigade because he and I made such a great team.

"'What do I say to Colonel Lindsay?' I asked. 'Besides since I am the ranking command sergeant major in the brigade, it is only fitting that I be at the brigade level.'

"He agreed, and apologized for not considering what was best for me. James E. Hargraves succeeded me as battalion command sergeant major. When Colonel Lindsay left the brigade to become the 82nd Airborne Division's chief of staff, he was succeeded by Colonel Jarold Hutchinson.

"Colonel Hutchinson and I shared a memorable experience one morning with a rattlesnake in our tent at Yakima, Washington, where we were taking part in field training exercises with the Ninth Infantry Division from Fort Lewis. I was awake at first light, when I heard Colonel Hutchinson whisper, 'Don't move. There's a rattlesnake next to your sleeping bag.'

"I assure you that I was not about to move. I stayed absolutely still. The colonel hit the snake with a trenching tool, which sent it slithering out of the tent. He jumped up, followed the snake and finished it off with the tool."

Maj. Gen. Dan K. McNeill, who was a captain at that time, was responsible for awakening Ted and Colonel Hutchinson that morning.

"There wasn't enough light to see well," General McNeill said, "but I stuck my head in and called to Colonel Hutchinson and Sergeant Major Gaweda that it was time to get up. There was movement and whispering inside the tent, so I left the flap up and headed back to the brigade Tactical Operations Center.

"I then heard some yelling and rushed back to see what was going on. I bumped into Sgt. Victor White, the brigade commander's driver, and he told me that Colonel Hutchinson had just killed a rattlesnake lying next to Sergeant Major Gaweda's sleeping bag."

"I served with Colonel Hutchinson for thirteen months," Ted said, "but I knew that my time at Fort Bragg was running out. In the late summer of 1976, I was ordered to Korea. Again, Command Sergeant Major Hargraves followed in my footsteps, replacing me at the Third Brigade."

CHAPTER SIXTEEN

Korea III

"In September 1976, I arrived in South Korea for my third visit," Ted said. "It was twenty-three years ago to the month that I first came to this land. As my airplane was making its final approach to Seoul's Kimpo Airport, I thought how much my life had changed since that first trip.

"In 1953, I was a young private, not very articulate in English, and with less than six months of service in the army. Now I was reporting for duty as the command sergeant major of the 2nd Infantry Division's 1st Brigade, known in the Army as the Iron Brigade.

"My first boss at Camp Casey was Lt. Col. William H. Roche, but after two months he was replaced by the colorful Col. Alvin Ornstein, an officer to whom I related very well. However, that was not the case with a number of officers on his staff.

"Colonel Ornstein was a tough, demanding commander who came down hard on his subordinates if they displeased him. In many ways, he was like Gen. George S. Patton in World War II.

"He would ask a battalion commander, 'Can you do this?' If the officer showed even the slightest hesitation, Colonel Ornstein would say, 'Well, if you can't do it, I will find somebody who can.'

"On many occasions, I acted as a buffer between the colonel and his staff. He would chew out some of his commanders furiously. They would then come to my office to find out if they were about to be dismissed. I told them to just keep doing their jobs and not to worry. In effect, he would fire them, and I would tell them they had been rehired.

"The colonel never said anything to hurt me in any way, but there were times when he was embarrassed at what he had done. He would say, 'I'm sorry, Sergeant Major, but I just had to do it.'

"When he was sharp with me one time, I smiled and said, 'Sir, can you believe that the army made me command sergeant major, assigned to this brigade, and also made you a colonel and assigned you as commander? We really have to live with one another.'

"One of my favorite officers at Camp Casey was a young captain who was the brigade's aviation platoon leader. Capt. Henry 'Hawk' Ruth's job was to support the brigade with four Huey and two OH-58 helicopters. He also was the best chopper pilot I ever flew with.

"Captain Ruth, who now is a colonel, and I shared some hair-raising experiences in our Korean tour. Late one winter afternoon, Hawk, Colonel Ornstein, and myself were up at Nightmare Range near the demilitarized zone (DMZ) between North and South Korea, when the wind chill factor was forty below zero."

Captain Ruth recalled that Colonel Ornstein wanted to return to Camp Casey, even though by now it was snowing heavily. "It was getting really bad," he said, "when the colonel and Sergeant Major Gaweda came running across the tarmac about 11:00 P.M. and jumped in the helicopter.

"Meanwhile, I had asked one of the tank commanders to light up the area with his huge Zeon searchlight, because we had to take off and go through two big rocks, fly directly toward a mountain wall, and climb hard to the right. Even on a clear day, it was extremely dangerous.

"The young warrant officer in the right seat asked to fly the bird. I was trying to build confidence in the kid, so I told him, 'Okay, but I'll be watching the controls.'

"As we cranked up the aircraft and lifted, the tanker turned on his searchlight. The kid got a big fixation on the white light and immediately went into vertigo. The chopper began to sway and dip. Colonel Ornstein started yelling from the back as we started into the clouds. I'm telling you, it was a scary situation.

"We were on our way to hit the mountain when I grabbed the controls, dropped the nose, turned the bird around, and landed.

"'Okay,' I said, 'that's it.'

"My poor warrant officer was devastated. His confidence, which I had been trying to build, went the opposite direction. It took me a month to get him comfortable again. It was a heart thumper, it really was.

"Sergeant Major Gaweda didn't say anything while we were in the air, but he later said, 'I'll be the first to tell you, my heart tightened in my chest. I was sucking air.'

"I think everybody was glad they were down. It's better to be on the ground wishing you were in the air, than in the air wishing you were on the ground.

"It was a cold, windy, miserable night, so I huddled around a stove in a small warm-up tent. The sergeant major came by and asked, 'Are you doing okay?'

"'Yeah,' I said, 'I'm doing fine.'

"'What's that I smell?' he said.

"'I don't know,' I answered. Then I looked down. One leg of my heavy jump suit was smoldering. It was melting from the heat. We got a good laugh out of that.

"By the next morning, it had stopped snowing, so I told Colonel Ornstein and the sergeant major, 'I'm not going to promise you guys anything, but I'll see if I can get us out of here.' Instead of flying the old pattern through the giant rocks and toward the mountain, I flew down Nightmare Range and climbed straight up through the clouds.

"As soon as I got above the cloud layer, I couldn't see the ground, so I hung a left and picked up a heading that I knew would take us home. After a forty-five-minute, white knuckle ride, we landed safely at Camp Casey.

"My relationship with Sergeant Major Gaweda was not just professional. It also was personal. I learned early in my career, particularly after being in Vietnam, to have great respect for senior NCOs, and that if you were ever going to be successful, you had to pay attention, listen to them, and talk to them. Ted had command sergeant major written all over him, and I knew that I had better pay attention and not screw up.

"Because the road network in South Korea was still quite primitive, we were always going somewhere together by air. The First Brigade was responsible for three of the twelve radar sites along the DMZ, and the sergeant major and I would fly up there every Saturday or Sunday."

"Those were my days off from normal duty," Ted explained, "so I went to the radar site with Captain Ruth on my own time. I would bring mail and other things that might help morale at those hazardous and isolated locations. I would bring apples, oranges, and whatever else the mess sergeant at Camp Casey could spare.

"The radar stations were right on the edge of the buffer zone. Although many people assumed there was a fence along the DMZ, that was not the case. There was a kind of fire break with a hedgerow, and beyond that, a no man's land that extended for almost three miles to the North Korean frontier.

"The radar, which picked up everything that moved on the ground or in the air, was an early warning system for any infiltration or surprise attack from North Korea.

"The radar stations were manned jointly by GIs and hand-picked soldiers from the South Korean Army, also known as KATUSA, which means Korean Augmentation to the U.S. Army. For the most part, they were from affluent families who considered their sons' selection to serve with American troops an honor.

"There were not many luxuries, and all the men slept in the same room. I made an emergency trip up there one night with Captain Ruth because the Americans and the South Koreans were battling—throwing rocks and fist-fighting over some silly disagreement.

"We took two Huey helicopters and a squad of eight or nine U.S. infantrymen up there and quickly secured the site. I ended up replacing an American sergeant who was responsible for letting things get out of hand."

Colonel Ruth remembered fondly Ted and his visits to the radar stations. "After the sergeant major made his rounds," he said, "we would walk around, checking things out. We would talk and spit chewing tobacco, spit on each other's foot, that sort of thing. I was around him for seventeen straight weeks because one of the brigade's battalions was in the field for that amount of time, which meant that we would visit the training areas two or three times a week.

"Ted would bring by a soldier and say, 'Sir, please take this man out of here. He has frostbite.'

"I remember evacuating a number of frostbite cases. I Medivaced one soldier who had lost his fingers when an artillery simulator exploded in one of his hands. Ted and I spent a lot of time sleeping in tents because he wanted to be with his troops. He was always with the soldiers, talking to them, relating to them, taking care of their problems.

"He always knew what was going on. Colonel Ornstein was a relentless boss, but Ted was the perfect sergeant major for him. Anyone else would have folded under the colonel. He was a commander that put the fear of God in people. He was tough, I mean he was as tough as a woodpecker's lips."

After twenty-seven years of service, Ornstein retired from the army in November 1977. Speaking from his home in Killeen, Texas, he said, "Running the First Brigade in Korea was the greatest assignment of my military career, and the principal reason for my feeling that way was the presence of Ted Gaweda as my command sergeant major.

"It was clear to me from the beginning that Sergeant Major Gaweda was a great soldier. He also was a great friend who got me out of more scrapes than I could ever recount. Ted was there the day I assumed command.

"The mayor of Tonduchon, a small town just outside Camp Casey, was in the audience on that occasion, and at one point, I spoke directly to him, saying, 'Mayor, I am responsible for what my soldiers do or fail to do, and I do not make this statement lightly.'

"The very next day, the second day of my command, Sergeant Major Gaweda came into my office and said, 'Sir, the mayor and his interpreter are outside and want to see you.'

"'What do they want to see me about, Sergeant Major?'

"'Well, it's about something you said yesterday.'

"'Okay,' I told him, 'send them in, but don't you leave me alone. Stay in the office with me.'

"So they came in, and after the usual courtesies were exchanged, the interpreter looked me squarely in the eye and said, 'Sir, did you mean what you said at yesterday's change of command ceremony? The mayor wants to know if you are a man of your word.'

"'Absolutely!' I declared.

"'The mayor wants to know what you are going to do about 3,000 orphans in and around our community, who were fathered by American soldiers stationed at Camp Casey,' the interpreter said.

"I don't know what came over me, but without batting an eye, I said, 'I'll tell you what I'll do. I can't accommodate all 3,000, but if you will find me a piece of land, the soldiers of this brigade will build an orphanage, and I will personally raise money for the children's other needs.'

"Sergeant Major Gaweda asked me, 'Colonel, sir, how are we going to do this?'

"'That's your problem,' I said. 'I made the promise, and now you have to go make it happen.'

"'Okay,' he responded, I know we can do it. We'll make sure your promise is kept.'

"Ted had outstanding command sergeants major leading our three battalions, and they worked wonderfully well under his tutelage."

"There was a school and primitive quarters on the site chosen," Ted said, "so we had something with which to start. We incorporated the housing into the new building. The Second Infantry Division's engineers gave me all the cement, two-by-fours, plywood, and nails that I wanted. They also provided plumbers, who built the showers, sinks, and sanitary facilities.

"Without the dedicated help of Command Sergeants Major Alexander Freitas, Freddie J. Weston Jr., and Douglas Hayes, I never could have fulfilled Colonel Ornstein's promise. We finished the job in sixty days, and some two hundred orphans moved into the new building. We named it Ahshin Orphanage. I'm sorry to say this, but the children of American servicemen were not very well accepted by the Koreans. The average age of the kids was about eight.

"Because of their Korean teachers, they were well-mannered and well-trained. I remember going into one of their classrooms, and the kids all stood at attention until the teacher told them they could sit down.

"The brigade sent over a monthly supply of rice, flour, and cabbage. Also, the GIs contributed between six hundred dollars and nine hundred dollars a month, which was exchanged for Korean money and used to shop the local markets."

"I have visited the orphanage on several trips back to Tonduchon," Ornstein said, "and I am pleased that every subsequent brigade commander has picked up the baton and kept the orphanage going.

"You know, Sergeant Major Gaweda was a great, great teacher and an admired leader. He would tell me that every soldier had a sergeant and that he was mine. I implemented a policy that required every new lieutenant coming into the brigade to spend his first day with the sergeant major.

"Ted would come by with a driver and a jeep and spend a full day showing the lieutenant around. Officer after officer told me how much they appreciated what the sergeant major had done to get them started on the right foot.

"There is a funny story about Ted Gaweda and two young lieutenants. The brigade had a night machine-gun firing exercise on one of the ranges. Ted picked me up in a jeep and we went to the range to observe. The range officer gave us a briefing and then began making announcements about clearing the range.

"'Are we clear on the right?'

"'Clear on the right,' came the answer.

"'Are we clear in the center?'

"'Clear in the center.'

"'Are we clear on the left?'

"'Not clear on the left.'

"The range officer waited a moment, and then asked again, 'Are we clear on the left?'

"'Not clear on the left,' again was the response.

"'Sir, Ted asked the range officer, 'do I have permission to investigate and attempt to solve the problem?'

"'Go take care of it, sergeant major,' he said.

"So Gaweda double-timed it to the left side of the machine-gun range. Picture this, there were two frustrated lieutenants struggling to remove a spent cartridge from the barrel of an M-60 machine gun. They had no idea how to unjam the weapon.

"'Sirs,' Ted asked courteously, "may I take control of this situation and solve the problem?' The lieutenants were more than happy for him to take over. Ted straddled the machine gun and proceeded to dismantle it. He put the front end of the barrel in his mouth, blew and the expended cartridge fell out the backside.

"He ran back to the range officer and said, 'Sir, the range is now clear.'

"By the time I got back to the officer's club, the dumbfounded lieutenants had already spread the word, telling their incredulous listeners how Sergeant Major Gaweda had blown in the barrel and cleared the round.

"Of course, over time, the story was somewhat embellished, and Ted's reputation soared. He could do no wrong. The young officers were in awe of him. He was the epitome of a noncommissioned officer.

"I really did not blow the cartridge out the barrel," Ted said later. "As I quickly dismantled the gun, I ran a wire through the barrel, which pushed the cartridge into my hand. I then blew into the barrel, simultaneously raising my hand to show them the expended cartridge.

"It happened so fast that the two lieutenants were convinced that I had literally blown the cartridge from the barrel, which is what I wanted them to think. It was a bit of trickery on my part, but it made for a good show.

"I pulled a similar stunt on the rifle range one day. I had been working with the First Battalion of the 17th Infantry or Buffalo Regiment. Once a month, the regiment held a ceremony, where new members were required to drink 'buffalo piss,' a terrible concoction of tomato juice, salt, pepper, onions, garlic, and God knows what.

"I frequently attended the party, and I spoke at several of their affairs. I also drank my share of 'buffalo piss.' To prepare for my trickery on the rifle range, I had the machine shop drill a hole the size of a rifle slug in the center of a nickel.

"With the nickel in my pocket, I went to the range to watch the shooting. There was one soldier who was having a hell of a time hitting his target. 'Let me see that rifle,' I said to him. 'You must not be aiming it properly.'

"He handed over his M-16, and I gave him a perfectly good nickel, saying, 'Throw this as high in the air as you can, and I'll see if I can hit it.'

"He sent the nickel soaring, and I blasted away with the M-16. It didn't take me long to 'find' the nickel with the hole in it. I had transferred it from my pocket to my hand. Now, it was simply a matter of bending over and exclaiming, 'Here it is.'

"The soldiers were really excited. 'Did you know that Sergeant Major Gaweda shot a hole in the center of that damn nickel?' they repeated over and over. I said, 'There's nothing wrong with your rifle, son,' as I handed back the M-16."

"Ted and I had a lot of good times together," Ornstein said, "but on a more serious side, he would give me personal advice on morals, ethics, and integrity. I would say to myself, 'My God, this is a sergeant major talking to me,' but I really never took it that way.

"This was a friend, a guy who cared for me. He wanted me to succeed, not do anything stupid. He felt responsible for me. I think the world of Ted. I would do anything for him. I mean that's how much love I have for the guy.

"An example of how he protected me took place on New Year's Eve, the last day of 1976. We were going to have a party at the brigade officers club at seven that evening, and I had invited Major Gen. Morris Brady, Second Infantry Division commander, and his two assistant commanders.

"The mayor of Tonduchon had asked Sergeant Major Gaweda and I to attend a town festival, which began at 3:00 P.M. 'Okay, we'll go,' I told Ted, 'but we have to get back to meet the general at seven.'

"We got to town about 4:00 P.M., and began celebrating. We were having great fun with the mayor and the community leaders, telling stories and drinking Korean sake. Ted and I were trying not to drink too much because neither of us had eaten anything. I also knew I had to function later at the brigade party."

"We were sitting on the floor at the mayor's house," Ted said, "participating in the Korean custom of toasting our friendship with each glass of the warm rice wine and constantly bowing to one another. By the time dinner was over, all had agreed on a plan to whip the North Korean Army. To say the least, it was a memorable afternoon."

"Well, I was getting kind of looped," Ornstein recalled, "and I was really beginning to feel it. Ted knew it too. At about 6:00 P.M., he jumped to his feet and declared, 'Sir, we must depart.'

"He told the mayor, 'The colonel must leave now. He has a very important meeting.' He had made a telephone call, and my sedan and driver were out front. He got me out of the house and into the car, and took me to my quarters, where he pulled off my coat, stuck my head under the shower, and turned it on.

"It was all so amazing how he got me somewhat sensible again. He telephoned the brigade XO (executive officer) and said, "You meet General Brady at the front door. I'm bringing the colonel in the back door.'

"Ted physically pushed me through the back door, handed me a cup of coffee and said, 'Drink this.' After I finished the coffee, he told me, 'Now, go out there and meet the general.'

"He had already told the XO, 'Give the colonel about 15 minutes of free time before you bring General Brady back here to say hello.'

"The XO had already picked up the party line, which was, 'General Brady, you always get to see the colonel. This is your opportunity to meet and visit with the lieutenants and captains.'

"As a matter of fact, almost an hour passed before I saw General Brady as we were getting ready to sit down and eat. That was Ted Gaweda, the finest noncommissioned officer with whom I served.

"One of his great attributes was that he was always calm in the midst of a crisis. We had a tragedy in the brigade about a week after New Year's Day 1977, when a soldier went berserk and started shooting people. I wanted to go talk to the man, who was holed up with an M-16 rifle in the orderly room of the First Battalion's Charlie Company, 17th Infantry Regiment.

"'Sir,' Ted said, 'you are going to stay right here in your office, even if I have to tie you to your chair. That's exactly what this guy wants. If he is going to go out, he would love to take a brigade commander with him. If anybody goes, I'm the one who will do it.'

Captain Ruth remembered, "I was talking with Sergeant Major Gaweda in his office when a young lieutenant with an M-16 in his hand burst through the door and called out, 'Sir, be careful. One of the soldiers has gone crazy, and he's shooting all the officers and NCOs he can find.'

"Knowing there was no hospital at Camp Casey and the Medivac ship wasn't due for more than an hour, I sprinted to my helicopter and told the new fuzzy-cheeked warrant officer I had with me, 'Crank it up and stand by.' The kid looked startled. He was so new he was still pissing stateside water.

"Ted, meanwhile, had run toward the orderly room. As I headed in that direction, I could hear rifle shots. Sprawled across the sidewalk in front of the building was a platoon sergeant with a large hole in the middle of his chest. I knelt down beside him and used my I.D. card to try and stem the flow of blood from his sucking wound. He was starting to get yellow on me."

"As I entered the orderly room," Ted said, "I saw the gunman chase the company commander out the back door. I didn't see him again until he was taken into custody fifteen to twenty minutes later. I stopped to give first aid to the first sergeant, who was bleeding from three or four wounds.

"He had held a hand out, palm up, in an attempt to stop the shooter, but the crazed young soldier fired anyway, hitting him in the upraised hand.

The bullet exited from his wrist and slammed into one of his lungs. Another platoon sergeant and a staff sergeant also had been hit. By this time, there were ten to fifteen other GIs there, trying to help out.

"I shouted to the chopper's crew chief, 'We got a mess of casualties here. Get the goddamn seats out of the helicopter so we can load the wounded.' The crew chief removed or collapsed the seats, and we loaded the four victims in less than two minutes. Despite what I had told him, Colonel Ornstein was there helping.

"'Get the hell out of here,' I told Captain Ruth. He broke every record in the book to get those men to a hospital as quickly as possible."

"Well, it was a tough event," Ruth recalled. "As soon as I was aloft, I called the Seoul air controller and said, 'I've got casualties aboard, and I have to get to the military hospital at Yonson garrison.' Most of the perimeter of Seoul was a restricted zone for air traffic.

"Fearing the possibility of incoming North Korean warplanes, machine guns were mounted everywhere. I knew, however, there was an opening, called a keyhole, that I could pass through to get to the hospital, but I quickly realized that I didn't have time to hunt for it.

"I told Seoul Air Control that I was coming in and proceeded to shortcut the keyhole. I didn't know the exact location of the hospital, so I told the people there to light up the damn place.

"They illuminated the building and told me to land on the seventh green of a golf course, next to the hospital. Someone had forgotten to take down the flag stick, which I cut in two as I landed. The normal flight time for my trip was thirty-five minutes, but I made it in less than fourteen."

"The platoon sergeant who was lying on the sidewalk with the gaping chest wound was dead on arrival at Yongson," Ted said, "but because of everyone's fast reaction, the other three men survived. The gunman apparently ran out of ammunition and was captured by the military police. He was a skinny kid, who stood about five feet, eight inches tall and weighed about 130 pounds. He looked to me like he was on something.

"I had never seen a person so full of hate. When his company commander read him the charges, the soldier looked at the captain and exclaimed, 'What? I am surprised you're still alive.'

"After the prisoner heard the charges, Colonel Ornstein told Captain Ruth to fly the prisoner to the U.S. Eighth Army stockade at Camp Humphries, about an hour away by chopper. I was in charge of the detail, which included two MPs who chained the prisoner to a seat. The flight to Camp Humphries was without incident. Two MPs and I later escorted the prisoner to Camp Casey, where he was court-martialed and sentenced to life in prison at Fort Levenworth, Kansas.

"I recommended that Captain Ruth be awarded the Soldier's Medal and that eleven GIs who helped with the wounded receive the Army Commendation Medal. The Soldier's Medal has to be approved by the Department of the Army and is the highest award for valor during noncombat action."

"About a year later," Ruth said, "I was in a cavalry squadron with the 101st Airborne Division at Fort Campbell, Kentucky, when my squadron commander telephoned and said, 'Hawk, I'm going to have breakfast up here at the division with some senior officers, and I would like you to join us.'

"So I go to the breakfast, and I notice right away that I'm the only captain in this room with all the brigade commanders and Division Commander Maj. Gen. John Brandenburg, whom I served as aide-de-camp. I said to myself, 'What the hell am I doing here?'

"General Brandenburg stepped forward and pinned the Soldier's Medal on my blouse, shook my hand, and gave me the citation, which Ted had prepared. He made that happen, and I shall always be grateful. You know, I always felt that if I got in trouble, I could go to Sergeant Major Gaweda, and he would rescue me."

"In January 1977," Ted said, "I had put in for a fifteen-day, mid-tour leave to the United States in February. I wouldn't have to pay airfare because my flight would be aboard a military aircraft. It appeared that I was all set, when Colonel Ornstein came to me and begged me not to go.

"There was a brigade review scheduled for one of the days I would be on leave, and General Brady and twenty-two Korean Army generals and field grade officers were to be special guests. 'You can't go,' Colonel Ornstein said, 'because you are the only one I can rely on to make the review a success.'

"So I stayed and trained two companies from each of our three battalions—about 350 men in all—for the review. It went perfectly. After General Brady inspected the troops, he came up to me, took off his glove, shook my hand, and said, 'Sergeant Major, that was a smart formation, with good-looking soldiers.'

"I took my mid-tour leave in March and had a wonderful time with Edith and my sons. There was only one problem. Since no military transportation was available, it cost me seven hundred dollars to fly commercial.

"Korea was a great place to train soldiers because there were little or no distractions. Colonel Ornstein was a superb trainer, and under his leadership our brigade was always combat ready. The brigade maintenance program was the best I have ever seen.

"All units passed the army training test and the annual division inspector general inspections. Our soldiers were mentally and physically tough. We were combat ready.

"When it came time for me to leave Korea, Colonel Ornstein came to my office and to my surprise asked me to stay two more months so we could depart Korea together. I was shocked and said to him, 'I can't believe you are asking this of me. I have served my twelve months and I want to go home to my family.'

"He did host a party for me at the Officers Club, where he said that I had helped him significantly improve the entire readiness of the brigade. The NCOs also held an affair in my honor at the Service Club. Colonel Ornstein presented me with my second Meritorious Service Medal. I was grateful for the recognition.

"In September 1977, I flew home to Fayetteville, where I would face new challenges."

CHAPTER SEVENTEEN

Signal Duty and Another Gender

"WHILE still in Korea, I received a telephone call from Col. Jarold Hutchinson, who was my boss when I was command sergeant major of the Third Brigade at Fort Bragg," Ted said. "He had since become chief of staff at West Point.

"For me, his news was not good. He told me that my next assignment would be at the army military academy. I said that all I wanted to do was to return to my family in Fayetteville and rejoin the 82nd Airborne Division at Fort Bragg.

"'Can you help me?' I asked.

"'I understand Ted,' he replied, 'I'll see what I can do.'

"Even though Colonel Twitchell had recommended me for the position of sergeant major of the army in 1975, I was prepared to take whatever job was available."

Kenneth Merritt, a World War II veteran of the Normandy landings on D-Day 1944, was command sergeant major of the XVIII Airborne Corps at the time. He also had been corps sergeant major once before—from 1962 to 1966.

"I had ten or twelve excess command sergeants major," Merritt said, "but I really wanted Ted back at Fort Bragg because he was such a great soldier. About the only thing I had to offer was at the battalion level. The

50th Signal Battalion needed a new command sergeant major, and Ted was told the job was his if he wanted it.

"It didn't bother Ted if he outranked the brigade command sergeant major. He could work under you or over you. It didn't matter that much to him. As far as I was concerned, the 50th Signal Battalion was filth, and I knew Ted could straighten it out, even though he had never been a signalman in his life."

"By now," Ted said, "Edith was selling real estate and my two sons were in high school. I felt the need to become a full-time husband and father, so I was pleased to accept the signal battalion post, and I did so, with gratitude, in the late autumn of 1977.

"It was another chance for me to show what I could do. The battalion was in miserable shape, with poor discipline, slovenly soldiers, and little leadership. After the Vietnam tragedy, there was a period of very low morale throughout the army. Officers and NCOs were not enforcing army standards.

"Once I began enforcing policy and demanding that army standards be met, I was able to weed out the undesirables. I told substandard soldiers that if they did not want to be in the 50th Signal Battalion, I could arrange for their quick departure. Taking advantage of the army's early-out programs, I arranged for a number of problem cases to receive general discharges. We had 12 percent turnover a month.

"As an infantry guy, I was accustomed to getting honest answers from my subordinate NCOs, but all I heard in the signal battalion were excuses. I would be told, 'Sergeant Major, this piece of equipment doesn't work because it's old,' but in many cases it didn't work because it had not been properly maintained. I didn't know that much about signal equipment, but I knew soldiers. Those guys were bullshitting me.

"I took the entire battalion, except for officers, to the field for seventy-two hours and told the troops that as soon as they established communications with other units of the XVIII Airborne Corps and maintain communications for twenty-four hours, they could break down their equipment and return to Fort Bragg. All of a sudden, I had soldiers trying to outdo each other so they could get the hell out of the field. The exercise worked well.

"I insisted on strict adherence to army regulations, right down to haircuts. I almost had a mini-revolt on my hands when I told my sergeants that the short-hair policy also applied to them. Soldiers who failed to show up for the 6:00 A.M. formations were punished with extra duty. Three-time losers were discharged.

"I set up Saturday sessions for soldiers who were deficient in various things—ill-fitting uniforms, improper haircuts, slovenly appearance, bad attitudes, inability to march correctly, and so on. The first sergeants of the battalion's four companies—men who had fifteen to twenty years in the Army—supported me 100 percent, and showed up every Saturday.

"The supervising sergeant of each private ordered to appear at a Saturday session also had to be there. The first inspection was at 8:00 A.M., followed by a forty-five-minute lecture by me on basic soldiering. About 75 percent failed the inspection. Those who passed went home.

"Those who failed were given an hour to correct their deficiencies, and were reinspected at 11:00 A.M. There was a break for lunch, and those who didn't pass the 11:00 A.M. inspection were again inspected at 1:00 P.M. Some GIs were there all day.

"The word got around quickly to the troops. If they didn't look and act like proper soldiers, they and their sergeants would have to show up at Gaweda's school until they did.

"I held only four Saturday sessions. By then, everyone was looking good. It was the turning point for the 50th Signal Battalion, which went on to become the top-rated battalion in the 35th Signal Brigade.

"I established regular weekly meetings with company first sergeants. One of my meetings was about to begin, when I noticed that one of the first sergeants was not present. I asked my clerk to telephone him and remind him of the meeting. The clerk came back and told me, 'The first sergeant is busy with the company commander.'

"I told my clerk to have the man come by my office. He showed up about 4:00 P.M., and I asked why he failed to attend my meeting.

"'I was shooting the shit with the company commander,' he told me.

"'You can't be serious,' I said.

"'Yes, I am,' he answered.

"I looked into his eyes and said, 'You are no longer first sergeant of the headquarters company. You have between now and 1800 hours (6:00 P.M.) to empty your desk and report for duty to the 35th Signal Brigade command sergeant major.'

"He was shocked. He couldn't believe it. He appealed to his company commander, who went to Col. John F. Markham, the battalion commander, but my decision stuck.

"My assignment to the 50th Signal Battalion brought me my first experience with women soldiers. We had forty-six enlisted women in the battalion and two female officers. I was determined to treat them like soldiers.

"When I first came to the battalion, the women were in a different building from the men. When I went to inspect their quarters, some woman yelled, 'Man on the floor,' like it was some sorority house. I had never seen anything like the condition of their barracks in all my time in the army.

"'This place looks like a Dempsey Dumpster,' I said, and ordered the women to clean the place for reinspection. So, what do you think the girls did? They got fifty guys over there to clean the place for them. The men did the whole nine yards, washing the windows and everything. I later put the women in the same building as the men, with separate rooms and washroom facilities.

"I would not tolerate any mistreatment of women because of their gender. Early in 1978, a woman soldier came to see me. As she entered my office, I could see that she was in terrible pain. She was crying.

"'First of all,' I told her, 'before you cry in my office, go to the restroom, fix your hair, wipe your face, and put on some make-up.'

"When she returned, she was much more composed. 'I don't know how to say this,' she said, 'but my company commander calls me three or four times a week and asks me for dates. I don't want to go out with him, Sergeant Major. What can I do?'

"'You did the right thing coming to me,' I assured her. 'I promise you that your company commander will never call you again, unless it is in the line of duty.'

"I telephoned the company commander, who was a captain, and said, 'Sir, please come to my office. I have an important message for you.'

"As soon as he entered my office, I said, 'Sir, one of the women soldiers under your command has informed me that you have been calling her for dates over the last two months. I am sure that you would not do anything like that, being a married man, but if I ever find out that you are trying to date the women or any other woman soldier in this battalion, I'm going to have your ass, and that, sir, is a promise. That's all, Captain.'

"After two weeks had passed, the captain stuck his head in my office and said, 'Thank you.'

"'For what?' I asked.

"He just looked at me, smiled, and said, 'Thank you' again. He was thanking me for not reporting him to the battalion commander.

"On another occasion, I was preparing an all-enlisted retirement ceremony for two senior NCOs, in which the battalion would march on the parade ground. A woman soldier disagreed with my instruction that all soldiers, including women, must wear pants in the parade.

"She took her complaint to the inspector general of the XVIII Airborne Corps, who, to my surprise, said he agreed with her position, that women soldiers should be given the option of wearing skirts.

"He called for the battalion commander, but when told the colonel was not in his office, he asked to talk to me. When he gave me his opinion about what the women should be permitted to wear, I said:

"'Sir, you are a staff officer. You are not battalion commander. Your job is not to set battalion policy, but to listen to complaints and report those complaints. If you can't do that, I suggest you tell that to the post commander, so he can find someone who can.

"He asked me for my full name, which I gave him. I never heard from him again. The female soldier was reprimanded for not utilizing the chain of command and departing her place of work without proper authority.

"It seemed that every time I turned around, I was facing 'new army' problems which I had never before confronted, like nepotism, for example. Wilbert Brown, the first sergeant of the headquarters company, told me that an enlisted clerk-typist was working for her husband, who was a captain, in the battalion operations section.

"'You're kidding,' I said. 'I didn't know that. Go see the woman right now and tell her to pack her bags and move to the headquarters company as a clerk-typist in operations.

"It wasn't long before her captain-husband showed up at my office. He was boiling mad, and said, 'Someone has made a mistake, a cruel mistake. I will not put up with anyone messing with my wife.'

"After a while, I asked, 'Are you finished, sir?'

"'Yeah, I'm finished,' he said.

"'Well,' I began, 'let me tell you my side of the story or, to put it a better way, the army's side. You don't act like you're in the army. You must think you're a civilian employer, who has hired his wife.

"'In the army, a wife does not work for her husband, and a husband does not work for his wife. I'm surprised you've gotten away with it this long. If you find my position unacceptable, go talk to Colonel Markham.'

"The captain left the army about ninety days later, and his wife soon followed. I was having the worst year of my life. Combat had been easier than this. However, before it was over, it was the best year of my life because of how the unit had progressed to become combat ready.

"For the first time in my army life, I had to deal with the pregnancy of a soldier. After a young woman was absent without leave for several days, I telephoned her mother, who told me that her eighteen-year-old daughter had come home because she was pregnant. She was thinking about an abortion, her mother said.

"'If your daughter is not back here in sixteen hours,' I said, 'she will have some serious problems. As for abortion, we have a fine military hospital at Fort Bragg whose doctors will do the abortion for nothing. After it is over, she can continue her military career.'

"The mother put her daughter on a bus to Fort Bragg, and the soldier had her abortion. Not long after, she left the army for 'non-suitability' and received a general discharge."

Retired Command Sgt. Maj. Kermit Short was a platoon sergeant in Charlie Company when Ted came to the 50th Signal Battalion. "We heard," he said, "that an infantryman was going to be our sergeant major, and as signal people we were kind of apprehensive.

"About his second day with the battalion, he brought all the NCOs together and told us his philosophy as to what our outfit should be. He made us feel comfortable with him right away. He told us to be proud of ourselves, and to act and look like soldiers.

"In my twelve years in the army to that point, I had never seen a sergeant major lead from the front. He met with a company or a platoon every morning for physical training. If we had a road march, he was there. If we were doing a ten-kilometer run, he was not only there, but he was always up front. Sergeant Major Gaweda was visible and easy to talk to.

"I noticed that he would never walk by a piece of trash. Without saying a word, he would bend over and pick it up. Before his arrival we were not really disciplined. For example, there were paths crisscrossing the grass everywhere. The sergeant major made us walk on the sidewalks.

"In a matter of six months we were a different organization. Here was someone at the top who supported and cared for us. Looking back, I realize that Sergeant Major Gaweda's coming to the battalion was the best thing that ever happened to us. We were proud to serve with him.

"Wherever my later tours of duty took me, whenever I faced a problem, I would ask myself, 'What would Sergeant Major Gaweda do?' He had more influence on my thirty-year career than anyone else in the Army.

"I've told this story a hundred times, but it is a wonderful example of Ted's strong feelings about the importance of NCOs. I was at headquarters—and I'm not sure the sergeant major even knew I was there—when I overheard a company commander say:

"'Such and such a sergeant's no good, and I'm going to get rid of him. I don't need NCOs like him.'

"'Sir,' Sergeant Major Gaweda said, 'just listen to what you are saying. That sergeant makes you look good. Captain, if you and other officers think you are so great, I'm going to ask the colonel to declare a holiday for all NCOs. You wouldn't know where to start. You couldn't even put together a formation. You would fall on your face. Let the NCOs do their jobs, and if you have problems, sit down with them and talk about it.'

"That captain was mad when he came to the sergeant major's office, but he left with an education. There was another occasion when a young second lieutenant was upset about one of the sergeant major's decisions. Sergeant Major Gaweda said, 'Sit down, Lieutenant, and have a cup of coffee with me. You know, sir, you're absolutely right. I should have handled that situation differently, but let me tell you what I was trying to do.'

"The lieutenant was loving it, but then the sergeant major went on to tell him a number of reasons for his decision on whatever the matter was. When the lieutenant came out of the office, he said to me, 'God, I sure looked stupid in there, didn't I?'

"'Yes sir,'" I answered.

"In my personal judgment," Ted said, "a second lieutenant knows nothing. He is in the army to learn and is no different than a buck private. As the second lieutenant matures, he advances to rank and position. If he makes a mistake, I don't blame him. I go looking for his sergeant, whose job it is to make sure second lieutenants don't screw up.

"I used to tell officers, including generals, that every soldier has a sergeant. Sometimes they would ask, 'Sergeant Major, who's my sergeant?' and I would reply, 'I am, sir.'

"I later wrote a speech entitled 'Every Soldier Has a Sergeant,' and it seemed to be very popular with all ranks. In the talk, I said:

"'Every soldier has a sergeant, even the chief of staff of the army. A soldier should have to look no further than his sergeant for guidance, training, enthusiasm, and assistance of all types. A soldier must be able to communicate with his sergeant.

"'Each soldier's behavior must be given individual attention, be it commendation or a fitting punishment. The sergeant must help the soldier to stabilize himself and provide him with a foundation for future growth. The sergeant is the soldier's primary source of information.'"

Retired Staff Sgt. Timothy Inch was the legal clerk when Ted came to the 50th Signal Battalion. "It was rather evident to me that the sergeant major had been involved in much higher levels of command. I was a young buck sergeant then, and to have a conversation with him was an opportunity because he always imparted knowledge.

"His positive attitude was infectious. He would come in the morning and say, 'Hey, isn't this a great day? Isn't this the best day of the week?' Personal morale soared, and everybody felt good about what they were doing.

"He would walk up to a soldier who presented a sloppy appearance and say, 'You're the ugliest soldier I've seen today. You ought to be ashamed of yourself. You should take pride in yourself and your unit. Go and do something about the way you look.'

"Frequently, the soldier being criticized would get tears in his eyes. Given the way Sergeant Major Gaweda handled the situation, most usually realized that they deserved his rebuke and would straighten themselves up. On the other hand, the sergeant major would tell a smartly turned-out GI, 'You're the finest-looking soldier I've seen today. You make me and the army proud.'

"That soldier would feel so good that his feet would hardly touch the ground the rest of the day. Sergeant Major Gaweda would write forty to fifty letters a month commending people for a number of good things that he had observed.

"He was a great organizer, a diplomat, and part-time psychologist. He also was a career planner for the soldiers, preparing them for promotion to higher ranks. I believe a Gaweda-trained soldier always had an edge over the competition.

"He made a number of great speeches. I remember an indoctrination talk, when he told the troops, men and women alike, 'Do not get AIDS in the military. No one will love you. You'll be rejected by your sergeant, your father, your mother, your sister, and your brother.'

"One time, I helped him write a speech for delivery to a group of artillery officers at Fort Sill, Oklahoma. He had a million ideas rolling around in his head, so many things he wanted to say.

"Those things in his head were coming directly from his heart. He just needed help in expressing his thoughts. Pretty fluent in the English language, I took his ideas and put them into proper English.

"The sergeant major rehearsed the speech into a tape recorder and watched himself in the mirror, so he could check out the gestures and body language."

"It was an outstanding experience," Ted said. "I spoke to more than two hundred captains, who were taking an advanced artillery officers' training course. My topic was 'The Relationship Between Officers and Senior NCOs at the Battery Level.'

"They gave me one of those microphones that you hook on your shirt, so I didn't have to stand at a podium. I just walked around naturally and delivered my speech. Among other things, I told them:

"'Commanders must be satisfied to command and senior leaders satisfied to lead, so the sergeants and soldiers can prove their worth to their leaders and themselves. It is at this level where the mission is accomplished ... These philosophies must be paramount in your dealing with noncommissioned officers.

"'As battery commanders, your job will be rewarding, extremely taxing, and loaded with frustrations, for you command the soldiers at the doer-leader level, not the battalion commander. You are the top of the bottom of the heap.

"'Let me acquaint you with your senior NCOs at the doer level:

"'Your motor sergeant's job is to maintain your vehicles, so they can pull the guns to their firing locations 100 percent of the time. It is not the job of the battery motor officer!

"'Your supply sergeant's job is to provide your soldiers with boots, socks, ammunition and whatever is necessary to win the battle in the first round—not the battery supply officer!

"'Your communications sergeant's job is to establish and maintain your communications with the fire direction center and all other parties necessary to accomplish your primary mission—not the battery communications officer!

"'The chief of the firing battery is responsible for the implementation of your battery's firing mission from gun emplacement to the jerk of the lanyard that puts the round in the air. So the infantry soldier can trudge forward under the sound of your guns. He is your chief of smoke—not the battery executive officer.

"'Your mess sergeant's job is to insure that the coffee is hot in cold weather, that there is ice in the Kool-Aid when the weather is hot, and that the food your soldiers eat tastes just like Mom used to make—not the battery mess officer!'

"When I finished, a full colonel came up and asked me for a copy of my remarks, which I later mailed to him.

Sgt. Maj. Fred Dabney, who was a corporal and a buck sergeant when Ted Gaweda was command sergeant major of the 50th Signal Battalion, said, "My wife and I will always remember the sergeant major's positive impact on our lives.

"As an NCO family support representative, my wife attended monthly meetings at the NCO Club at Fort Bragg. All the spouses would be there, from the commanding general's wife on down. After three months of listening to the officers' spouses talk about the 'little enlisted wives,' she blew her top, and said, 'I am sick and tired of hearing about the little enlisted wives.

"'I've never heard anyone talk about the little officer's wives, you bunch of biddies, clucking hens, and so on.' After she said her piece, she stormed out of the room, came to the company area and told me what she had done.

"I told her to tell my first sergeant about it, so he wouldn't be blindsided. She saw him and then went home. Later in the day the first sergeant called me and said, 'Gina needs to see Sergeant Major Gaweda at 7:30 tomorrow morning at battalion headquarters.'

"Of course, Gina was quite nervous about all this and decided she would not go. 'Well,' the sergeant major said, 'I'm going to send a car and driver for her, because I really want her to come and see me.'

"With great trepidation, she accepted the ride to battalion headquarters. Sergeant Major Gaweda came out of his office, put his arm around her, and said, 'Thank you for coming to see me. I've always liked a woman with spunk. Mrs. Dabney,' he told her, 'I want you to know that I spoke with Col. Swede Nelson, deputy chief of staff of the XVIII Airborne Corps, and that based on your actions, the council will no longer use the words "little enlisted wives." I am proud of you.'

"He gave Gina a tour of the place, showing her all the plaques the battalion had been awarded and the pictures of army leaders who had served there, after which she was driven home. She has never forgotten that.

"Sergeant Major Gaweda was my mentor when it came to social affairs. After inviting Gina and me to a dinner-dance at the NCO club, he said, 'Fred, go out, buy your wife a party dress, and come to this affair.

"He helped teach me the social graces. Later in my career, Gina and I attended a number of regimental balls and other parties, and we always felt comfortable because of what we had learned from the sergeant major at Fort Bragg.

"As his clerk, I saw him do some amazing things. One day a company commander, who was a captain, came to the battalion to see the commander, and the sergeant major wouldn't let him in because his uniform was sloppy and kind of soiled, his boots were dirty, and he needed a haircut.

"'Get out of my way. I'm going in anyway,' the captain told him.

"Sergeant Major Gaweda stood in his doorway and said, 'No, sir, you are not going in. Please go home, sir, put on a clean uniform, get a haircut, and then come back.'

"So the guy came back and went in to see the battalion commander. He complained about the sergeant major's actions, whereupon the commander threw him out of his office.

"On another occasion, we were trying to get a hardship discharge for a soldier with family problems, but it was being stalled at a higher level. Saying, 'The officers don't know how to handle this,' Sergeant Major

Gaweda telephoned the sergeant major of the adjutant general unit where the discharge was being delayed.

"He got the guy on the phone and said, 'Hey, this is Ted Gaweda over at the 50th Signal Battalion. How are you doing, my friend?'

"They talked and talked, and finally they worked everything out. I thought the other sergeant major must have been a close friend of Sergeant Major Gaweda.

"After he hung up, he turned to me, smiled, and said, 'Well, I got it done, and I didn't even know that sonofabitch.'

"Sergeant Major Gaweda always watched over his soldiers and kept track of many of them, no matter where they went. I was attending a Primary Leadership Development Course at Fort Bragg in April 1979, and we were about to break for lunch when one of the senior people came to me and said, 'You have a visitor. He's standing out there.'

"I looked across one of the fields, and there he was. With that erect stance and military bearing, there was no mistaking him. I double-timed it out there, and we talked for ten or fifteen minutes. He wanted to know how things were going, was I doing okay, and all this good hurrah stuff. I was pleased and flattered that he had stopped by to check on me.

"When I returned to the building, one of the soldiers asked, 'Who was that general you were talking to?'"

CHAPTER EIGHTEEN

Homecoming for Edith

"After I fled from East Germany in the summer of 1955, letters were the only way I could communicate with my parents for years," Edith said. "Sadly, my father died at home in Ilmenau in 1966, without my ever having the chance to hear his voice once more.

"Beginning in the early 1970s, however, I was able to telephone my mother on Christmas Eve. I think the Communists softened their normally hard position at that time of year. Most times the calls would go through, but occasionally they did not.

"But in 1976, after the United States recognized East Germany and the two nations opened embassies in each other's country, I applied for and received a visa to visit my family at Ilmenau. We knew that this softened position on the part of East Germany was only for selfish reasons, because they badly needed any kind of Western currency. The East German mark was not recognized anywhere in the world and, therefore, could not buy anything.

"As an American soldier, Ted was not permitted to go. In fact, before Ted and I left Europe after our marriage, my mother had sent me a visitor's visa, but I could not go because it was against army regulations.

"I had been away from Ilmenau for more than twenty years when my visa was approved in 1976. I was going to take both boys to East Germany with me, but George was sixteen, and had just received his driver's license. He preferred to stay home with his dad, because he would have a chance to drive my car for four weeks.

"To be honest about it, I said to myself, 'Well, maybe traveling with two fighting and arguing teenagers is a bit too much anyway,' so I took Gregory, who was fourteen.

"He was very adventurous-minded and wanted to see new things all the time. We flew to Frankfurt, and then boarded a train for a two-hour ride to Fulda on the East German border. The train seemed to have on board only retired people.

"The Communists had a rule, saying that once someone was sixty years old, they could travel back and forth between East and West Germany to visit relatives. By then, they didn't care if the older ones escaped or not. The East German government probably was happy when it happened, because it would not have to keep paying benefits such as Social Security.

"Because we were foreigners and the only young people on the train, everyone was eyeing Gregory and me. The East Germans, many of whom had not been out of their country since the war, wanted to know where we were from and what life was like in America. They really were very nice.

"It would be hard for any Westerner to understand what took place behind the so-called 'Iron Curtain.' On the last stop before the East German border, people were throwing newspapers, magazines, books, Bibles, and Western literature from the train.

"Those items were forbidden, as were coins, electronic items, cameras, and any other currency not declared. East Germans returning home from visits with relatives in the West would spend their last West German mark to buy oranges, bananas, chocolate, and coffee from vendors at the train station. Fresh fruit was hard to find in the East.

"The train passed through many miles of no-man's land, where there was endless barbed wire with weapons pointing to the West. I could see heavily guarded watchtowers on top of the hills. Field glasses were directed toward incoming trains.

"The tensions in the railway cars rose to a high level. All conversation had stopped, and the only thing I could hear was the rattling of the train. At the East German frontier, border policemen with shepherd dogs began inspecting the train. You could hear them walking on top of the cars. I saw them poking underneath the train with twenty-foot poles and assumed they were looking for persons attempting to enter the country illegally, maybe even spies. It gave me an eerie feeling.

"The train's next stop was the town of Eisenach, famous for Wartburg Castle, where Martin Luther ignited the Protestant Reformation. As a young girl, I had visited there a number of times. My sister and her husband, Manfred, whom I had once dated briefly as a young girl, met us at Eisenach with his car.

"He was one of the few East Germans who owned a private car, because he was a scientist and a university professor. When I saw my sister for the first time, I was so happy that I cannot describe it. We embraced on the station platform, cried, and kept looking into each other's faces. Since we had exchanged photographs over the years, there was not a problem with recognition.

"However, I had not heard my sister's voice in more than twenty years, and it sounded strange to me. All of a sudden, I had a problem. Here I was, a person who could read, write, and speak German fluently, unable to get out a word in my native language.

"I stuttered like an idiot. I kept saying, 'Excuse me, excuse me,' but every other word came out in garbled German and English. Because of my excitement, I just could not make any sense, and it took me about two days to start saying what I really wanted to say.

"After a ride of about an hour and a half, I arrived at my mother's home. There was this big scream, 'yeahhhhhh,' that seemed a mile long, when my mother and I saw each other. We hugged and cried and laughed with joy. It was the high point of my life, far more so than anything I had ever encountered.

"Everyone we met in Ilmenau was very polite to Gregory and me, and many wanted to practice their English with us. For example, Gregory came down with an eye infection from dust. I took him to an eye doctor's office even though I didn't have an appointment.

"When we walked in, the waiting room was full of people. It looked like we were in for at least a two-hour wait. I told the nurse, 'I am visiting here from America, and my son has an eye problem. Can I arrange for him to see the doctor?'

"In a really loud voice, one that everyone in the waiting room could hear clearly, she said, 'Oh, you must be the lady that called earlier for an appointment.'

"I didn't catch on right away. I was slow, but then I realized I was getting special treatment. Within ten minutes, Gregory and I were in the doctor's office. He gave Gregory a thorough examination and gave him medicine for his eye infection.

"But then, he wouldn't let us go. He wanted to practice his English on us. His dream was to visit the United States. He had encountered American soldiers as a World War II prisoner of war, somewhere in Italy, I believe. We became so friendly with him that I considered sending him a postcard when I came home.

"We met many people who were curious about the United States and wished they could travel here and to the rest of the world, but in 1976 they were trapped behind the Iron Curtain.

"When our visit came to a close, I again left my family behind with a heavy heart and many tears on both sides. There always was the hope that I would return soon. Fortunately, they could not hear the sigh of relief when Gregory and I left this beautiful but imprisoned country.

"Gregory had received an education in what freedom really means that no teacher could have taught him. Later, he wrote a thesis in college on communism. It had been the ultimate sacrifice to leave my loved ones behind, not knowing if I would ever be able to return.

"But I could not imagine having stayed. I marveled at the goodness of my Maker and thanked Him for steering my life in a different direction. Fortunately, I was able to return to East Germany and my family three more times."

"When I returned in 1980, the Communists had tightened restrictions on foreign visitors. A woman border guard was very impolite. She searched me, tipped over my suitcase and emptied it. I'm sure she did it on purpose.

"My relatives, with the exception of my mother, had to get permission to receive a Western visitor in their homes. My mom didn't have to because she was already on Social Security and a widow's pension. The Communists only worried about the younger generations.

"On my next visit, in 1984, it was obvious that East Germany had visibly tightened the noose around its people. The customs agent told everyone in my compartment to leave, so she could search the American visitor without witnesses. Again, my suitcase was dumped on the floor. Every compartment in my wallet was examined and my address book was carefully studied.

"I was treated like a suspected spy. After it was over, I sat there exhausted and drenched in perspiration. I had seen customs agents take visitors off the train for no reason at all.

"Meanwhile, my sister's husband had been instructed not to have any contact with Westerners, and certainly not in his house. He and my sister defied these orders and I stayed with them many times. As before, as a Western visitor I had to report to the local police station within twenty-four hours. No one dared to disobey these orders. They were posted everywhere.

"Your passport was taken and you were seated in a room by yourself, as if in preparation for an interrogation. The East German officials searched their network to see if your name appeared on any of their suspected spy lists. Those were always tense moments. Without your passport, you were at their mercy.

"Since my mom lived in an apartment, my next step was to register in the Communist party boss's visitor book, which listed every apartment and residence. This way, your comings and goings were closely monitored. As a visitor, you could not leave the city shown on your visa. During my early visits, we traveled to many, many places, but always under the protection of my brother-in-law. Scientists then had special privileges, but all that had changed by 1984.

"One day my sister and I were strolling leisurely downtown, arm-in-arm, when she suddenly disengaged herself from me and started walking twenty feet away. She had seen a party chief from her husband's university approaching and did not want to jeopardize his job. I tried to understand. I felt sorry for them, but at the same time I was furious that such a police state was allowed to exist.

"My sister and brother-in-law were one of the few two-car families in East Germany. Only Communist party members, sports personalities, entertainers, and the intelligentsia had that privilege. The average citizen, even if he or she had money, had their names on a ten-year waiting list for an automobile.

"All other living conditions were difficult. Long lines for the most basic necessities were everywhere. People on the streets hardly ever smiled. Of course, there wasn't much to smile about. In contrast to other conditions, alcoholic beverages were always available and in abundance. Many Communist countries had a high rate of alcoholism. The alcohol helped the people drown out their miserable lives.

"There were double standards everywhere. Some had the luck to have Western currencies from relatives. For these people, there were so-called 'Inter-Shops,' where one could buy Florida orange juice for eight D-marks, or four dollars, a can. There also were the 'Exquisite shops' for citizens with high incomes, where imported goods were available. Of course, the average citizen could not afford any of that.

"When Mrs. V.I.P. called the butcher shop for a special cut of meat, it was ready when she arrived. For the rest of the population, the shelves were always empty. This was communism, not hearsay. I have lived it and seen it with my own eyes.

"My departure that year from East Germany resembled a criminal being smuggled out of the country. The place where the Inter-train left to take me across the East German border to catch my flight at Frankfurt was two hours away from Ilmenau by car. Since my brother-in-law could not be seen with me, my sister took me on a forty-five-minute drive to what appeared to be a deserted barn, which was in front of a closed gasoline station.

"By then my brother-in-law had arrived in a second car. My sister parked her car and all three of us got in his automobile, which took me to my destination. It was like a scene from an old spy movie, and I kept thinking, 'If only someone in Fayetteville, North Carolina, could see me now!'

"Had it not been for my family, I would have never gone back.

"Years later at the Brandenburg Gate in Berlin, our president of the United States, Ronald Reagan, said these words: 'Mr. Gorbachev, tear down that wall.' No one had ever said that before. The events that followed will be forever etched in our hearts and minds. They became another high point in my life.

"In October 1989, the Berlin Wall came down as the old Soviet Union began collapsing. There was now a great deal of free movement between East and West. Because of this, Ted and I visited my family together for the first time in 1990.

"By then, Gregory was an Army captain stationed in Berlin, so we were able to visit with him and his family before my sister and her husband drove us to Ilmenau. It was the first time they had ever seen Ted. It was quite exciting as we drove through the ruins of the infamous Checkpoint Charlie, which was once the gateway to freedom in the West and the entrance to repression in the East.

"There was much happiness at my mom's apartment when Ted met his mother-in-law for the first time, even though he had been married to her daughter for thirty-one years. He asked her how she felt about all the changes that had taken place, now that almost everything was available.

"Her answer was: 'Well, before we had only one kind of cheese in the supermarket. Now, there are fifty kinds. It is all so confusing. And now, I am too old to travel.' So for the older generation, which had paid for Hitler's war, the freedom came too late.

"Manfred made his first visit to the United States when he attended a scientific meeting in New York City in March 1993. Ted and I wanted to buy him an airplane ticket to Fayetteville, but he said he wanted to see more of the country than just Wall Street and Broadway.

"We told him he would regret it, but he came by Greyhound bus. He must have seen a lot of the country, because it was a fourteen-hour ride. He didn't seem the worse for wear, and we had a nice family visit.

"Ted and I continue to travel to Ilmenau, making our most recent trip in August 1998. For years we had offered to buy and pay for the installation of a telephone for my mother, but the entire apartment building was not wired for phones. The only one there was in the office of the Communist superintendent.

"That changed in February 1996, and now my eighty-seven-year-old mother has her very own telephone, and I can talk to her as I please. That certainly is an improvement over those once-a-year Christmas Eve calls of the past."

"Above our desk at home, Ted and I keep a framed piece of rock from the Berlin Wall, which Gregory brought us. Strangely, our younger son stood on that collapsing wall during those eventful days. It seemed that fate had come full circle."

CHAPTER NINETEEN

Battalion to Brigade

"Lt. Col. Richard Earle replaced Colonel Markham as commander of the 50th Signal Battalion in the spring of 1979," Ted said. "Before his departure, Colonel Markham became the second officer to recommend that I be advanced to the position of sergeant major of the army.

"He said some nice things about me, writing: 'Command Sergeant Major Gaweda is the most professionally competent and dedicated command sergeant major I have ever known . . . His outstanding contribution has been his training of junior leaders. He conveys to them his own high standards of discipline, appearance, and job performance.'

"Retired Maj. Gen. Leon Childs, who was a colonel commanding the 35th Signal Brigade, endorsed Colonel Markham's recommendation. In all, I was considered for the position of sergeant major of the army three times. In each case, my name was out on a list of men to be selected for the post. Since I was never chosen, I assumed a better person was selected. Nevertheless, I was deeply honored even to be on the list.

"'The color guard which Command Sergeant Major Gaweda trained has won groupwide competition for three consecutive quarters. Command Sergeant Major Gaweda is an excellent public speaker and an invaluable practical advisor to the commander and all principal staff officers.'"

"Before taking command of the signal battalion," Earle said, "I was cooling my heels at the headquarters of the XVIII Airborne Corps, when Ted wandered by my office. I think he wanted to be sure that he approved of me.

"I tried my best to convince him that I could live up to his standards, and at the same time I wanted to see if I approved of him. We both came to the conclusion that we would get along well, since our personalities meshed so nicely.

"I don't recall our ever having a contradiction, much less an argument. From the beginning, we seemed to understand what the other was thinking and feeling. Everything was as smooth as it could be.

"Ted acted differently than other sergeants major I had known. He grabbed hold of responsibility and ran with it. The best description I can think of is 'self-starter.' You never had to tell Ted what to do. In fact, I don't think anybody ever did. Well, maybe his mother did, or maybe his wife, Edith, does.

"Intuitively and instinctively, Ted always did the right thing. He instilled pride in the soldiers. No man fights for just the dollar, and no man fights for himself. He fights only for pride. It's the only damn thing that keeps you going when you're cold, hungry, tired, and maybe even sick. If you are a proud man, you'll keep fighting, but if you are a wimp, you'll run like hell or surrender.

"Ted and I were about forty-six or forty-seven years old, which meant we were pretty much out of the fighting business. I didn't figure I would be running around again with a rifle in some jungle. We were training young soldiers to pick up that duty. We owed the army that.

"I told Ted recently, 'Now that we are in our sixties, I feel pretty damn good about things. I have friends who spent the greater part of their lives working in a bank room or something similar and now are concerned about being too old to do the things they always dreamed of.

"I would say that Ted Gaweda and Dick Earle did the things they dreamed about—travel, adventure, comradeship, and dedicated service to country. I also remember all the fun we had, although at the time we may not have thought so.

"My wife used to make rum cakes, and she was very generous with the rum. I would take them to battalion headquarters, and Ted would eat a whole cake all by himself."

"Yes," Ted interjected, "I ate all of this damned rum cake one time and jumped in a jeep to go home. An MP stopped me and gave me a breathalyzer test. 'Look,' I told him, 'I haven't even seen any booze, only rum cake. I guess I ate one slice too many.'"

"Ted and I shared the experience of commanding women soldiers," Earle said. "The two of us took the approach that, first of all, they were soldiers, but we also knew we had to use common sense with the women. For example, we would not station one by herself at a lonely guard post in the middle of the night.

"When we did push-ups at the physical training exercises in the morning, no one ever stood over them, counting. They might not have done as many as the PT leader, but nobody does. After six months in the battalion, the women were in great physical condition, and many could outrun and outmarch the men, and I'm talking about four-mile runs and ten-mile marches.

"You know, there is always some shithead who doesn't like another soldier because of race or gender. People like that normally do not get very far in the army because they are found out by their contemporaries. Then they get to become civilians.

"Some exceptions had to be made for women soldiers. One of those was the difference in upper-body strength between men and women. I was on a night jump one time when I noticed a small soldier standing next to me who was loaded down with gear.

"After a few moments, I realized the soldier was a woman. She had been assigned to carry a huge bag that went all the way down to her boots plus other paraphernalia. Adding to the weight, of course, was her parachute.

"She was bent over, trying to carry some 160 pounds of weight on her shoulders and back. She simply couldn't do it. It was the dumbest goddamn thing I had ever seen. It made no sense at all.

"You had to be prepared for almost anything in the army. I remember getting up one Sunday morning when the battalion was in the field and marveling at the beautiful day. The sky was clear and the birds were chirping. Everything was just perfect.

"But then Ted walked up to me with a worried look on his face and said, 'Sir, I need to talk with you. We've got a problem.'

"'Ted,' I said, 'we can't have a problem, not today.'

"Then he told me that one of my company commanders, a captain, had solicited a sergeant and had actually made a pass at him. The sergeant bolted and told Ted what had happened. This was not a male-female thing. Both individuals in this situation were men.

"I was dealing with a gay captain. When it came to getting him out of the army, we were on shaky ground. First off, we did not have a witness. The options were to keep him in command and have an investigation, which would have lasted six months and destroyed the morale of the company, or relieve and transfer him.

"I confronted the captain with the accusation and told him I was transferring him to corps headquarters.

"'But I didn't do it,' he said.

"'Well, Captain,' I said, 'I don't believe you. I worked with this sergeant in another assignment, and I don't believe he would make up a story like that.'

"He was sent to corps and then to Germany. It is my understanding that he left the army after he was caught in a room with another soldier. Someone told me that he ended up in Hollywood as an actor. So much for a perfect day."

"In December 1979, I left my many friends in the signal battalion," Ted said, "and became the command sergeant major of the 35th Signal Brigade. Colonel Earle was very kind in his last efficiency rating, saying, 'Command Sergeant Major Gaweda is a man of integrity. He is clearly the finest soldier and the most outstanding noncommissioned officer I have known during my twenty-three years of military service.'

"To add frosting on the cake, Col. Thomas B. McDonald III endorsed Colonel Earle's rating and added, 'The brigade will benefit in great measure from this man of inspiring character and strength.'

"I had only been at the brigade for eight or nine months when First Sgt. Wilbert Brown, my former Headquarters Company first sergeant at the 50th Signal Battalion, showed up at my office. You could see the pain in his eyes, which were shedding tears.

"A young woman company commander had given him a poor efficiency rating. He was on a list to go to the Sergeant Major Academy, and if the rating stood up, his army career would be at a dead end. Colonel Earle had not yet seen the report.

"Brown told me that someone had poured piss in her ear about his not being loyal to her. I knew him well enough to know that someone was lying and it wasn't him. I found out that actually he was teaching her and trying to be her mentor, and there was resentment. She was the first woman company commander in the battalion, and everyone treated her with kid gloves.

"I told Colonel Earle what I knew. He called the company commander to his office and told her that she was being unduly harsh with this talented soldier. When she resisted amending the report, the colonel said that if she refused to make a change, she would be given a similar report card. The report was amended.

"I transferred Brown to the brigade headquarters company, where he was the first sergeant. He went to the Sergeant Major Academy and was graduated with honors."

Now retired, Brown said of the incident, "I owe my life to Sergeant Major Gaweda, because he saved my ass. Without him, none of the good things in my Army career would have happened. He was the type of person that could be either liked or hated, but the large majority of the guys who served under him not only liked him, they loved him.

"If you were right, he would go to bat for you. He had a tremendous sense of fairness. I retired in January 1990 after thirty years and two months of service to my country."

Maj. Gen. Childs said of Gaweda: "I often thought that if he could train every noncommissioned officer in the army, we would have an unbelievable army.

"He displayed outstanding poise, confidence, and professionalism. He was distinctly a cut above, unique and special. Ted would take junior officers aside, never in front of anyone, of course, and tell them what they were doing wrong. As a consequence, we have a lot of fine field grade officers today.

"He led by example, and no matter what he did, you could count on it being flawless. There is no question that part of my success was due to having Sergeant Major Gaweda helping run one of my hot battalions."

"When you've been in the army for a long time," Ted said, "you learn that many veteran soldiers know at least one person you know. This really came home to me because of my long-time acquaintance with a soldier named Joe Lupyak, whom I had served with off and on at Fort Bragg.

"In 1968, I went to Sydney, Australia, on a five-day R & R leave from Vietnam. A couple of us were having a beer in the hotel lobby bar, when we struck up a conversation with several long-haired civilians who looked like hippies.

"One young man with long blond locks, who obviously was an American, asked what outfit I was with. 'I'm with the Special Operations Group at Nakhon Phanom, Thailand,' I answered.

"'Oh yeah,' he said, 'I used to be in that outfit. Did you come out of Fort Bragg?'

"Somewhat startled, I said, 'Yes,' but I was even more surprised when he asked, 'By the way, do you know Joe Lupyak?'

"'Of course I know Joe Lupyak, and I have for a long time,' I replied. The young man had been on Joe's team in Vietnam.

"Eleven years later, I was in Tokyo waiting to catch a military flight back to Fort Bragg, when I struck up a conversation with an Air Force colonel who was a C-141 pilot. As I was telling him about my Fort Bragg background, he suddenly asked, 'Do you know Joe Lupyak?'

"'My God,' I said, 'everyone knows Joe Lupyak.'

"It turned out that the colonel piloted the plane that carried Joe and other Special Forces raiders in the daring attempt to rescue some seventy American prisoners from Son Tay Prison in North Vietnam. The raid was unsuccessful because the prisoners had been moved.

"Now retired, Joe works at Fort Bragg as chief of the training division at the Special Forces school. Every time I see him, we both laugh about his being the man everyone knows, and he loves to tell the story to anyone who will listen."

CHAPTER TWENTY

Korea, Last Tour

"It was October 1981," Ted said, "and my retirement from the army was only eighteen months away. It was a bittersweet time for me, as I dreaded the day that I would give my last salute. Yet I knew that Edith needed me at home, more than ever now that our older son George was married and Gregory was away at college.

"But all of that changed when I received a telephone call from Sergeant Major of the Army William Connally, who told me I had been selected to serve beyond the thirty-year mark. It was a tremendous honor, and I could not turn it down.

"Prior to the mid-1960s, there was no limit on years of service. You could stay in the army almost as long as you wanted, if you could continue to pass the required physical examination. But in the latter half of that decade, a new policy was issued, saying that retirement was compulsory after thirty years.

"But there was an exception. The Department of the Army, based on its needs, would select a handful of people to serve beyond thirty years. When I was chosen, I was one of five or six soldiers so recognized. My God, I was proud.

"Now that I would not be retiring in eighteen months, I faced another overseas assignment. It turned out to be Korea, for the fourth and last time!

I said good-bye to my many friends in the 35th Signal Brigade and left for my new post in February 1982.

Colonel McDonald, the brigade commander, gave me a hell of a send-off, filling me with pride when he said, 'Command Sergeant Major Gaweda is the finest soldier I have ever known. In his every word and action, he exemplifies what it means to be a professional leader of men. He should be the sergeant major of the army.'

"My new assignment in Korea was command sergeant major of Special Troops, Combined Field Army, which was made up of both American and Korean soldiers. It was a brigade level position. This was my sixth one-year overseas tour without my family.

"I felt pretty gloomy flying into that mountainous and mostly barren land on a cold February day. I swear that Korea can be the hottest and coldest place on earth. In August, temperatures can top more than hundred degrees, and fall to thirty below zero in winter.

"Edith and I resumed our ritual of writing daily letters to each other and tearing dates off the calendar. I guess that was what kept us going, but it was a tough time for us, particularly for her because she was now alone in the house.

"My new boss was Col. William V. Johnson, who was a top-notch commander. I was responsible for about twenty-five hundred men and women at eleven installations scattered across South Korea. Shortly after my arrival at Special Troops headquarters at Camp Red Cloud, I asked Lt. Gen. James B. Vaught, commander of the Combined Field Army, what were his priorities for me as the post command sergeant major, what were the things he most wanted me to do.

"I had known General Vaught for many years, but had never served under him directly. He told me he was concerned about the appearance of the soldiers, their conditioning, and the lack of military courtesy. The men and women in the unit were not bad people. They just had not been properly trained and disciplined.

"Out of shape, with bad haircuts, wearing sloppy uniforms with unshined boots, and lacking military courtesy, they lacked basic soldiering skills. Add to that those who were badly overweight, and I did not have many troops fit for combat. The whole purpose of the army is to have physically fit troops immediately deployable when called upon.

"With the solid backing of Colonel Johnson and General Vaught, I took the bit in my teeth and jumped right in. I quickly established a weight-loss program. There were 350 men and women at Camp Red Cloud. Every soldier had to be weighed quarterly. After the weigh-ins, the medics declared twenty-four men and three women overweight.

"For those who could not run the required two miles in sixteen minutes during morning physical training or PT, I organized extra PT sessions at night. I had the mess hall prepare special fat-free menus for these people.

"The overweight soldiers had to come to my office every Saturday morning to be weighed. I know it was embarrassing, particularly for the women, but at the end of six weeks, all twenty-seven soldiers had met their ideal weight.

"I told the men with bad haircuts that they were the ugliest soldiers I had seen in my long military career. I showed them pictures of what a regulation army haircut looked like. I mean I had those guys in tears.

"I told the barbers—and there was one at every installation—that only three haircut styles would be acceptable: the Sergeant Major Gaweda cut, the Colonel Johnson cut, and the command general cut. General Vaught, who was balding, wore his hair a little longer than me, but we both were neatly trimmed. The soldiers could choose which one they wanted. I also said there would be no more block haircuts, where the hair is not tapered on the back of the head and neck.

"When I saw a soldier with a really lousy haircut, I would say, 'Send your supervisor to see me.'

"'My supervisor is Colonel So and So,' one master sergeant told me.

"'Well, send the colonel to see me,' I responded.

"The colonel came to my office with the master sergeant, and I showed him a copy of army regulations concerning haircuts. He pointed out that the regulations said a block haircut was permissible if done in the 'modern way.'

"'Sir,' I said, 'I am the interpreter of what is the modern way. I am the only one being paid to interpret army regulations. You, sir, are not being paid to do that. This soldier needs a haircut, and, by the way, sir, so do you.' I told Colonel Johnson what happened. However, the colonel never talked to Johnson. Needless to say, the colonel and the master sergeant got themselves two good-looking haircuts.

"I also held monthly NCO development meetings, where we would have an open exchange of ideas between several hundred sergeants. In all, six command sergeants major supported me in this endeavor.

"We operated an NCO academy at Camp Jackson, where we put 150 NCOs through the program every four weeks. It was a requirement that someone from each NCOs chain of command make a visit to the academy at least twice during the training. Of course, I was over there at least three times a week.

"I told the command sergeant major running the academy that all visitors, regardless of rank, must look as good as the trainees, who were being taught to present a smartly dressed and clean-cut appearance.

"'If a visitor shows up needing a haircut or wearing an improper uniform and boots not shined,' I said, 'he should be refused admittance. And if someone doesn't like it, have them call me.'

"Several high-ranking officers were turned away and they were mad as hell. Their sergeants major telephoned my office to complain, but I said, 'All they have to do is meet the army standards. If they want to file a formal complaint, let them do so with Colonel Johnson or General Vaught.'

"I was really upset when an obese master sergeant reported to me for duty at Camp Red Cloud. He was at least sixty-five pounds overweight, which meant he never should have been sent overseas.

"'Let me see your clearance papers,' I said.

"He handed them to me, and I saw that some warrant officer in the States had signed them, certifying that the master sergeant met all the requirements for an overseas assignment.

"'Look,' I said, 'I don't know who this warrant officer is, but he must be your friend. Obviously, he isn't familiar with army regulations, which state that a soldier cannot be deployed overseas if he or she is overweight.

"'Therefore, I am going to send you back to where you came from. You will not be allowed to sign in here, because you are not properly fit.

"He just couldn't believe it. I mean he just could not believe it.

"'Look,' I said, 'I'll tell you what I am going to do. I'm going to send you to the sergeant major of the Eighth Army, Roosevelt Martain. If he has a job for you, fine.'

"I told the sergeant major, 'I don't want to take the responsibility of writing this man's next of kin after he collapses and dies during physical training. He has twenty-two years in the army, so he is fully qualified for retirement.'

"I never heard a word back from the Eighth Army sergeant major, but I do know the man was sent back to the States, where he did retire. He had made that long trip over the ocean on an airliner and then had to turn around and go right back. What a waste of taxpayer's money.

"It was my job to monitor the behavior and mental state of my soldiers, just as it was to make them combat ready. In fact, the two were intertwined. They couldn't be 100 percent combat ready if they were in a poor mental state or feeling guilty about their behavior.

"I would always arise early and begin running at 5:00 A.M., an hour before I would join the soldiers for regular PT. There was a rule that everyone had to be off the streets between midnight and 5:00 A.M.

"As I was running I would see senior NCOs returning from passes, kissing, embracing, and holding hands with their Korean girlfriends just before they came through the compound's main gate. I didn't worry about the single men, as long as their hanky-panky took place during off-duty hours and they didn't make a spectacle of themselves.

"But when I saw the senior NCOs, whom I knew were married, it upset me. They would try to hide their faces behind newspapers and magazines, but I knew who they were, which meant they were due for an office call with the command sergeant major.

"I usually would call the NCO by his first name, saying, 'Jim, David, or whatever, you probably wonder why you are here.'

"'Yes, that's true, Sergeant Major,' was the usual reply.

"'The reason you are here,' I would say, 'was that it was brought to my attention that yesterday, at such and such a time, you were seen showing affection to a female Korean national. You were holding hands with her and more. There is nothing wrong with being attentive to a woman, but I happen to know that you are married and your wife is somewhere in the States. All the soldiers in your charge know that this is not the right thing to do.

"'I also know you receive mail from home on almost a daily basis. I don't think what you are doing with that Korean girl is right. Do you think it's right?'

"This question almost always brought forth a mumbled, 'No, Sergeant Major.'

"'Then why are you doing it?' I would ask.

"'Well, I got lonely,' the soldier would say, and then go into the age-old song and dance about needing female companionship and on and on and on.

"'Look,' I would inquire, 'do you believe that your wife at home is not lonely? I hope I never see you again with a woman that is not your wife. Do you have anything to say?'

"'No, Sergeant Major' was the normal meek reply.

"I must have had that kind of meeting every week. I am sure there were repeat offenders, but never within my eyesight. They knew where I stood.

"General Harold K. Johnson, while chief of staff of the army, said that 'the individual who cheats on his wife will also cheat on me.'

"Think about that. It is true. In combat you must be able to rely on those around you that you lead and those you follow. Anything that diminishes your own self respect creates a hardship for your family, such as attempting to support both a family and a girlfriend. It creates adversity which impacts on both your family and the soldiers under your charge.

"Colonel Johnson told me that I was the most authoritarian person he had ever known, military or civilian. After my first six weeks on the job, everyone hated me, but six months later they loved me. They had become proud of their physical fitness and military bearing.

"I wasn't at Camp Red Cloud long when I learned that soldiers getting ready to go home were being ripped off by a Korean tailor on the post. He would collect the GI's money for a new civilian suit, but never had it ready when it was the soldier's time to leave. I could understand one mistake, maybe two, but when you get fifteen complaints, that's another matter. The guy was a thief.

"I did not have the authority to fire the little bastard, so I declared him a security risk and told the military police to refuse him admittance to the post. After that situation was ironed out, if you'll forgive the pun, I hired a new tailor and warned him that if he ever tried to cheat a GI, he would be history too.

"'Oh, don't you worry,' he said in good English. 'I will provide good service to the soldiers,' which he did.

"As usual, I took charge of the color guard and outlined my normal requirements for a soldier to be in the guard. Each man had to be six feet, two inches tall and have a waist of thirty-two inches or less. Since we were a Combined Field Army, made up of Americans and South Koreans, I wanted a Korean to carry his national flag.

"The Korean sergeant major, my counterpart, failed to provide me with a soldier who met my specifications. They were all too short. 'Well,' I told him, I'll just have to have an American carry your flag.'

"'No, no, no, you can't do that,' he said. 'It is not permitted.'

"'Then find me somebody,' I answered.

"I don't know where he found him, but suddenly I had a six-foot, one-inch Korean soldier, who carried his country's flag. Everywhere I went, I carried a set of army dress blue uniforms that I got years ago from the United Nations Command, Eighth Army Honor Guard Company.

"A first-class color guard, marching with a band, is a real asset to a post. It can lift a soldier's morale and fill him with pride and patriotism. I received countless letters of appreciation and commendation from commanders at almost every place I served.

"I viewed Camp Red Cloud as my town. One time the president of South Korea announced he was going to pay us a visit. His security people said that when he arrived, everyone had to be off the streets and away from the windows.

"'Hey, this is my Dodge City,' I protested. 'What do you mean that I have to be off the streets? I am the command sergeant major of this post, and I will go anywhere I please. The security team relented and said that everyone had to be off the streets and away from the windows except me. I could go wherever I wanted.

"Colonel Johnson was reassigned in early July 1982 and replaced by Col. William Orlov, a highly educated officer. Before Johnson departed, I held a farewell dinner for him at the Papason NCO Club, which was hosted by the NCOs of Camp Red Cloud.

"I was most grateful for what he did before departing. He wrote in my Enlisted Evaluation Report: 'Command Sergeant Major Gaweda moved into his assignment with vigor, enthusiasm, and authority rarely seen in soldiers of any grade—officer or senior noncommissioned officer . . . At his insistence, the NCOs have been given meaningful responsibilities and are performing admirably . . . His advice and assistance are sought by officers, NCOs, and junior enlisted personnel. There are no responsibilities too great for him to handle.'

"It took me about twelve seconds," Orlov said, "to figure out that Ted was a soldier's soldier, because of his appearance, his demeanor, and the way he interacted with the troops. I had a number of young captains that needed grooming and Ted was an ideal teacher. He was the soul of tact when it came to letting junior officers know that they were not doing something in the proper way.

"When Ted saw a soldier doing a great job, he would come by my office and say, 'Let's go give a soldier a medal.' It wasn't a cheap thing by any means. He had a nose for spotting truly outstanding people.

"I would ask the adjutant to write up the award, which usually was for an Army Achievement Medal, and I would do the honors. It was a tremendous morale booster and caused other GI's, I am sure, to say to themselves, 'Hey, if I do a good job, maybe I'll get a bit of recognition too.'

"Ted Gaweda and I bore an awesome responsibility, which was that American mothers and fathers had entrusted us with the welfare of their sons and daughters. It was our job to honor that trust and do our best to return our soldiers safely to their families."

"We worked hard to provide recreation on the post," Ted said. "I remember sitting in a staff meeting where there was a discussion about adding nine extra greens to our little nine-hole golf course. The idea was to put a second green off each fairway, which meant that a golfer could go around twice and play eighteen holes. An engineer estimated that it would cost three hundred thousand dollars to build the additional nine greens.

"'Three hundred thousand dollars in Korea?' I said incredulously. 'You must be shitting me. You can buy half of Korea for three hundred thousand.'

"'Well, that's what is required,' the guy said. 'You're talking about moving one hundred twenty tons of sand, a like amount of gravel, and one hundred tons of topsoil.'

"'Wait a minute,' I said. 'Before you commit any money, let me look into it.' We controlled the nearby Injum River, which would provide the sand, and the U.S. Eighth Army Engineering Battalion had trucks.

"I spoke to the battalion sergeant major about hauling sand from the river, and he said, 'No problem, I'll give you six 20-ton trucks. In fact, it will help me because some of our young drivers need training on navigating the big trucks. This will give them some practice. You'll have a sergeant and driver for each vehicle.

"Now things were beginning to look up. I also was able to 'borrow' a front-end loader and diesel fuel to operate it. I found the gravel and rocks almost under my nose. A Korean contractor was installing a new sewer and water system at Camp Red Cloud. He was excavating tons of rock to put pipes under the ground.

"'What are you doing with this stuff?' I asked him.

"'Oh, I'm hauling it over to the Injum River,' he said.

"When I asked how much it was costing him to do that, he gave me a large number. 'You can save a lot of money,' I said, 'by just piling the rocks in the area which I have outlined with engineering tape at Camp Red Cloud.' He thought that was a great idea. We had nine piles of rocks, which served as foundations for the new greens.

"I also got a real break on the topsoil. A Korean colonel with the Combined Field Army very graciously told me I could take topsoil from a farm he owned. The engineers' twenty-tonners hauled the free topsoil to the golf course.

"All supplies were in place by the Fourth of July 1982, and two months later we had an eighteen-hole golf course. It cost absolutely nothing. No money was exchanged anywhere.

"Colonel Orlov had a charming Korean secretary, whom everyone called Miss Kim. The name Kim was as common in Korea as the name Smith in the United States. She had started working for the army in 1954 and was about fifty-five years old. Colonel Orlov didn't give her a great deal of correspondence.

"When I started loading her up with things that required a lot of typing, she became angry at the increased magnitude of her work. I spoke to Colonel Orlov about this, and he suggested I ask her what she wanted for her upcoming birthday, which I did.

"Without hesitation, she picked up the post exchange catalogue and pointed to a picture of a pearl necklace that cost seven hundred dollars. 'I would like to have this,' she said, adding, 'I don't expect you to buy. I get the money.'

"Given post exchange prices, there was no way she could afford to purchase pearls of that quality in Korea. They would have cost many times seven hundred dollars. I telephoned the PX manager, who also was named Kim, and asked about the availability of the necklace.

"'Sergeant Major Gaweda,' he said, you are a very lucky man. There is in Korea right now a sales representative of the company that offers this necklace. You also very lucky because it is on sale for four hundred dollars.'

"So Miss Kim got her pearl necklace. I'm not sure if she paid for them or not. It would not surprise me to learn that Colonel Orlov paid for them, because he wanted to get her something for her birthday and she was very loyal to him. Anyway, she stopped complaining about how much correspondence I was giving her.

"On this overseas assignment, I was asked to organize the first Korean chapter of the Association of the U.S. Army. The organization's annual convention was held in October 1982 at the Sheraton Hotel, Washington, D.C.

"I was honored to accompany the new Korean chapter to our nation's capital. I also was delighted because Edith drove to Washington with members of the Fayetteville chapter. We had three wonderful days together.

"I was informed by the Department of the Army in the first week of January 1983 that I again was being considered for the post of sergeant major of the army. This had happened twice before. Lt. Gen. Vaught, Colonel Orlov, and Gen. Robert W. Sennewald, commander-in-chief of U.S. forces in Korea, strongly endorsed my nomination.

"When General Vaught announced his retirement in January 1983, the noncommissioned officers held a farewell dinner for him at the Papason NCO Club. It was handled entirely by NCOs. There were 250 sergeants there, and among the officers present was the deputy commander of the Combined Field Army, a Korean major general.

"Other than General Vaught, I was the only speaker. I said, 'Because of men like General Vaught, the army is in its highest state of readiness in the nation's history. His frequent family separations on combat assignments had not been easy for General Vaught and his family. His army years were filled with sacrifice and achievement, performed with honor for our country and its people.'

"We gave the general replicas of the unit colors and other mementos. When the dinner ended, the Korean general couldn't believe that it had been arranged totally by American Army NCOs.

"The day before General Vaught's retirement ceremony, I went to his office and briefed him on the sequence of events. He was in a cheerful mood and after I finished, he thanked me and said, 'Ted, that was a superb briefing.' Before my departure, he handed me the following letter:

"'As I leave Korea, I want to thank you for your dedicated service in support of our Combined Field Army (ROK/US). As the post sergeant major, your outstanding job performance increased the operational readiness of the Combined Field Army.

"'I have been fortunate in my career to have had the honor and pleasure to serve with dedicated and professional soldiers like you. I commend you for your superior work and encourage you to continue. Press on!'

"I also organized and supervised the actual retirement ceremony itself, which was to take place in what we called the Little Green Village, a grassy area lined with trees in front of the Officers Club. The plan called for a fifteen-gun salute by a 105-millimeter howitzer. The Officers Club had a large picture window, which overlooked the Little Green Village.

"As we were preparing for a dress rehearsal, I told Brig. Gen. John 'Doc' Bahnsen, chief of staff of the Combined Field Army, that since it was only twenty degrees outside, I feared the sound waves from cannon blast would shatter the club's picture window. I suggested taping the glass.

"Nah, there's no need to do that,' General Bahnsen said. 'That window is not going to break.'

"When the 105 fired, the window came down like a curtain. I mean it just crumbled.

"'All right,' Bahnsen said, 'we'll replace it with plexiglass,' which they did, and the new window remained intact through all fifteen rounds.

"I had a great deal of respect for Doc Bahnsen. He was an American hero in Vietnam. As a battalion commander, he won the Distinguished Service Cross, which is one step down from the Medal of Honor, and multiple Silver Stars and Distinguished Flying Crosses.

"He was taken aback one time when, as president of the Enlisted Promotion Board, I voted against the promotion of his personal driver from buck sergeant (E-5) to staff sergeant (E-6). The young man had only been in the army for about three years, and was only a year away from getting out. He had no intention of making the army his career. Also, he had never taken an NCO training course. He was a time-server.

"He had been General Bahnsen's driver at Fort Hood, Texas, so Doc brought him to Korea with him, but he couldn't read a map.

"General Bahnsen called me and asked why the promotion had been turned down. 'You know,' he told me, 'we're not trying to make this man a sergeant major. We're not even trying to make him a colonel. We're just trying to make him an E-6.'

"'Sir,' I said, 'this man is only qualified to be a second lieutenant. That is all. If you want to get rid of a second lieutenant, give him a map and a compass and you'll never see him again.'

"The general laughed and said, 'Okay, okay.'

"I remember attending one of his staff conferences, where a woman army doctor, a captain, reported that the number of venereal disease cases among the soldiers had risen from eleven in October to fifty-five during the November-December holiday period of 1982.

"When I asked, 'What does that mean? Did troop morale go up or down?' everyone broke up laughing.

"My tour of duty ended in late February 1983, and I was anxious to go home. Colonel Orlov and Doc Bahnsen spoke at my farewell dinner, as did Lt. Gen. Louis Minitery, who had replaced General Vaught as commander of the Combined Field Army.

"Both Colonel Orlov and General Bahnsen were overly kind to me in what was my farewell-to-Korea Enlisted Evaluation Report.

"Colonel Orlov said, in part: 'Command Sergeant Major Gaweda is the most outstanding soldier I have ever known . . . As my trusted advisor, he was intimately involved in all of the unit planning and operational activities. He favorably influenced the decision-making process. He significantly improved the effectiveness of the organization because his program of NCO development was wise in concept and precise in execution.

"'The soldiers on this installation know that he cares and consequently he has earned their trust and confidence . . . I regard him as an outstanding example of great professional competence and class, coupled with an unequaled sense of dedication and commitment to the best interests of this unit, as well as to the U.S. Army. I am a better soldier for having been influenced by him.'

"General Bahnsen wrote: 'Command Sergeant Major Gaweda is absolutely the best command sergeant major I have known in over twenty-six years of service. He gets things done and takes care of soldiers. He knows how to train men and mold them into a cohesive unit and care for their needs.

"'Command Sergeant Major Gaweda is a tough, no-nonsense leader with impeccable personal qualities . . . No one could present a better image as sergeant major of the army. His dedication to his unit and his mission are truly outstanding. He is a 'take charge, do it now' NCO, whose drive and initiative kept him in the forefront of all the important activities conducted by his command. He is my top choice for command sergeant major of the army.'"

CHAPTER TWENTY-ONE

Grenada

"I was a happy man when the wheels of my airplane touched down at the Fayetteville airport in March 1983," Ted recalled. "It was a great homecoming. Looking radiant, Edith was waiting for me. My God, how I had missed her.

"I had leave time coming, so the two of us headed for the Florida beaches. There were delightful days in West Palm Beach, and at Daytona Beach we found ourselves in the middle of Spring Break. We must have been the only parents in town, but that didn't bother us. We were having a wonderful time on our second honeymoon.

"Rested and relaxed, I came home and reported to Fort Bragg, where I was assigned as command sergeant major of the 82nd Airborne Division's Third Brigade. In a way, it was a homecoming for me, because I had served as command sergeant major of the brigade under then-colonel James J. Lindsay in the mid-seventies. My new boss was Col. James H. Johnson."

Johnson, who retired as a three-star general after commanding the 350,000 soldiers of the U.S. First Army, said, "I had known Ted by reputation some eight years before we soldiered together, because I first came to the 82nd Airborne Division as a battalion commander in 1974, when Ted was command sergeant major of the Third Brigade.

"Later, he established a tremendous reputation with the 35th Signal

Brigade. Everyone in the XVIII Airborne Corps knew that Ted Gaweda was running the 35th, because he would not stand for anything less than perfect when it came to things that really count.

"The troops were in awe of him, and he had their utmost respect and admiration because he epitomized the professional noncommissioned officer, the top NCO. There was no one more professional than Ted Gaweda when it came to standards, when it came to discipline, and when it came to knowing what soldiering was all about.

"He could be intimidating to officers and enlisted men alike. Hell, he sort of intimidated me. He had a stern presence about him that caught everyone's attention. I was privileged to serve with him. If you're going to be a success in the army, you best listen to your sarge.

"He had this wonderful ability of saying to an officer, 'Sir, you know the way you are preparing for this ceremony is wrong. According to FM-22-5, chapter so and so, and page such and such, you are supposed to do this and this, and, of course, he would be right.

"I was in Croatia not too long ago, and I must tell you that foreign armies, particularly those in Eastern Europe, do not have a noncommissioned officer corps. They may have grade instructors, but they don't have what we have, and they are worse off for it.

"Our NCOs enforce standards and discipline and train and develop soldiers from the squad level on up. That's something the officer corps could never do. I don't care how long they talk about it, legislate about it, and rule on it, it will never change. You need an NCO corps to carry out its role in running the army.

"Leadership skills are not necessarily born to one. I believe they are learned. We have developed a noncommissioned officer education system that mirrors that of the officer corps and covers basic and advanced leadership. We have recognized that it is as important in the NCO corps as it is in the officer corps, if not more so. Sergeant Major Gaweda has been in the forefront of that program."

Col. Timothy Scully remembers well Gaweda's arrival at the Third Brigade. "I was a young captain, the brigade adjutant," he said, "and I looked up to sergeants major as god-like figures. Sergeant Major Gaweda was in civilian clothes the first time I met him, and I wondered, 'Who is this well-dressed gentleman visiting brigade headquarters?'

"So I very gingerly asked him how we could help him. He told me who he was and said he was just in for the day, checking out the place where he was going to work. He was in sharp contrast to the man he replaced, a classic NCO bulldog of a man. With Ted, we went from a bulldog to a gentleman.

"'So, where have you been, Captain? What have you done?' he asked.

"I told him that the first company I had commanded was the Old Guard in Washington, the famous honor guard company that everyone has seen performing on television at Arlington National Cemetery.

"'Then you can march,' he said.

"Anyway, the next day the sergeant major showed up with two sabers. 'Come here, young captain,' he said, 'let me show you something.' We went out in the hallway and he went through the saber drill, demonstrating that he really did know the saber manual.

"He gave me the other saber, and we marched up and down the hall together until he pronounced that I indeed could march. I passed his test and I was okay. From that point on, it was a great relationship. Later, when I commanded a battalion, I used him as a standard for the way I dealt with my NCOs.

"He was the sergeants major's sergeant major. He set the standards which all the others were measured against. He was intimidating to junior officers, but he worked with them in a masterful way. He would quickly determine who was a player and who was just passing air.

"He was a wonderful teacher. I never saw him raise his voice, and I would always laugh to myself when I saw him correct a young soldier or officer. He would do it in the most diplomatic way I had ever seen or heard.

"He might whisper in an ear, 'You are the ugliest soldier I have seen today,' and then add, 'I know you can do better because I've seen you do it.' No screaming, no yelling, but at the same time building the man up.

"Ted is the honorary command sergeant major of the 505th, the most famous regiment in the 82nd Airborne Division. That's a significant honor, which shows how he is respected by both those of World War II vintage and the present airborne leaders. The late Gen. Jim Gavin of Normandy fame was once the honorary colonel. People in the 505th today know who Ted Gaweda is because he remains active and attends many events at Fort Bragg.

"So he's not really retired. He may have retired from active service in the army, but his legacy is not only to those who have been fortunate to serve with him and have seen his leadership, but to today's soldiers who are aware of his reputation and see his presence. We're lucky to have him so close to Fort Bragg."

"When I was training young lieutenants," Ted said, "the first thing I would tell them was, 'In order to be effective talking to soldiers, you have to understand weapons. Effective tomorrow evening, you're going to assemble and disassemble this machine gun while the soldiers are watching out their windows.'

"Over the next several days, I would go through the same drill with a hand-held rocket launcher, a .45-caliber side arm, and an M-2 carbine. And all the GIs watched from their windows, and they gained respect for the lieutenant, which meant they would have confidence in him for combat situations.

"For example, he would ask a soldier about the head space in the .30-caliber machine gun. Some soldiers didn't know what he was talking about, but qualified machine gunners knew that the head space is the distance between the face of the bolt and the base of the cartridge, fully seated in the chamber. After all, the army's mission is not just to march in parades, it is to fight and win against America's enemies, when called to do so.

"One time, a colonel approached me and asked if I would teach him to salute the way I did. I rehearsed him in front of a mirror, first in slow motion, and then in normal motion. After four or five days, he had it down perfectly. I was glad to help.

"Colonel Johnson left the brigade in July 1983 and was replaced by Col. James T. Scott. Colonel Scott had been a Ranger battalion commander and was a paratrooper and qualified jumpmaster."

Scott, who retired as a lieutenant general, recalled, "Although I didn't know Sergeant Major Gaweda personally before taking over the Third Brigade, I knew of his reputation as one of the army's premiere senior NCOs. I learned quickly that he was an absolutely remarkable individual.

"He did two things right away that put me at ease. 'Look, sir,' he said, 'every soldier needs a sergeant and I am going to be yours.' I knew what he meant by that. He would tell me when he thought I was wrong, or when he believed I should do something or not do something to keep me straight.

"And that's what he was telling me, and he did just that, you know. He gave me extremely good advice on everything from officer personnel to policies and tactics. He was generally right, and everything he said was based on many, many years of experience.

"Ted was one of the few people I met in my more than thirty years in the army who had no personal agenda. He just didn't have one. He was totally wrapped up in the unit and the soldiers. He ran an out-of-his-pocket training program for soldiers in the brigade who had been selected for promotion from specialist to sergeant.

"It was the first time I had seen that done inside a brigade-size organization. What it did was help the young soon-to-be sergeant learn how to be an NCO and break ties with old buddies in the barracks, who were about to be his subordinates. It is something our system has never done well. It is very tough for any soldier to assume the added responsibility and the new status associated with being a sergeant as opposed to being a specialist.

"Ted ran a marvelous little school for all of our guys who were selected for promotion to E-5, which assisted them in making that transition. He also carefully monitored each one of their assignments, making sure they were not in a position of telling their former buddies what to do. In other words, he moved people around to make an ideal fit.

"He asked for my support of his program, which I gave him. I would ask somebody to give him more help than they were giving, because the program was not universally acclaimed. But I thought it was absolutely great. I believe there are a lot of NCOs in the army today who are much better leaders for having gone through Ted's little school.

"I often wish I had known Ted earlier, but we met sort of late along the way. There is a picture on my wall of the two of us in Grenada, and everyone can see that I value that picture because it is only one of four that I have hanging.

"You know, Ted was physically very strong. He was probably the oldest man in the brigade, but he could outrun 75 percent of the troops. He would run six-to-seven minute miles without breaking a sweat.

"Even though I was younger than him, he could flat run me into the ground, which is no big trick, but the amazing thing was that he smoked cigarettes and still outran us all. I could not do both—run and smoke cigarettes—but he could, and everyone marveled at that."

In October 1983, approximately ninety days after Scott took over the brigade, three Third Brigade battalions were dispatched to the Caribbean island of Grenada, where revolutionaries had killed Prime Minister Maurice Bishop and seized power.

There was fear in Washington and the region itself that Cubans were supporting the rebels in a move to export Castro-style communism throughout the Caribbean. On October 23, the Organization of Eastern Caribbean States asked President Ronald Reagan to "assist in a joint effort to restore order and democracy to the island."

Reagan ordered Marines, Army Rangers, and the 82nd Airborne units to invade Grenada, saying the landing was necessary to restore law and order after "a brutal group of leftist thugs violently seized power," adding that U.S. objectives were to protect U.S. citizens, evacuate anyone wishing to leave, and "help in the restoration of democratic institutions in Grenada." There were some one thousand Americans on the island, including six hundred U.S. students at St. George University's School of Medicine.

"We landed on October 26 at Port Salines on the southwestern tip of the island," Ted said. "Supported by helicopter gunships, we advanced under sniper fire, and by the end of the day our troops had overrun most of their objectives.

"Along with Colonel Scott, I watched the artillery bombardment of a rebel camp from a helicopter. When I boarded the chopper, I was surprised to see that the pilot was Lt. Col. Robert N. Seigle, who, as a lieutenant, had been my company commander in 1967. He had become commander of the 82nd Airborne Division's Aviation Battalion.

"I couldn't see a single person in the camp, and that also was the case when we entered it. The rebels apparently had fled during our advance. We did discover a gigantic underground bunker, filled with explosives. There must have been between one hundred thousand and two hundred thousand pounds of the stuff. If one of our artillery shells had made a direct hit on the bunker, the resultant blast would have destroyed the entire island.

"On October 27, I managed to capture my own personal prisoner. After seeing movement in a bush near our command post, I unholstered my .45 automatic and was about to fire when a rebel soldier jumped out and said, 'Don't shoot, I'm your friend.'

"On October 28, the First Battalion, 505th Parachute Infantry regiment, found the two hundred-plus American students who had not been accounted for and requested assistance for their immediate evacuation. Lt. Col. George A. Crocker told me the students' reaction when they first saw the U.S. paratroopers.

"'They were so excited,' he said, 'that they hugged and kissed our soldiers, and cried and laughed at the same time. It was a very happy moment for the students and our troopers.'

"By the next day, most of the rebel resistance had ceased. Our units escorted all the American students to safety. After the university was captured, we set up a command post there for about two weeks. One of our heroes was then Captain Scully, because he flew in with our mail every day.

"Some six hundred Cubans, many of them military advisors to the rebels, were rounded up by American forces, and six warehouses full of Russian-made small arms ammunition and weapons were seized.

"I truly enjoyed watching the evacuation of the Russian embassy personnel from Grenada. There was a single line of about sixty men, women, and children waiting to be photographed and have their personal belongings inspected by U.S. Customs agents before being put aboard a Mexican airliner.

"One woman refused to be photographed, so the military police escorted her to the back of the line. She was screaming, kicking, and crying, but at the end she too was photographed. Some of the Russians' baggage was loaded with AK-47 assault rifles and ammunition, which was quickly confiscated.

"Colonel Scott and I went inside the embassy, which was full of Communist propaganda—films, books, and posters of Karl Marx and Lenin, bearing the hammer and sickle emblem. It was with great satisfaction that I visited the Cuban embassy shortly after it was captured by the First Battalion, 508th Parachute Infantry Regiment.

"The Cuban ambassador complained to me that he and his staff had been mistreated by our soldiers. He claimed that he was cursed, that his hands were tied behind his back, and that his people were forced to lie face down in the hot sun for almost an hour. He said this happened after he introduced himself to one of our sergeants and showed him his diplomatic passport.

"'Sir, I said, 'I don't see any evidence of physical harm done to your person, your people, or your building, so you should consider yourself fortunate. Our soldiers are trained to kill our enemies and destroy things, and I don't see anything here destroyed.'

"At that point, I walked away. I went looking for the sergeant to congratulate him on a job well done."

Command Sgt. Maj. Franklin Fowler, who at the time was a sergeant first class, senior communications specialist, remembers Command Sergeant Major Gaweda as a man who made things happen.

"On the morning of October 27," Fowler said, "he took me and ten other troopers to recon for a new location for the Brigade Tactical Operation Center (TOC). When we arrived at a possible site, we fanned out to check for booby traps. It was then that Sergeant Major Gaweda captured a prisoner who had been hiding in the bushes. He told the prisoner to drop his trousers down to his ankles to make sure he wasn't hiding any explosives.

"We set up the TOC in the house of Grenada's prime minister. There was an additional house below the main house, which was the servants quarters. I went down there with two other sergeants to check it out. We found medical supplies including morphine, new television sets, VCRs, large quantities of food, and cases of Cuban rum.

"Sergeant Major Gaweda ordered us to break every bottle of liquor. We looked at him like he was crazy, but when he said it again, we knew he meant it. He also told us not to use our weapons, but to smash the bottles against rocks. So we broke every bottle—well, almost. We did keep two of them.

"Sergeant Major Gaweda was tough but respectful and completely professional. I remember on one occasion he stepped between two captains who were about to come to blows in front of the enlisted men at Pearls Airport. He told them, 'You haven't done anything wrong yet; get back to work,' which they did.

"Sergeant Major Gaweda was a slick devil with his tongue. He talked the manager of the only hotel in town into letting us use the facility for our TOC. He was always looking out for the troops."

"In the first six days of combat," Ted said, "our meals consisted only of C-rations, but the morale of the soldiers was remarkably high. Then, without advance notice, we were issued new rations, which were called Meals Ready to Eat (MREs). Immediately, the morale dropped to rock bottom, because, unlike C-rations, the MREs had no cigarettes.

"When I visited our units, the soldiers let me know right away that they wanted their tobacco products in the worst way. I talked to Capt. Joseph Pitts, our brigade logistics officer, who called himself the 'beans and bullets man,' because he could supply both.

"I asked him if he could get us some cigarettes or switch back to C-rations. The next day, Lt. Col. Bowman Olds, the brigade executive officer, told me there were no more C-rations in the inventory.

"But then I lucked out. As Colonel Scott and I were on our way to the Division Tactical Operation Center, we ran into a female captain dressed in full combat gear. Colonel Scott and I were amazed that she was on the island, because no women soldiers were allowed in a combat zone.

"After exchanging salutes, I asked her what she was doing on Grenada.

"Without hesitation, she cheerfully replied, 'Sergeant Major, I am here to help you guys win the war.'

"'In what capacity?' I asked.

"'My name is Capt. Paige Kellogg,' she answered, 'and I am the morale, welfare, and recreation officer for the XVIII Airborne Corps.'

"'That's great,' I said. 'When can we get some cigarettes for our soldiers?'

"'This issue has been addressed,' she said. 'We have a contract with a firm in Atlanta, and the shipment should be here in two or three days.'

"With cigarettes being the most priceless commodity on the island, Captain Kellogg was right. Her contribution to the morale of our soldiers led to the swift end of the war on Grenada."

Scott said, "Having Ted in the brigade on Grenada was like having another lieutenant colonel around because of his experience. Whenever I left the command post, I would try to leave Ted in charge, and he always handled it very well. Oh, he let the senior lieutenant colonel, the executive officer, or whoever was there think they were in charge, but Ted and I both knew that he was running the brigade in my absence.

"That was invaluable to me. I had never encountered a situation before where I could just wander off and do whatever I needed to do, and leave a command sergeant major essentially in charge of the organization, but Ted had a lot of talent. He had the expertise and the situational awareness of what the tactical and operational objectives were, so I never worried about taking off when he was around.

"Whenever I think of Ted Gaweda, I think of absolute professionalism. He was the most professional guy that I ever ran into. If there was anything about soldiers or soldiering, or tactic and equipment that he didn't know, I never saw it. He really knew his job.

"He was equally good with officers and soldiers, which is a rare skill.

His principal legacy to the army was that of a magnificent role model for the NCO Corps, but not far behind that was his relationship with officers as a teacher and a friend.

"You don't find those two characteristics combined in very many people. I have seen guys who were one way or the other, but you rarely see one that is both. It wasn't just to me as the brigade commander; it wasn't just that he was my friend, confidant, teacher and helper; he treated all officers in a sensitive way—friendly, firm, and always right. He was even better, I think, with the soldiers.

"Perhaps I was oblivious to it, but I never found any officer resentment against Ted. There was some minor NCO resentment because some sergeants major, I believe, felt threatened by him. It certainly was not anything that he did, but some probably were troubled that he enjoyed such a close relationship with his soldiers and the officers."

"I left Grenada in late November 1983, getting home just in time for Thanksgiving," Ted said. "A month later, I was awarded my second Bronze Star."

In Ted's evaluation report, Scott wrote: "Command Sergeant Major Gaweda is a positive, dynamic leader whose charisma and example make every soldier want to do his best. He is mentally and physically tough, but compassionate and concerned where soldiers and their families are involved.

"During the Grenada campaign he demonstrated personal courage and leadership. His tactical advice was always sound. He had a complete grasp of the friendly and enemy situation, and thoroughly understood the missions and requirements. In summary, Command Sergeant Major Gaweda is the epitome of what a command sergeant major should be.'

Brig. Gen. Peter J. Boylan, assistant commander of the 82nd, endorsed Scott's remarks and noted, "Command Sergeant Major Gaweda is the best brigade level command sergeant major in this division . . . He is one of the first few on whom I would call during combat."

Boylan then did a rare thing in an official army report, when he added, "He also has an extremely supportive wife."

Col. Joseph Hunt, who was a major in Grenada, said when he witnessed Ted's performance on the island, there was no doubt in his mind "that Sergeant Major Gaweda was going to move up in the world," and that "the brigade position was just another stop on the way to the top."

"I remember the junior officers would panic over an issue and start running around a little crazy, and then Ted would come in and get us back to what exactly it was that we were trying to accomplish and what direction the old man wanted us to go.

"It had a calming effect on all of us when he would say, 'Come on, gentlemen, let's think about what we are trying to do here and then do it.' He would help us come to the right decision on many occasions."

"A few days after the Grenada invasion, scores of congressmen and senators, accompanied by their aides and a fleet of reporters arrived on the island. As they were briefed by Maj. Gen. Edward Trobaugh, 82nd Airborne Division commander, a congressman from California consistently interrupted him with derogatory remarks.

"Sen. John Tower of Texas appeared to be one of the very few who supported the invasion. He asked the California congressman to make his opinion known to President Ronald Reagan and not to General Trobaugh.

"The reporters also were unhappy because they had not been allowed to accompany the invading forces. After the briefing, Senator Tower requested some time with the paratroopers. Colonel Scott asked me to take the senator wherever I felt it was safe and also to lunch with the paratroopers.

"We dined with the Company C, First Battalion, 508th Parachute Infantry Regiment. I introduced our visitor as a World War II veteran with two years of combat in the U.S. Navy, who was only thirteen grades away from being an admiral. The senator got a kick out of that and so did the soldiers. He really knew how to relate to the troops.

"The lunch consisted of 'sun-heated' C-rations, but Senator Tower seemed to enjoy it. I was very proud of our soldiers. Morale was extremely high, and the senator noticed that too.

"By November 12, only the Third Brigade remained on Grenada. All other units had left. Two battalions from our brigade and the brigade command group left on November 23. The Second Battalion, 505th Parachute Infantry Regiment, remained until the end of December 1983.

"When we arrived at Pope Air Force Base, adjacent to Fort Bragg, we were greeted by the 82nd Airborne Division band as well as wives, sons, daughters, and parents. They had come from every part of the nation to welcome back the soldiers.

"You could see the smiles on their faces and the tears in their eyes. It was a very happy occasion, one that will forever be etched on my mind."

CHAPTER TWENTY-TWO

Armed Forces Day, Chicago

"IN May 1984," Ted said, "I was asked to take my hand-picked Third Brigade color guard to Chicago to represent the 82nd Airborne Division in an Armed Forces Day parade.

"All sixteen men in the guard had served with me in Grenada. We were told there would be protesters along the parade route, who might try to disrupt the march by throwing animal blood on us and pushing cars into our path.

"I told my soldiers, 'Make sure no one touches the colors of the 82nd Airborne Division, and, by no means, does anyone touch the national flag.'

"We assembled and began the long march. As we approached a group of screaming protesters, a man suddenly rushed from the curb and tried to grab the American flag. Almost without missing a step, a member of my color guard planted a paratrooper boot in the protester's backside."

Marching in the color guard that day was Sgt. John Gleason, who as a member of a scout platoon saw Ted almost every day in Grenada. Recalling the incident in Chicago, Gleason said, "After the protester got his butt stroked, he was face down as we marched over him. As soon as we passed, he hightailed it out of there. There was some yelling from other protesters, but no one else tried to attack our formation.

"So the trip got off to an exciting start. It was something to tell a war story about. After the parade was over, Chicago Mayor Harold Washington invited our contingent to dinner. Representatives of every branch of the U.S. Armed Forces were present, and Mayor Washington asked that someone from each branch get up and speak.

"I can't even remember what the air force guy said, and the next speaker said the Navy was just happy to be there. The guy from the marines got a double clap, and that was about it.

"I was posting the colors in the back of the room when Sergeant Major Gaweda got up to speak. People were looking at their watches, and I could tell by their faces that they were saying to themselves, 'Oh God, now we have to listen to this soldier.'

"The sergeant major started one of those rousing, from-the-heart speeches of his, and before he was halfway through, the attitude of the whole room had changed. No one looked at their watches anymore. Instead, they were on the edge of their seats. Patriotism was flowing like a river, and when he finished he received a standing ovation.

"I mean he had them rocking and rolling. He didn't look at a single note, and he seemed to make eye contact with every person in the audience. He owned that place. There were generals and admirals slapping each other on the back. They were just proud to be there.

"After Mayor Washington finally quieted the enthusiastic crowd, he said, 'I am very happy that Sergeant Major Gaweda is not running for public office in Chicago, because if he did, I would leave town.'"

In recalling the dinner, Ted said only, "Oh, I just gave a short speech and gave the mayor a memento of the 82nd Airborne Division. During my three-day visit to the Windy City, I hired a cab and visited some of the places I had lived before joining the army.

"I was horrified at the appearance of what had once been a pleasant neighborhood. It had become a slum. I told the driver not to stop. It was like the end of an old chapter."

"On our last evening in Chicago," Gleason said, "I went to a party for servicemen, knowing full well that I had to be on a bus to the airport at 7:00 A.M. 'If you're not there, you'll have to find your own way home,' Sergeant Major Gaweda told us.

"I had quite a full evening with the ladies. I awakened with a start at about 6:30 A.M., roused the young lady next to me from a sound slumber, and said, 'Get up, get up. I have to go.'

"Well, I was all the way across town, so I was working hard to get into my uniform. We jumped into her car and took off. Meanwhile, I could see my army career flashing before my eyes. I could see Sergeant Major Gaweda standing in front of the hotel with my fate in his hands.

"I dashed into the hotel, only to learn that everyone had left. My buddies, all being good soldiers, had grabbed my gear and taken it with them. After my cry, 'Which way to the airport?' was answered, the young lady and I roared off, hoping to catch the bus.

"I already was in deep shit and felt like I was chasing my career. But I was in luck, because after about five minutes on the highway to the airport, we spotted the bus. The young lady drove alongside, I waved my arms frantically, and the bus pulled off the road. I jumped out of the car, gave the young lady a fine salute, and boarded the bus.

"Sergeant Major Gaweda had his glasses on and was reading something. The rest of the troops were watching, thinking, I'm sure, 'Boy, we are going to watch Gleason get his butt caved in.'

"The sergeant major didn't say anything for a long time, so I made my way to the back of the bus. The longest ten minutes of my life went by before the sergeant major motioned for me to come to him. He pulled his reading glasses down, looked at me over the top of them, and asked:

"'Sergeant Gleason, did you show that young lady what a paratrooper is all about?'

"'Yes, Sergeant Major, I did,'

"'Okay,' he said, 'that's all I wanted to know.'

"Being around Sergeant Major Gaweda influenced me to stay in the army after my second tour. The years of watching and listening to him helped me tremendously. He gave me confidence in my own abilities when it came to dealing with the troops.

"For example, when a first sergeant is addressing soldiers, he can't show any nervousness or appear to be wavering. Soldiers see that, and some of those guys are like vultures. They'll jump on anything, and your image of leadership goes down the drain.

"There is an old saying, 'Never let them see you sweat.' Because Sergeant Major Gaweda was my mentor, that sort of thing never happened to me. He taught me to lead from the front."

CHAPTER TWENTY-THREE

Corps Sergeant Major

"I was at home on leave in early August 1984," Ted said, "when I received a telephone call from Marie Allen, secretary to Lt. Gen. James J. Lindsay, commander of the XVIII Airborne Corps. She said the general would like me to come to his office for an interview.

"'I am on leave,' I told her, 'and I really don't want to be interviewed right now.'

"'General Lindsay really wants to see you,' she answered. 'Can you come by for a cup of coffee?'

"Okay,' I said. 'I'll come by for a cup of coffee.'

"I drove to corps headquarters and upon arrival was promptly ushered in to see the boss. General Lindsay and I were old friends. I first knew him when, as a colonel, he took command of the Third Brigade in 1973. At that time, I was sergeant major of the First Battalion of the 508th Airborne Infantry Regiment. I later served briefly as his brigade command sergeant major.

"At the time of our conversation, General Lindsay had been corps commander for about four months. Over coffee, we discussed the mission of the corps and the things that needed to be done to successfully accomplish that mission.

"The basic mission of the corps was and is: **'To Provide a Strategic Response Force Manned and Trained to Deploy Rapidly by Air, Sea and Land Anywhere in the World; Prepared to Fight Upon Arrival and Win.'** That meant we had to train and develop a strong chain of command; confident leaders; physically fit, tough, and competent soldiers with a capability to fight at night. Our goal was to get most of our units in the air no later than eighteen hours after a first alert.

"My meeting with General Lindsay was an enjoyable and relaxing discussion between two veteran soldiers talking about their favorite subject—achieving the highest possible standards for the corps and the army.

"Four or five days later, August 16 to be exact, I received my new assignment instructions, sending me to the XVIII Airborne Corps as its command sergeant major.

"I couldn't believe it. I felt like I was walking on a large body of water without getting my feet wet. It was the highest honor that could be bestowed on a career paratrooper. For me, it was the pinnacle of my chosen profession. Suddenly, this one-time poor Polish immigrant was the top NCO of some 84,000 elite warriors. I felt proud, but also humbled by the experience. In my new job, I would travel the world, visiting soldiers, meeting dignitaries and many other wonderful people.

"Besides the 82nd Airborne Division, the units of the corps included the 101st Airborne Division at Fort Campbell, Kentucky; the 10th Mountain Division at Fort Drum, New York; the 24th Infantry Division at Fort Stewart, Georgia; the 194th Armored Brigade at Fort Knox, Kentucky; and the 196th Infantry Brigade at Fort Benning, Georgia

"As all of this was happening, Edith was visiting her family in Germany. When she returned a week or so later, I surprised her with the news."

"He was excited and so was I," Edith said. "He deserved the recognition because he had worked so hard. The boys also were so proud of him. Our life would change, of course. On some days, for example, he would leave the house at 3:30 or 4:00 in the morning and be halfway around the world by the time I had breakfast.

"On one trip, he was to make a one-night stopover at Ramstein Air Force Base near Frankfurt, Germany, on his way home from Egypt. He was supposed to be home for dinner the next day. I arose that morning to learn that a terrorist bomb had exploded at Ramstein. Of course, I was worried sick. It turned out that he and General Lindsay had taken off an hour before the blast."

Colonel Scott was one of the first to know that Ted was going to corps. "I had just returned from General Lindsay's assumption-of-command ceremony," he said, "when the telephone rang. It was General Lindsay, who said, 'Terry, what's it going to do to you if I take Gaweda?'

"'Well, sir,' I replied, 'it's going to set me back. But on the other hand, it would be for the greater good to have him at corps, where he could do good for a whole lot more people. In the long run, that probably would help me out about as much as if he stayed here.'

"'Well,' General Lindsay said, 'I really want to do this, but I hate to hit you with it so quickly.'

"'Well, sir, I answered, 'when you mentioned Ted Gaweda's name three times in your change-of-command speech, I knew it was coming. I didn't expect it would happen so quickly, but this does not catch me totally by surprise.' We got a good laugh out of that."

"In October 1984, General Lindsay and I attended a first anniversary observance of the invasion of Grenada, where I had the opportunity to meet and talk with Secretary of Defense Casper Weinberger. I also accompanied Deputy Corps Commander Maj. Gen. Jack Farris to Holland for a fortieth anniversary commemoration of the Normandy landings in France.

"Upon my return, I drove to Fort Campbell to meet General Lindsay, where we both attended the air assault course. It was the first time that a corps commander and a corps sergeant major had taken the course together. We made quite a splash among the youngsters, all of whom were half our age. All their eyes were on us. General Lindsay showed them how tough he was when he almost broke the record for a twelve-mile road march.

"After qualifying, he ran in the grueling Boston Marathon in 1976 and 1977. The soldiers called him the 'Road Runner.' General Lindsay also loved to jump, and when he jumped, I jumped with him. As a general officer, he stayed on jump status for fifteen years. He did more for the airborne than any general officer I have known.

"The general and I averaged about two jumps a week. Many of our jumps were at night, which meant getting home late. One time I asked a paratrooper, 'Have you made many night jumps?'

"'Sergeant Major, everyone I make is a night jump,' he answered.

"'How's that?' I inquired.

"'I make all of them with my eyes closed,' he said.

"I told him that soldiers who do night jumps in the daytime can get themselves killed. There were cases where paratroopers jumped with their eyes closed and went straight in, not knowing whether their chutes opened or not. That can happen when you leave an aircraft at less than six hundred feet."

"During the time I commanded the Third Brigade," Lindsay said, "I had become very fond of Ted. I thought he was a real fine soldier. I would meet him in the field off and on, and we would talk about the tactics and objectives. I also came to know Edith, and we all became good friends.

"When I became commander of the 82nd Airborne Division I almost brought Ted up, but it didn't work out that way. So when I went to the XVIII Airborne Corps, I knew who my sergeant major was going to be. I had seen sergeants major who were egotistical and self-serving, but Ted was anything but that. I was impressed with his loyalty and his total commitment to the army.

"To a civilian outside looking in Ted might look rigid; he might appear ramrod straight, a real tough guy who could be difficult to talk to. But the fact of the matter was that soldiers found out very quickly they could talk to Ted Gaweda and he would listen. He also handled his relationship with officers, with NCOs, and with the soldiers as well as anybody I have seen.

"The example he set as a selfless, dedicated, and committed professional is his legacy to the army. If you'll look within the various units of the corps, you will see a whole lot of successful NCOs who modeled themselves after Ted."

David F. Ralston, who was sergeant major for the adjutant general when Ted came to the corps, said, "Oh God, what a soldier Ted Gaweda was! This guy, I mean, he was just the epitome of a soldier. The troops just loved him. He would go out of his way to take care of them. I don't know of anybody that spoke ill of him. He was a man who led by example, and his troops admired him for that.

"When I was a student at the Sergeants Major Academy at Fort Bliss in 1985, he was invited to speak. He came over from Fort Bragg and put on a dynamic presentation. I mean he had numerous standing ovations.

"Sergeant Major Gaweda let people do what they were supposed to do, but if they had a problem, he would take care of it. I would go to him and say, 'Sergeant Major, I've talked to everybody and his brother, and I can't get anyone to agree with this particular assignment.' He would pick up his telephone and call the sergeant major of the army or whoever and get it done. God, he helped so many people with assignments at Fort Bragg."

"In the first week of April 1985, General Lindsay suggested that I visit our soldiers of the First Battalion, 508th Parachute Infantry Regiment, stationed in Egypt's Sinai Desert. The battalion commander was Lt. Colonel Bowman Olds, who had served as executive officer for the Third Brigade in Grenada.

"The unit was part of the Multinational Force and Observers (MFO), which was created by treaty of peace between Egypt and Israel signed on March 26, 1979. President Jimmy Carter brokered the agreement at Camp David. The First Battalion, 505th Parachute Infantry Regiment, was the first unit deployed to the Sinai in July 1982.

"It was a delightful visit. Colonel Olds and the battalion command sergeant major, Arthur Adams, accompanied me to each of the outposts in two helicopters. I saw that the morale of our soldiers was extremely high and the command climate was at its best."

Colonel Olds later said, "Duty in the Sinai Desert can be lonely and desolate. With the series of outposts and checkpoints, which stretch from the tip of the Sinai Peninsula at South Camp on the Red Sea to the heart of the Sinai Desert two hundred miles north, soldiers patrol, secure, and maintain the peace as required under the Camp David Accords.

"Unlike many assignments for soldiers overseas, this lonely and isolated six-month tour of duty has more visitors than most places, from statesmen and general officers of every nationality to groups of observers and civilians interested in the life and time of soldiers along the desert frontier.

"In all of my travels and having to cater to visitors from every walk of life, none of these hundreds of visitors from my perspective ever made much more of an impact on soldiers than the visit by the command sergeant major. And as fortunate as it was, no visitor made more of an impact on my tour of duty in the Sinai than the visit of Command Sergeant Major Gaweda. As I remember one young soldier telling me at an outpost overlooking the Gulf of Aqaba after a series of dignitaries had come through during a week-long visit, 'When the general speaks, we hear what he is saying, but when the command sergeant major speaks, we listen.'"

"In May 1985," Ted said, "I faced a daunting task. I was invited to be the keynote speaker at Duke University's ROTC commissioning ceremony, where the graduates would become army second lieutenants. Initially I was apprehensive. Who was I, a Polish immigrant, to speak at such a highly acclaimed institution of learning.

"I spoke to General Lindsay about the invitation, and he said, 'Go do it, Sergeant Major!'

"I made the trip to Duke in one of our helicopters, taking off from and landing at Fort Bragg's Athletic Field. I wished that my late father could have seen that.

"I told the new second lieutenants that it was an honor and privilege to be 'the first noncommissioned officer to address the future leaders of our nation,' saying, 'The greatness of the officer corps, the courage of our soldiers, and the strength of the noncommissioned officer corps are inseparable . . . As future leaders, I say to you: As the quality of the NCO corps goes down, so does the quality of our army.

"' . . . Leadership is not the inherent right of the officer or noncommissioned officer. It is the ability to inspire others to follow you, regardless of the difficulties encountered or the danger involved.

"' . . . One of the army's major strengths is based on leadership provided by the noncommissioned officer corps. No other army in the world enjoys this reputation. Therefore, we must maximize this strength and exploit it to its fullest potential. When this is done, we will have made the good better and the better best.'"

"When I finished, I received a standing ovation.

"Several months later, at my recommendation, Captain Scully, my old friend at the Third Brigade, became General Lindsay's aide-de-camp in the summer of 1985. It was great to serve with him again."

"Of course, I knew I had a friend in court when I arrived at corps," Scully said. "I knew that no matter how much trouble I would have with the boss or how much I messed up, Sergeant Major Gaweda would take care of me."

"One of the saddest days of my army career and in the history of the XVIII Airborne Corps was December 12, 1985. Two hundred and forty-eight soldiers of the 101st Airborne Division lost their lives that day when their airplane crashed on Newfoundland. They were coming home for Christmas after six months of duty in Egypt's Sinai Desert.

"By 8:30 A.M., General Lindsay and I arrived at Fort Campbell to see for ourselves what was going on. The families were assembled in a gymnasium, waiting for the arrival of their loved ones, when word was received that all had perished. I accompanied General Lindsay to Fort Campbell for a memorial service on December 16. President Ronald Reagan flew in on Air Force One and delivered a very moving speech."

The president told the grieving families and friends:

"We are here in the name of the American people; the passing of American soldiers killed as they returned from difficult duty abroad is marked by our presence here.

"At this point the dimensions of tragedy are known to almost every person in the country. Most of the young men and women we mourn were returning to spend the holidays with their families. They were full of happiness and laughter as they pushed off from Cairo, and those who saw them at their last stop spoke of how they were singing Christmas carols. They were happy; they were returning to kith and kin.

"And then the terrible crash, the flags lowered to half-staff, and the muffled sobs, and we wonder: How could this be? How could it have happened and why? We wonder at the stark tragedy of it all, the enormity of the loss. For lost were not only the 248, but all the talent, the wisdom, and the idealism that they had accumulated; lost too were their experience and their enormous idealism.

"Who else but an idealist would choose to become a member of the armed forces and put himself or herself in harm's way for the rest of us? Who but the idealist would go to hard duty in one of the most troubled places of the world and go not as a matter of conquest, but as a force that existed to keep the peace?

"Some people think of members of the military as only warriors, fierce in their martial expertise. But the men and women we mourn today were peacemakers. They were there to protect life and preserve a peace, to act as a force for stability and hope and trust. Their commitment was as strong as their purpose was pure. And they were proud. They had a rendezvous with destiny and a potential they never failed to meet.

"Their work was a perfect expression of the best of the Judeo-Christian tradition. They were the ones of whom Christ spoke when He said, 'Blessed are the peacemakers, for they shall be called the children of God.'

"Tragedy is nothing new to mankind, but somehow it's always a surprise and never loses its power to astonish. Those of us who did not lose a

brother or a son or a daughter or father are shaken nonetheless. And we all mourn with you. We cannot fully share the depth of your sadness, but we pray that the special power of this season will make its way into your sad hearts and remind you of some old joys. Remind you of the joy it was to know these fine young men and women; the joy it was to witness the things they said and the jokes they played, the kindnesses they did and how they laughed.

"You were part of that, and you who mourn were part of them. And just as you think today of the joy they gave you, think for a moment of the joy you gave them and be glad. For love is never wasted; love is never lost. Love lives on and sees us through sorrow. From the moment love is born, it is always with us, keeping us aloft in time of flooding and strong in the time of trial.

"You do not grieve alone. We grieve as a nation, together, as together we say good-bye to those who died in the service of their country.

"In life they were heroes; in death, our loved ones, our darlings . . . And so, we pray: Receive, O Lord, into your heavenly kingdom the men and women of the 101st Airborne, the men and women of the great and fabled Screaming Eagles. They must be singing now, in their joy, flying higher than mere man can fly and as flights of angels take them to their rest.

"I know that there are no words that can make your pain less or make your sorrow less painful. How I wish there were. But of one thing we can be sure—as a poet said of other young soldiers in another war—they will never grow old, they will always be young. And we know one thing with every bit of our thinking: They are now in the hands of God."

"When the President finished, he went down into the crowd and embraced many of the mourners," Ted said. "Everyone was weeping, including myself."

"General Lindsay, Ted and I made a number of wonderful trips to many interesting places," Scully recalled. "However, a trip we took to Honduras in the spring of 1986 turned out to be a disaster for Ted and an embarrassment for me. We flew there for a training exercise that had been planned for some time, but coincidentally, the Sandinista rebels in Nicaragua had launched an Easter offensive that had pushed into what was called the Las Vegas Salient of Honduras.

"The Monday after the incursion we were preparing for a highly visible daylight drop. Earlier, I had asked a helicopter pilot to recon the drop zone. He reported that when he landed in the zone, he didn't raise any dust, which meant that the ground was extremely hard.

"General Lindsay and Sergeant Major Gaweda jumped from the lead aircraft. General Lindsay hit the ground without a problem, but I had a big cut on one of my legs, where I landed on my pistol. My trousers were torn and there was blood everywhere.

"General Lindsay laughed at me, and Ted Gaweda was laughing the most, but not for long. He had broken his right foot and was Medivaced to the hospital. Our timing was great, however. The Sandinistas withdrew from the Las Vegas Salient.

"General Lindsay and I spent the remainder of the day with the troops, evaluating the exercise. Just before dark, we returned to the airfield and went to the hospital to see how Ted was doing. As we walked into the door of the treatment room, we saw him sitting on an examination table, wearing a white jump boot and a nondescript baseball cap.

"'What's with the cap?' General Lindsay asked.

"'I don't deserve to wear an airborne beret,'" he replied.

"I was embarrassed and depressed," Ted said. "I felt that by breaking my foot I had let down General Lindsay, the corps, and the army. I had been on jump status for more than twenty-five years with hundreds of successful jumps behind me. If I could no longer compete physically with my peers and set an example for the soldiers, then maybe it was time for me to leave the army.

"The army already had too many persons in all ranks who could not run one-half mile with the troops. I had seen too many goldbrickers in my career whose only interest was serving time. Those people were not well respected. I was not going to be one of them. I firmly believed that if I couldn't perform up to the high standards I had set for myself, then I should retire. General Lindsay said that was nonsense and gave me a pep talk."

Sgt. Maj. Johnny Kitchens, Lindsay's senior executive assistant, said, "I sort of took care of Ted until we could send him home. He didn't want to leave Honduras, and I kind of had to keep him down. He had a pretty severe break and didn't want to leave the soldiers in that condition. He wanted to go to work and do things with the general. I don't know why he was embarrassed about the break. That ground was harder than concrete."

"When I returned to Fort Bragg," Ted said, "I put Edith's exercise bicycle in my office so I could stay in shape. Because my foot was itching, I took the cast off after twenty-four days, even though it was supposed to stay on for six weeks. Thirty-four days after the accident I jumped again and ran six miles in forty-eight minutes. I was back. Edith's bike went home."

Retired Maj. Gen. Claude Ivey, who served as deputy commander of the XVIII Airborne Corps under both General Lindsay and his successor, Lt. Gen. John W. Foss, said, "Ted Gaweda made me a better general. If you could play God one day and say to yourself, 'I want to create a model soldier, one who fellow soldiers, peers, seniors, subordinates—the whole enchilada—would respect and admire in every measurable category, from physical fitness to technical proficiency, that model soldier would be Ted Gaweda.

"Our relationship—our personal relationship and our professional relationship—from the first moment we served together was one of mutual respect and admiration.

"I was sort of a chairperson of a host of people who would greet two or three hundred newly arrived soldiers every Thursday morning at one of the Fort Bragg chapels. After the administration guys did their thing on where to draw their pay, post facilities, and so on, I would be introduced.

"I would talk to them about my responsibilities to them and theirs to me, and then say something like, 'You fine young men and women are blessed to be joining the XVIII Airborne Corps. There's no other unit like it, never was and never will be. It's the national strategic rapid reaction force, and what makes it so good is not only our officers, but our noncommissioned officer leadership.

"'In just a few moments, I'm going to introduce you to the best soldier I have ever served with in my army career. He inspires me every day. He will inspire you this morning, and he will inspire you every day that you have the honor to serve this great, great parachute corps.'

"Ted would step forward and deliver one of his rousing speeches. He had those soldiers in the palm of his hand. You, know when Ted walks into a room, even now in civilian clothes when he's coming off the golf course, he commands the room. He is fit, he is a good-looking guy, and just beyond all of that, he is very highly respected. I was really surprised that he wasn't selected to be the sergeant major of the army, but, on second thought, I don't think he would have traded the XVIII Airborne Corps for one of those four-star billets.

"Was he Superman? Hell, no. Nobody expected him to be Superman, but he was an exceptionally effective senior noncommissioned officer who lived his job. Someone once asked me to describe in two or three words what Ted Gaweda is. I thought for about two seconds and said, 'Incredible competence.'"

"Despite an increased load of administrative duties in my job," Ted said, "I tried to get away from my desk as often as possible to spend time with the troops. And when I saw a sloppy soldier, it still raised the ire within me.

"I recall standing in the back of a formation with Sgt. Major Joe Turner, when I saw a soldier whose long hair looked like it had been packed down with grease. He also was wearing jungle boots that looked like they had been spray painted.

"I said, 'Joe, look at that awful-looking guy up there in the Headquarters Platoon. Tell him to report to me.'

"Joe walked up and tapped him on the shoulder, and said, 'The corps sergeant major wants to see you.'

"When the man turned and looked at me, I saw that he was an NCO, a staff sergeant. I couldn't believe it. He came over to me, and I just walked around him. His hair was at least six inches long.

"'You are the ugliest soldier I have ever seen,' I told him. 'I want you out of my army. I want you to put in for your discharge today.' The man did what I asked and left the service.

"Unless there was a blatant disregard of army regulations, as there was with the staff sergeant, I tried to be fair and help soldiers who had problems. For example, when I was president of the re-enlistment review board, a guy came in with a terrible gap in his front teeth.

"'You're going to have to get your teeth fixed,' I told him. 'We can't have someone with teeth like yours representing the army.'

"I called in his NCO, who said, 'He's just got a big gap in his mouth. I can't help it.'

"'He's going to have to get his teeth fixed,' I said. 'We have fine dentists here at Fort Bragg who can take care of that.' About a month later, the soldier came back, and his teeth looked great. He thanked me and went on with his army career.

"One of the best things I did as a relatively new corps sergeant major was to put Henry Spell in charge of the NCO Academy. I had become impressed with Sergeant Major Spell when he was the spokesman for the United States Forces Command at a hearing before the House Armed Services Committee.

"A chemical warfare expert, he urged the committee to fund the procurement of new nuclear-biological-chemical equipment, on the basis that old equipment could be hazardous to soldiers' lives. Because of the testimony of Spell and others, the funding was approved.

"When I telephoned him about the academy job, he reminded me that he had been a command sergeant major designee for eight months and wanted very badly to become a command sergeant major. He also wanted to disassociate himself from the Chemical Corps.

"The academy position required a command sergeant major who had served as a CSM for a colonel or above. Obviously, Henry did not meet these requirements. Nevertheless, when I told General Lindsay that I wanted him, he said, 'You have my approval. Go ahead and do it.'"

"So I received my command sergeant major wreath," Spell said, "and twenty-seven days later, with Corps Sergeant Major Gaweda's magnificent support, the academy was accredited by the Training and Doctrine Command. I remember attending a meeting of command sergeants major from every level in the corps, and Corps Sergeant Major Gaweda telling them, 'I want the best noncommissioned officers on the post sent to the NCO Academy as instructors, and I always will be grateful for your support.'

"When I started, the failure rate for trainees was between 12 and 15 percent. With hard work, we were able to get that down between 4 and 5 percent. We learned how to do things better. We brought in the new instructors, who improved the quality of teaching, which meant that the soldiers retained more.

"With the approval of General Lindsay, Corps Sergeant Major Gaweda mandated that the speakers for our various graduations had to be a CSM. Besides the primary leadership development course, we taught infantrymen, mortarmen, anti-tank soldiers, combat engineers, artillerymen, computer guys, and so on.

"Every noncommissioned officer who came to Fort Bragg had to take a two-week senior leadership refresher course that Corps Sergeant Major Gaweda developed to provide commanders with all the information they needed to know about those soldiers' skills. There were no exceptions. The only way you could get out of taking the course was to die. Think what a great thing this was for the soldiers' commanders.

"There were between five hundred and six hundred men and women on campus at any time. We had 105 names on our list of instructors. Corps Sergeant Major Gaweda spoke at a number of graduations, and when he finished his remarks, the soldiers were totally inspired.

"He tried to attend every graduation he could, even when he wasn't the speaker. I well remember one time when he was at a graduation and the guest speaker walked to the podium and collapsed.

"I had just introduced him when I heard these noises next to me, followed by a crashing sound. I looked around and there was the guest speaker, if you will excuse my expression, flat on his ass.

"He had fainted, and as it turned out, he suffered only a few bruises. Sergeant Major Gaweda immediately came to the podium and handed out diplomas. After everyone returned to their seats, he delivered a dynamite graduation speech.

"He just blew those soldiers away. He inspired the hell out of them. As I was leaving, I overheard a soldier say to one of his comrades, 'I'm sure glad that other guy fainted.'"

CHAPTER TWENTY-FOUR

Citizen Gaweda

"Since Fayetteville, North Carolina, just outside Fort Bragg, was my home for most of my military career," Ted said, "I tried—with the help of the Army—to give back to the community as much as I could.

"I often helped the Fayetteville Chamber of Commerce with its events and worked with townspeople in soliciting corporate members for the AUSA (Association of the United States Army). The AUSA was founded some thirty-five to forty years ago to watch over the interests of the army. Although it is not a registered lobby, the organization supplies information to Congress that, hopefully, will help the members to make the right decisions as far as the army is concerned.

"The bulk of the membership is made up of active-duty army officers and the enlisted ranks. I am pleased to say that the Braxton Bragg chapter had 20,325 members in 1985, which made it far and away the largest chapter in the world. I always believed strongly in the AUSA, and felt it was my duty to solicit memberships from both the military and business world.

"When I was the command sergeant major of the Third Brigade in 1984, I told Colonel James T. Scott, the brigade commander, that the annual AUSA membership drive was coming up, noting, 'Sir, we had better jump on the bandwagon and get this thing kicked off early.

"'The Braxton Bragg Chapter will pay for breakfast at the NCO Club for about 250 soldiers, including yourself, sir, to talk about the AUSA.' So I made the arrangements. At the last minute, Colonel Scott received an assignment that prevented him from attending.

"'Perhaps we ought to call off the breakfast,' he said.

"'Sir,' I answered, 'we should go on with the breakfast. I have the NCO club reserved and the invitations have been sent out. You go ahead and do your mission, and I will take care of the membership drive.'

"The breakfast went ahead as planned, and thirty days later we had 1,750 new AUSA members and the dues money in hand. Later, at a conference of the 82nd Airborne, Maj. Gen. Edward Trobaugh, division commander, told the other brigade commanders, 'Look here, only the Third Brigade met its quota on AUSA members. The rest of you did nothing.'

"Colonel Scott told me that General Trobaugh congratulated him and said, 'It seems that Scott is the only one who knows what's going on in this division.' That made me damned proud."

Ted also was proud in September 1985, when he received an Award of Patriotism from Secretary of the Treasury James Baker III for his service to the U.S. Savings Bond program.

When Ted was the XVIII Airborne Corps sergeant major, local businessman Fritz Healy said, "I was president of the Braxton Bragg Chapter of the AUSA, as well as president of the Fayetteville Area Chamber of Commerce. I remember going to General Lindsay, the corps commander, and asking him for some help on one of our parades, either on Memorial Day or Veterans Day.

"He turned me over to Ted, and within twenty-four hours everything was taken care of. He provided us with the 82nd Airborne Division band and a fifty-foot flatbed trailer for the band and reviewing dignitaries to sit on. We draped the flatbed with flags and bunting and it looked just great.

"Fayetteville's relationship with Fort Bragg is like that between a college and the community in which it is located; for example, the so-called town and gown relationship that exists between, let's say, Yale and New Haven, Connecticut.

"We were having a huge community outing one time and there was a threat of rain. Suddenly, out of nowhere, Sergeant Major Gaweda showed up with this mammoth parachute that the army uses to drop tanks, trucks, and other vehicles. It must have been one hundred feet square. A light, but steady rain fell, but the giant canopy saved the day.

"It seemed that Ted could somehow find about anything we needed. He and I accompanied a group of Fort Bragg troops to Washington for some AUSA function, and Ted, who couldn't spend AUSA money, would scrounge up for the soldiers sandwiches and potato chips from some bread company and beer from a friendly distributor. He was the most honest, polite and efficient Sgt. Ernie Bilko (of television fame) that I ever knew.

"Another thing I noticed about him was that he never would say to his people at Fort Bragg, 'The general wants this done.' Instead, he was the type who would say, 'We would like this done this way,' or, 'I really think this is the right way to do it.' The soldiers didn't perform their tasks because of what the general wanted. They did them because Tadeusz Gaweda said so.

"In his military role, he really could arouse your patriotism. One time we had the governor of North Carolina and some bigwig from Washington at one of our community affairs. When Ted and his breathtaking color guard paraded by, he looked up and, I swear, I had never seen that many ribbons and decorations since General Douglas MacArthur. He could make you feel great about your country.

"Not only was Ted a great soldier, he also was a very good citizen who always was interested in doing things for his community. I am chairman of the governor's Military Affairs Committee and, as such, put together an observance of the fiftieth anniversary of World War II.

"As a civilian, Ted volunteered to serve on the committee. It was a hell of a lot of work, and as usual he did a great job. After it was over, he sent me a handwritten letter, complimenting me for the job I did. I didn't receive a letter like that from any other damned soul."

Ms. Kay Leonard, a former Fayetteville banker who preceded Healy as president of the Braxton Bragg Chapter of the AUSA, said, "The community leaders thought Ted was just wonderful. Anytime they needed something from Fort Bragg, he never wavered. I was his civilian partner when the two of us would solicit local business for memberships in the AUSA.

"We would go around on our route, and at each stop Ted would give a little five-minute speech without using a note, which was very impressive. We urged the business owners and managers to join, pointing out that many of the some forty thousand soldiers at Fort Bragg were their customers.

"You know, some sergeants major are not as polished as others and have problems dealing with the civilian business community, but Ted was the epitome of a well-rounded and articulate sergeant major. Some sergeants major had trouble fitting in with the downtown group, but Ted could and did fit in everywhere.

"He also is the most patriotic person I have ever known. He is a patriot from the word go, who loves his flag and who loves America. To me, he was the Lee Iacocca of the enlisted world. He appreciated the civilians in the community. He felt, I believe, that Fayetteville had sort of adopted him. He was a wonderful diplomat for the army.

"In 1986, I left my banking job and became the civilian protocol officer of the XVIII Airborne Corps. When Ted retired in 1988, I sent out more invitations for his retirement ceremony than I had for many generals. Because he had so many friends, I must have sent out somewhere between eight hundred and one thousand invitations."

CHAPTER TWENTY-FIVE

A New Boss

"In October 1986, Major General Ivey, deputy commander of the XVIII Airborne Corps, called me to his office and told me that General Lindsay would be leaving the corps for another post. He added that in a telephone conversation from Washington, General Lindsay made it clear that he wanted me to organize the change of command ceremony.

"General Lindsay had indicated to General Ivey that he wanted a 'manila folder' ceremony, which meant plain and simple. I knew what he wanted. Because of inclement weather, the ceremony was held indoors at the William Lee Fieldhouse at Fort Bragg. The 82nd Airborne Division band was there, along with a group of command sergeants major, who presented the colors of the corps' various units. I was the commander of the formation.

"There were five hundred people present to hear guest speaker Gen. Joseph T. Palastir Jr., head of the Forces Command, the largest command in the army. After he finished, General Lindsay spoke and was followed by Lt. Gen. John W. Foss, the new corps commander, who had moved up from commanding the 82nd Airborne Division. And that was it, just like General Lindsay wanted. There was a nice reception afterward, where he was given a number of mementos.

"General Lindsay was selected to head the Special Operations Command at McDill Air Force Base, Tampa, Florida, which was responsible for joint operations between the army, navy, air force and Marine Corps. For example, the Navy Seals are part of that program.

"The assignment called for a four-star general, so he was promoted from lieutenant general to the top rank in a ceremony at the Pentagon in Washington. He invited me to attend, so I had the honor of flying to Washington with him. It was an impressive ceremony, hosted by Admiral William Crowe, chairman of the Joint Chiefs of Staff.

"I was immediately proud of him. As I said earlier, he was, as far as I was concerned, the American Airborne Caesar and a hero to his country.

"After the change of command I went to General Foss to ask about my future. I didn't know if he wanted to name a new corps command sergeant major or if he wanted me to continue.

"'What do you want me to do?' I asked.

"'I want you to be my command sergeant major,' he replied. 'I want you to do for me what you did for General Lindsay. I want you to tell me what is going on with the troops. I want to make sure that we take care of the soldiers.'

"Those words were music to my ears, of course. We quickly developed a fine working relationship. He too was a soldier's soldier and an outstanding infantry tactician."

Foss, who enlisted in the army as a private in 1951 and was commissioned upon graduating from West Point in 1956, said, "Officers tend to screw the troops without realizing they are doing it. They get focused on short-term operational issues and forget about soldiers living in barracks and things like that. Guys in the barracks need somebody to worry about them.

"As an example of what I am saying, in 1987 the barracks of the 82nd Airborne Division were more than forty years old. Mostly cinder block, they had been built shortly after World War II, and were in pretty bad shape, cold in the winter and hot in the summer.

"We ran down some money to do the job, but some of my staff officers said the funds should be used to improve the old machine-gun range, which had been earmarked for improvement in our spending program. One of my colonels said, 'Sir, we don't want to leave out the old machine-gun range. Can't we keep that in the program?'

"'No, no, no,' I said. 'We have a machine-gun range that works fine. We have to do something about the barracks.'

"'Oh, sir,' he said, 'I think we can live with that situation for another year.'

"'You don't live in the barracks,' I told him. 'I'm concerned about the soldiers who do live there.'

"That was the end of that. We burned about a quarter of the old buildings because they were beyond repair. Major improvements were made on the remainder, including putting in new latrines and painting everything in attractive color schemes. It had to boost the morale of the soldiers.

"I always have said, if you really want to know what's going on, eat in the mess hall every day. Ted Gaweda became my eyes and ears, and he knew there wasn't anything that the two of us couldn't talk about. That was a comfortable position for both of us.

"A good sergeant major will find out what's going on and advise the commander as to what actions he ought to take. Ted quickly found out that he could come in and tell me something, knowing that I wasn't going to pick up the telephone and say to another officer, 'Your sergeant major told my sergeant major so and so,' which is the worst thing that could happen. It's like two kids telling on each other.

"He might come to my office and say, 'Sir, the mess hall is serving the worst doughnuts in the world.' It seems like a silly thing, but not if you eat in the mess hall every day. The mess sergeants were putting the doughnuts in the refrigerator.

"When you put a sugared doughnut in the refrigerator, it will turn wet. The mess sergeants would drag them out and put them on the serving line. The soldiers hated the soggy doughnuts. Ted got into that and the mess sergeants were told to put the doughnuts in dry storage. Important? Very important to the soldiers, very important to maintain high morale among the troops. As they always say, an army travels on its stomach.

"Ted and I had a great career together. He was a terrific sergeant major. In my book, the best. Our relationship was one of total trust and confidence. We certainly didn't try to do each other's job. I didn't worry about where he went or what he did, because I knew he always was going to do the right thing.

"I came to know his values and he came to know mine. You can't hide those, because you have to live them. Once you have mutual respect, you can feel comfortable and free and easy about your relationship. Respect is the foundation for everything else.

"A corps commander and a corps sergeant major also can become good friends. You don't have to be good friends to have a good relationship, but you can be good friends when neither takes advantage of the other. That was the case with Ted and me.

"You know, there are a lot of noncommissioned officers in the army today who have a better understanding of their responsibility to the soldiers because Ted Gaweda was there. I believe the things he did will live on in the army for a long time. The XVIII Airborne Corps leaves a definite mark on the rest of the army, and the command sergeant major of the corps leaves a definite mark within the entire corps.

"Sergeant Major Gaweda set up luncheon meetings between me and the key sergeants major of the corps every six to eight weeks. It was a great opportunity to exchange views. I would tell them how I felt about certain things, and they would talk about problems and things they wanted to get done. It was a frank and open exchange that I enjoyed and appreciated.

"When you take over a post or a command, you talk about whether or not it is healthy, whether it's vibrant, and all of that. I believe that Fort Bragg was a pretty healthy place in those days. I mean, the sergeants, officers, and soldiers all were doing their jobs. It was just a delight. The army had recovered from those dark days of the 1970s and, in my opinion, our airborne units recovered first.

"I think some of the colonels on my staff were afraid of Ted because they were worried that he would rat on them, but a good sergeant major can be a great conduit of information, which Ted was. I think there was a concern on the part of the staff officers as to how bad news would be received.

"Good news travels very quickly, but bad news doesn't travel well. Whether you're in the army, industry, or whatever, the boss doesn't want to be the last guy to hear bad news, which often happens. If you are the last guy to hear it, it's usually too late to do something about it, and that's a big mistake.

"I am sure that some individuals felt that they would be thought less of if they were the bearers of bad news. In ancient Greece, the deliverers of bad news were often killed. I used to tell officers going into new commands, 'Kill the messenger the first time, and they'll send another one. Kill the second time, and that's the last time you'll ever hear from them.'

"Ted would approach bad news in a nice, indirect way, saying, 'Sir, we need to look at such and such.' And, you know, we might do this together, which didn't happen very often, or I would poke my fingers into the problem or ask the chief of staff to do it for me. That system worked quite well because of the trust and confidence that Ted and I shared.

"Ted and I didn't run around with each other all that much, but we did make two to three parachute jumps a week together. We also would run with the troops as often as we could. I enjoyed jumping. I mean, I enjoyed being with the troops."

"To my disgust," Ted said, "I had another jumping accident in February 1987, when a paratrooper above me suddenly guided his chute under me. I hit his suspension line, tumbled, and struck the ground in a spread-eagle position. I was conscious, but went into shock about two minutes later.

"I had a badly broken left ankle. I spent the night in the hospital, where they put my ankle back together with three screws. The pain was terrible. When General Foss came to visit me in the recovery room, I told him, 'Sir, I am no longer fit to fight.' He was very kind, saying, 'Ted, I need you, the corps needs you and the army needs you.

"He followed up with a personal letter, in which he said:

"'This is just a short get-well note to remind you of your importance to the XVIII Airborne Corps and paratroopers throughout the world.

"'Your courage and patience while injured were worthy of emulation and the mark of a true paratrooper. As a physically fit and very motivated soldier, I am sure your recovery will be swift.

"'May God assist you in a speedy recovery and place you back in the harness as the CSM of the XVIII Airborne Corps.'

"His words inspired me to press on. So I brought Edith's exercise bike back to my office and used it as a substitute for the running I could not do. The cast came off the ankle after twenty-seven days, and seven days after that I jumped again, wearing a special boot and a parachute that descended at twenty-eight feet per second instead of the normal forty-five. I still carry the three screws in my ankle as a reminder of that unfortunate experience."

Ted's position as Corps sergeant major put an extra burden on Edith, who found herself with greater responsibilities as a hostess. "I enjoyed it very much," she said, "but at the same time, I wanted to keep my own career in real estate.

"It was a very demanding situation, but I wanted and needed to participate in my husband's social activities. One time, when I was driving on a highway near Fayetteville, my office called on the car radio and a secretary said, 'Oh, Edith, I'm so glad I found you. Your husband wants to meet you at home because a general and his entourage are on their way to your house.'

"Of course, I was in shock. I rushed home and made sure everything was in Class A shape before they arrived. Our visitors were retired Lt. Gen. James B. Vaught and his wife, who were in town and just wanted to come by and pay us a friendly visit. I had met Mrs. Vaught, who was a lovely lady, at a meeting in Washington. Knowing the general and his wife made it a lot easier. We had an enjoyable afternoon together.

"Whether Ted and I were hosting a crowd or just a small gathering, I never brought in caterers. I would take a day off from work to shop and prepare food. I was not one to just throw a bag of potato chips on the table. I remember going to functions at Fort Bragg, where everyone was dressed up, only to find the food prepared in a sloppy manner and nothing but paper plates to put it on. I am not like that. I would polish and put out my best silver and china.

"When Ted was command sergeant major of the 82nd Airborne Division's Third Brigade, he came home one day and announced, 'The British are coming. We're going to have some eighty guests here for dinner this coming Sunday.' Naturally, I was taken aback. To make it worse, it was February, which meant we couldn't use our backyard swimming pool area."

"What had happened," Ted explained, "was that the brigade had established an exchange program with a British airborne regiment. The Brits sent a company to Fort Bragg, and the Third Brigade dispatched one of their companies to Great Britain.

"Altogether, there were about 140 British paratroopers at Fort Bragg. There was a long weekend approaching, and about sixty of these men really had no place to go. They had no agenda for the weekend.

"I called a meeting of battalion sergeants major and asked for volunteers to entertain two or three of our visitors in their homes during the upcoming weekend. I had no takers. 'Okay,' I said to myself, 'I'll invite all of them to my house,' which I did.

"That meant including Maj. Gen. Thomas Tackaberry, division commander; Col. Jarold L. Hutchinson, brigade commander; then-Colonel James Lindsay, division chief of staff; all the battalion commanders and sergeants major; and, of course, all of the wives."

"I worked quite hard putting together a stand-up buffet," Edith said.

"Obviously, I couldn't do a sit-down dinner for that many people in twenty-two hundred square feet. We even turned our laundry room into a bar, which, of course, was quite a popular place.

"It was a wonderful party and our British guests seemed to enjoy themselves immensely. We produced and paid for the whole affair. No one offered to help or participate, and we never asked. When Ted later accompanied General Tackaberry on a visit to England, he met the wife of one of the British paratroopers, who said, 'Oh, this is Sergeant Major Gaweda, the American millionaire.'"

Ted said, "General Tackaberry and I jumped from a hot air balloon, which was a great honor."

Tackaberry, who retired in 1981 after thirty-seven years of service, said, "I was not the least bit surprised when General Lindsay chose Ted to be the command sergeant major of the XVIII Airborne Corps.

"I would watch him in a crowd, where he would charm the ladies and officers and enlisted personnel alike. He also did the same thing with civilians. The old army had a lot of tough and rough-edged professionals who could not do what Sergeant Major Gaweda did.

"He trained a citizen army, and he did it in a magnificent way. He was a role model for officers and men alike and, as far as I know, was never challenged. He appeared more proud to be an American than those of us who are natives. His pride and patriotism exceeds that of many who take America for granted because they were born here and had all the privileges of American citizenship for as long as they could remember.

"One of the things I most remember about Ted came from one of my sons, who at the time was a colonel in the 101st Airborne Division at Fort Campbell, Kentucky. Ted, who was XVIII Airborne Corps command sergeant major, went up to Fort Campbell and delivered a speech about leadership.

"My son, who had spent a lot of time in the army and had been around a great deal, told me that Ted's speech was the most inspirational he had heard in all of his years in the army. And I must say that my son is not easily impressed. He's just not that kind of person. To me, that was a great tribute to Ted Gaweda."

"When you cut a man's hair for fifteen years, you get to know him pretty well," commented Travis Bell, one of the civilian barbers at Fort Bragg.

"You soon learn about his attitude and behavior. I have a Wall of Honor in my shop, and before Ted Gaweda became corps command sergeant major, the only photographs on that wall were of generals, most of whom had commanded the XVIII Airborne Corps.

"But after getting to know Sergeant Major Gaweda and listening to his soldiers talk about him, it didn't take me long to put his picture on my Wall of Honor. Anybody that makes my wall has to be a special person. I had seen a lot of corps sergeants major come and go in my time, but Ted was outstanding. He loved and understood his soldiers, and when mercy was required, he gave it.

"I remember one corps sergeant major who came into the shop twice and ripped apart soldiers right in front of everyone there. Sergeant Major Gaweda would never do something like that. He was strict with the troops, but he always was fair.

"I remember soldiers talking about him when I was cutting their hair. They spoke of him with great respect and admiration. Even when they had been punished, they felt they had been treated fairly. In fact, I've never heard anyone say a bad word about him.

"He was a stickler on the type of haircuts that were acceptable to him. Many of the soldiers wanted block haircuts, where the hair on the back of the head and neck is very full. Army regulations state that block haircuts are okay if the hair is tapered on the back.

"When I told the sergeant major that some of the soldiers didn't want their hair tapered, he said, 'Tell them to go downtown to get their hair cut.'

"The word on that got around real fast. When I told soldiers how Sergeant Major Gaweda felt about non-tapered haircuts, most of them would say, 'Okay, go ahead and taper it,' knowing that was the way to keep from having any problems.

"Ted still comes here to get his hair cut. He's a joy to be around, always joking and laughing. He is such a nice fellow. He still gets a decent haircut, but not as close as it used to be."

"In August 1987," Ted said, "General Foss and I traveled to the Egyptian desert to take part in a training exercise called Operation Bright Star. I had made the same trip with General Lindsay in 1985.

"One morning we were busily preparing for a parachute jump with Egyptian paratroopers. We were loaded and ready for take off when word came that there would be no take-off because the Egyptian airfield commander was still asleep and the noise of the airplane engines might wake him up.

"We waited for an hour-and-a-half under the blazing desert sun until the guy awakened and we were given permission to take off. I couldn't believe it. To the Americans, the whole thing was incomprehensible."

"The thing I remember most about that trip was the problem with food," Foss said. "We had no milk and we had no bread. All we had to eat were T-rations, which the soldiers called 'T-rats.' It was institutional food, of course. The T-ration came in a big flat can. To warm it, you would dip it in hot water and open the can.

"The army hadn't yet figured out how to properly distribute the T-rations to provide the troops with a semblance of a varied diet. Whatever the forklift operator picked up was what you ate for four days running. For a week we had lasagna for breakfast, lasagna for lunch, and lasagna for dinner. You found yourself hoping that the forklift operator would pick up anything but lasagna on his next trip to the warehouse. It was something else. We called it the Forklift Menu.

"After we were there for a couple of weeks, Ted stopped by one day and said, 'Sir, the food is terrible. The soldiers will not fight for this food. We must feed them better than this.'

"When I returned to Fort Bragg, I made sure Ted's statement was broadcast throughout the army. Everyone knew about his coming in and saying, 'Sir, the soldiers will not fight for this food.' I made sure the guys at the Department of the Army in Washington knew about it.

"I became famous in the army for my campaign to improve food served in the field. Field food was one of the things that the army cheated on. The food has become considerably better, but it is not as good as it should be. The soldiers still were complaining about the quality of the food, such as MREs (Meals Ready to Eat), in the Persian Gulf War."

"When I was with General Lindsay in Egypt," Ted said, "soldiers who ate in the XVIII Airborne Corps mess hall complained to me that they could not get Kool-Aid. A mess sergeant said to me, 'Every mess hall except ours is serving Kool-Aid.'

"'Do you have Kool-Aid here?' I asked.

"'Oh yeah,' he replied, 'we've got plenty of Kool-Aid.'

"'You say you have plenty of Kool-Aid, yet the troops are complaining they can't get Kool-Aid,' I said. 'Damn, this can't be. What the hell is going on?'

"It turned out that a well-meaning officer at corps headquarters had ordered that no Kool-Aid should be served because he didn't think it was good for the soldiers' health. When I spoke to General Lindsay about it, he asked, 'What do you want to do, Sergeant Major?'

"'Sir,' I said, 'I want the soldiers to have their Kool-Aid.'

"'Then do it,' Lindsay told me.

"I went to the mess hall and told the mess sergeant, 'Serve the goddamn Kool-Aid.'

"It may seem a small point, but when you are thirsty as hell in the desert and craving something refreshing, it becomes a big point, particularly when someone else is receiving what you are being denied.

"The exercises in Egypt prepared the army's airborne units for the Persian Gulf War. When that conflict started, our troops were deployed in the same way as they were in Operation Bright Star, only in different locations, and the eighteen-hour response time was not compromised.

"In September 1987, I was assigned by the Department of the Army to serve on the sergeant first class promotion board for thirty-three days. I didn't really want to be away from the troops that long, so I asked General Foss if I could be replaced on the promotion board.

"General Foss took off his glasses and looked at me with his 'infantry blue' eyes, smiled and said, 'Sergeant Major, you are the perfect person for the job. No one likes this kind of duty, but the army needs people like you to select our future enlisted leaders.'

"The next month I suffered my most painful injury as a paratrooper. General Foss and I were in Fort Chaffee, Arkansas, for a night jump with the troops. The aircraft was at about nine hundred feet when General Foss went out the door. I jumped right behind him.

"He slammed into a parked Hum-Vee vehicle and rolled off, suffering only bruises. I landed on a tree stump. I was hurting, but I tried to ignore it. After returning to Fort Bragg the next day, I went to Washington for a day. By now, my rib cage was thumping with pain.

"I came home only long enough to repack and take off in my car for a promotion board meeting at Fort Benjamin Harrison, Indiana. It was a fourteen-hour drive, and every breath I took resulted in overpowering pain. It was almost unbearable.

"At Fort Ben, I served as the senior enlisted member of the combat arms panel. Our mission was to select the best staff sergeants for promotion to sergeants first class. I am proud to say that every member of the panel was impressed with the high caliber of noncommissioned officers we have in our army. Of course, only the best of the best were selected for promotion.

"By the time I arrived at Fort Ben, I almost fell out of my car. I practically dragged my aching body to the post's medical center. There, X-rays showed I had two broken ribs, one of which was broken in three places. The medics expressed amazement that I had waited so long to be examined.

"They told me I could not engage in any physical exercise for a month. However, three days later I found that I could stand to run. In a month I was fine. My ribs had healed, and I was happy to go home to Edith and start parachuting again.

"In early March 1988, the XVIII Airborne Corps was ordered to provide a rapid response to the Republic of Honduras. It was known as 'Operation Golden Pheasant.'

"The mission was a reaction to growing intelligence that the Nicaraguan Sandinistas were violating Honduran sovereignty by crossing the border in pursuit of Contra rebel freedom fighters. The show of force included two battalions from the Seventh Infantry Division (Light) and two airborne battalions from the 82nd Airborne Division.

"Coincidentally, my son, First Lt. Gregory Gaweda, was serving in the Second Battalion of the 504th Parachute Infantry Regiment, the unit selected to lead the airborne assault. To his surprise and pleasure, he learned that he was to be jumpmaster on a flight where his first jumper was going to be Lt. Gen. John W. Foss, XVIII Airborne Corps commander, and his second jumper was to be his father.

"Only it was not to be, because the Pentagon would not permit General Foss to make the trip because of his high rank as a three-star general. Anyway, Gregory and I had that brief moment of joy.

"Nicaragua President Daniel Ortega withdrew any Nicaraguan soldiers operating in Honduras in spite of his declaration on the Cable News Network that his troops would 'annihilate the infamous 82nd Airborne Division.'

"General Foss and I visited the about-to-depart troops at Pope Air Force Base, along with scores of newspaper and television reporters. The morale of the soldiers was extremely high. My boss and I were terribly disappointed that we could not go with them.

"Gregory, who served as a platoon leader in the Supply and Transportation Platoon, remembered the mission well. We deployed on short notice, eager for combat. It was only natural for morale to sink in the wake of a withdrawing enemy.

"Creature comforts were in short supply, and the old problems with Meals Ready to Eat and no cigarettes cropped up again. I told General Foss that the troops wanted tobacco. In any high tempo operation, the number of tobacco users goes up, and no self-respecting tobacco user would ever smoke without offering cigarettes to his buddies.

"With the help of Fritz Healy, who was president of the Braxton Bragg Chapter of the Association of the U.S. Army, we were able to send three thousand cartons of cigarettes to Honduras. Gregory's platoon sling-loaded the first tobacco shipment flown there. When General Foss and I later visited the troops, we found the morale to be sky high."

CHAPTER TWENTY-SIX

Best of Days, Worst of Days

"WITH the last weeks of my thirty-five years of Army service rapidly winding down, I started in January 1988 the planning for my retirement," Ted said. "As Edith and I were looking through a 1988 *Farmer's Almanac,* we chose Friday, May 13, as the day for my farewell ceremony.

"According to the almanac, the weather was supposed to be good, and, besides, Edith said, 'Friday the thirteenth is your lucky day, because you were injured in two Friday the thirteenth parachute jumps, but survived. See, you were lucky that you didn't get killed.'

"Interesting logic, I thought. I could have taken the opposite view; that it was my unlucky day because I did get hurt. 'Oh well,' I said to myself, 'what does logic have to do with it anyway? I'll live with Friday, May 13.'

"Col. Tom Needham, who was the chief of operations at the XVIII Airborne Corps headquarters, was responsible for putting together the ceremony. It was not an easy task, given the coordination required and the number of personnel involved."

Needham, now a major general and current corps deputy commander, said, "Yes, I was responsible for the event, but I had a lot of help from some very good people, including input from Sergeant Major Gaweda. From General Foss on down we wanted to do something really top-notch for the sergeant major. Sergeant Major Gaweda may not have known everyone at Fort Bragg, but everyone at Fort Bragg knew who he was.

"We came up with a format that since has become the model for the big ceremony, such as a high-level change of command or major retirement. It was a colorful and impressive show, with twenty commands of brigade level or above represented, but what made it remarkable was the presence of so many general officers."

"Edith and I traveled to Atlanta on April 30, 1988," Ted said, "where I was honored as Airborne Man of the Year by *Static Line*, a monthly publication 'for, by and about paratroopers and men with airborne hearts.'

"As the countdown to my retirement day continued, I was becoming more and more nervous. It was a time of mixed emotions for me. I didn't really want to leave the army, but I had no choice.

"I received many telegrams and letters from retired and active duty officers and NCOs I had served with over the years, including a note from Army Chief of Staff Carl E. Vuono. General Scott, who as a colonel had been my Third Brigade commander for thirteen months in 1983 and 1984, wired from his Special Operations Command in Europe:

"'You will be sorely missed at Fort Bragg and throughout the army. You should take great pride in the number of soldiers you have trained in your time. From privates to generals, everyone you have worked with has benefited from your wise counsel and great experience. I will be forever grateful for your loyal and professional support to a young brigade commander who had not previously served in the 82nd Airborne. You are truly a soldier's soldier and an NCOs NCO.'

"A most moving letter came from my old friend, Col. Tim Scully, who had soldiered with me in the Third Brigade and the XVIII Airborne Corps. He wrote: 'I have thought constantly about how to thank you for everything you have done for me.

"'You watched over me for a long time. I am convinced that my success at Fort Bragg was largely due to your guidance and the words you spoke to the commander about me. I know that I got the job as General Lindsay's aide because of your help and influence. I know that you kept Colonel Scott (who retired as a lieutenant general) from killing me on more than one occasion. I am certain that you saved me time and again. I will forever be in your debt.

"'... You are a soldier that legends are written about... For years to come the best soldiers of our nation will be those who learned to serve from the finest paratrooper in the army—you! The highest compliment I can pay you is to try and serve our nation as well as you did.'

"On May 12, I made my farewell parachute jump with a distinguished group of soldiers. I had asked Maj. Gen. Claude Ivey, deputy commander of the XVIII Airborne Corps, who was the only general officer at Fort Bragg currently qualified as a jumpmaster, to serve in that role for my ceremonial final jump."

"I told Sergeant Major Gaweda that I would be honored," Ivey said. "I was pleased that he asked, because we had developed such a tremendous professional relationship. I'll never forget that jump. On my side of the airplane, Ted was the first man out the door. He was followed by his son, Lieutenant Gregory Gaweda, who in turn was followed by General Lindsay and General Foss.

"After that, it was two-star general this and two-star general that, followed by a line-up of senior sergeants major. They joked that the airplane was so heavy with brass on one side that the pilot had to put in a lot of right rudder to keep the plane level. It was a great day and a good jump."

"I was up early the next morning," Ted said, "and I felt so good that I went for a six-mile run with Brig. Gen. Daniel Schroeder, chief of staff of the XVIII Airborne Corps, and Specialist Alex Vega, my administrative assistant.

"As I put on my uniform for what I believed might be the last time, I thought, 'There's no turning back now.'

"The almanac had been right. Friday, May 13, was a picture-perfect spring day, with a cloudless sky and a warm sun. As Edith and I sat on the reviewing stand, I secretly wished I was there for a change of command ceremony or someone else's retirement.

"Colonel Needham had put together a grand ceremony, with a Green Beret parachute jump, the 82nd Airborne Division Band and Chorus, colorful flags, and some fifteen general officers on the reviewing stand, including my old mentor, General Lindsay.

"I was proud when General Foss pinned the Distinguished Service Medal on my uniform, and I was honored by the citation, which declared that I had been an 'effective voice of the soldier and an exceptional leader and mentor of the noncommissioned officer corps.'

"I laughed when General Foss said he considered himself my 'most recent trainee,' and I stood tall when he read a congratulatory telegram from Secretary of the Army John Marsh. I was thrilled when marching units bearing the colors of the twenty commands of the XVIII Airborne Corps passed before me in review, and I was filled with emotion when I experienced the never-to-be-forgotten honor of reviewing the troops, while standing in the back of a moving jeep.

"Despite all of the pomp and circumstance, despite the wonderful words being spoken about me, my heart was filled with melancholy. To paraphrase Charles Dickens, it was the best of days and the worst of days.

"It was time to say good-bye. I stepped to the reviewing stand podium and asked, 'Where do I go to re-enlist?'

"I told my listeners, 'There are days in everyone's life when their emotions run well ahead of their capacity to put them into words. Today is that day for me. I am genuinely proud to be an American, but I am equally proud for being able to wear the uniform of the United States Army for the past thirty-five years.'

"'It has been worth every success and failure, every exhilaration and disenchantment, and every joy and heartache. It has been worth every moment of every day, of every year, of every decade. Leaving the military today is certainly the hardest thing I have ever done.

"'... The greatness of the XVIII Airborne Corps, the courage of our soldiers, and the strength of the leadership are inseparable. This is the army I always dreamed of serving in. Other men have served their entire lives and probably have never known the sense of professional completeness I feel at this moment. To all those who contributed to it, I offer my profound thanks.

"'General Creighton Abrams, former commander-in-chief of all U.S. forces in Vietnam, said during the 25th Infantry Division change of command, and I quote, "There are those who believe that freedom is indivisible ... I believe that freedom is a perishable asset that must be defended at all cost. Our nation has what it has, and is what it is today, because of those men whose profound faith in the idea of freedom would carry on through the darkness of fear, indecision and travail," unquote.

"'... Ladies and gentlemen, as we look at the soldiers on the parade field, I say to you, our nation will always have whatever it takes to carry the torch of freedom that was once carried by those who served before us.

Because of you and those who served before you, Americans will continue to live in the land of the free and the home of the brave. Thank you for the memories. God bless you, and God bless America.'

"I was humbled by the standing ovation I received from all of those high-ranking officers and dignitaries after I finished speaking, and there were tears in my eyes when the band closed the ceremony with the playing of 'Auld Lang Syne' and the 'Army Song.' Edith and I attended a reception in my honor at the Non-Commissioned Officers Club, and after it was over, she left to take care of her real estate business.

"I drove home alone, reflecting on the day and all that it had meant to me. The house seemed exceptionally quiet. Only hours earlier I had been surrounded by hundreds of soldiers and friends, and music and marching. I was changing into civilian clothes, when it hit me, when it really hit me. My army career was over, and, therefore, my life no longer had any meaning. Suddenly, it was the saddest day of my life.

"My emotional pain was almost unbearable. I remember going to the backyard, sitting in the grass, and weeping. I did that several times, seeking comfort from Edith and trying to cope with my feelings of uselessness."

"I didn't really know how bad it was for him until he later told me about sitting in the backyard and crying, because he felt that he had no worth," Edith said. "As for me, I was very happy, because no longer would he have to go through the terrible hardships that had been part of his job—little sleep, long hours of duty, and extended overseas absences from his family.

"I had heard from other wives that his retirement would be a difficult time for me, because, all of a sudden, we would be together every day. 'Oh, now that my husband is home all of the time, he gets on my nerves,' one woman told me. But I tell you, this never happened to me, not for one hour of one day. I was just so happy to have him home, something I had not experienced in all our years of marriage. We did not have a single problem of adjusting to our new situation."

"After a week of sitting around and feeling sorry for myself," Ted said, "I received a telephone call from Maj. Michael Anderson, General Foss's aide. He told me that Trivett Lloyd, my successor as corps sergeant major, had broken a hip on a jump and would be out of commission for ninety days.

"Since I would not be officially mustered out of the Army until my 87 days of accumulated leave had expired, Major Anderson said that General

Foss would like me to return to active duty at corps headquarters and help him select an interim corps sergeant major, who would serve until Lloyd's return.

"'Oh, yes sir,' I told Major Anderson, 'I will be pleased to do that. I will be there the first thing in the morning.' So I put on my uniform and went back to work. It almost was as if I had never left. I recommended and General Foss approved naming Robert M. McLymore temporary corps sergeant major. McLymore already was on orders to go to Korea in about three months, so it worked out perfectly.

"Although my return to duty lasted only ten days, I managed to get in two more parachute jumps. I never maintained a running total of every single jump, but I ended up with somewhere in the neighborhood of twelve hundred.

"Those brief ten days helped lift me out of my deep depression. Although my mind would now and again experience that dark emotion, I was on my way to recovery from post-retirement blues. I took my final physical examination, signed all the required papers, and formally left the army in late June 1988.

"John H. Bell, civilian retirement services officer at Fort Bragg, personally handled the processing of my paperwork. As an army captain he had served with me in the Third Brigade in the 1970s, where he was the recruiting and retention officer."

"Sergeant Major Gaweda is one of my heroes, a straight shooter who always led from the front," Bell said. "He never showed a sign of weakness, nor did he ever speak of any. You know, if the situation called for it, he could have been a Rambo behind enemy lines.

"He was the kind of guy that if the going got tough, you knew he would not let you down. You could count on him 100 percent. He had so much strength within himself that he would never fold. Given the opportunity, he could have been another Audie Murphy." (Murphy was the most-decorated combat soldier of World War II.)

After Ted left the army, his older son, George, gave him some golf lessons. The game became his new passion, and he applied the same intensity to it that he did to everything else. He started going to the Fort Bragg courses almost every day. Despite taking up the game late in life and playing on a regular basis for only ten years, he has scored four holes in one.

"It was a joy for me to play with many comrades with whom I had served," Ted said. "It was like old home week, and the next thing you know, I stopped thinking about the army all of the time."

"He was enjoying life again," Edith said. "We planned our first overseas trip together and it was just great. I remember his sitting at the breakfast table and saying, 'I don't understand how I earned such a good life. I can do as I want.'

"And that's what we are doing—doing as we want—and that's all we need. We don't need riches and fame to be happy. We are thoroughly happy, and it's a wonderful experience."

"That's all true," Ted added, "but I will miss the army until the day I die."

Epilogue

IN retirement, I am happy to be living in a free country, without the perils of war. Of course, freedom is not free. Throughout the history of the United States, many have paid the ultimate price for it.

In 1990, I was named honorary sergeant major of the 82nd Airborne Division's 505th Parachute Infantry Regiment. When Desert Shield and Desert Storm came, I visited Col. Karl L. Johnson, who was operations officer of the XVIII Airborne Corps, and told him that since I was the regiment's honorary sergeant major, I wanted to go to Saudi Arabia to see my soldiers.

He didn't buy that, but I must confess that it was hard for this old soldier to sit at home and do nothing while the Persian Gulf War was raging. I had trained troops in the Egyptian desert for just such a conflict. When it appeared that the regiment would be going to Haiti to enforce civilian rule there, I visited Lt. Col. Jacob McFarren at the headquarters of the Third Battalion, 505th Parachute Infantry Regiment.

As I stood in his doorway, he said, "Sergeant Major, come in. It's so good to see you."

He was surrounded by a lot of hubbub, so as I sat down I said, "I won't take long. I just wanted to be with paratroopers today. Isn't this a great day to be a paratrooper?"

"God, Sergeant Major," he answered, "I wish you could go with us."
"I would go in a minute," I said.
"I know you would," he replied, "and you would beat me out the door."
It was a special moment.

I do not agree with some of the things that are happening in today's Army. When I left active duty in mid-1988, we had approximately 740,000 soldiers in uniform, and twelve four-star generals. As of January 1, 1998, the troop count was down to 480,000, but the number of four-star generals remained at twelve.

Our army has too many generals and field grade officers on active duty. It is small and getting smaller. We should purge the ranks so that every soldier on active duty is "fit to fight" and deployable on short notice.

All personnel with chronic medical problems, including those who test HIV-positive, should be discharged with disability pay or for the good of the service. There are too many soldiers who place an additional burden on the rest of the Army, when it comes to sending soldiers to overseas assignments or war.

We have an all-volunteer army, and, as such, every soldier should be combat ready. If soldiers fail to perform up to army standards, they should be immediately returned to civilian life. There is no room in the army for those who lack common sense, basic discipline, and self-motivation.

The qualifications for soldiering are simple. A soldier must be physically and mentally tough, and must be able to recognize right from wrong. Our Army has been and should continue to be very selective. Everyone is not qualified to serve and nobody is forced to serve.

Those who enter the service and declare themselves to be homosexuals should be discharged within two weeks. They should not be able to use the court system to interfere with the good order and discipline of our army. Those who believe in homosexuals serving in the armed forces either have never been in the military or failed to enforce standards of conduct when they did serve.

Army Gen. John Shalikashvilli, chairman of the Joint Chiefs of Staff, told the Senate Armed Forces Committee in March 1996 that discharging military service members with the AIDS virus would be unfair and waste money spent on training. He said there are thousands of people in the military who cannot be deployed because of such ailments as heart disease.

"We have some 6,500 men and women in uniform who for one reason or another are non-deployable," he continued. "To single out one group over another is how we look to treat them among all the nondeployables is, I think, unnecessary because the system we have works well."

I immediately fired off a letter to him, in which I said:

"Your testimony before the Senate Armed Forces Committee is an enormous disappointment to our nation and its armed forces. The key words are combat readiness, and members who test HIV-positive are never deployable. Your comparison with those who have other ailments such as heart disease is incorrect. Personnel with permanent medical profiles are being discharged with disability."

He responded five weeks later, writing: "The FY DOD Authorization bill requires the separation of any member of the military who is HIV-positive and, if this provision stands, approximately one thousand individuals will be discharged. As I said in testimony, this issue is one of fairness.

"The legislation singles out one group of service members for discharge, whether or not they are able to do their jobs when a physical evaluation system to determine fitness for duty is in place. Decisions regarding retention, as with other diseases, must be made on an individual basis. But, make no mistake, the readiness of our armed forces is my number one priority, and readiness today is at an all-time high.

"Your interest in the welfare of the men and women in uniform is understandable. Also, your contributions to the nation as a member of the army are greatly appreciated."

Despite his explanation, I still believe he is wrong.

Documented evidence of widespread sexual harassment in the army fills me with revulsion. So much so, that I think the army should give serious thought to sending men and women to separate basic training programs. It appears that most of the harassment of women occurs at the basic training level, where, being brand new to the army, they are the most vulnerable.

I have no respect for any officer or noncommissioned officer who would use his position to sexually harass women soldiers. They should be court-martialed as speedily as possible and slapped with dishonorable discharges.

I was terribly distressed when a veteran female sergeant major alleged that Sergeant Major of the Army Gene C. McKinney had sexually harassed her. I know McKinney and he knows who I am, because he has an airborne background.

I wrote to him on February 9, 1997, saying:

"The allegations of sexual assault and harassment against you are an enormous disappointment to the noncommissioned officer corps, as well as to the army. Regardless of the outcome of the investigation, you will not be able to represent the enlisted forces or be an effective advisor to the chief of staff of the army.

"The code of honesty, integrity, and moral conduct has been breached. You should ask to be replaced, and be allowed to retire at the earliest possible date."

Single parents also are a big problem in the army. In my opinion, there is no room in our army for a single parent, male or female. Single soldiers, who take their dependent children to a day care center in the morning and pick them up at the end of the day, are kept from the most-demanding assignments. That places an additional burden on those soldiers who are subject to call twenty-four hours a day, seven days a week.

I have rarely reviewed an army-mandated "family care plan" in which I had any confidence. I believe a pregnant soldier should be administratively discharged until her child is at least three months old. She should be allowed to return to active duty only when a solid family care plan is presented.

My son Gregory, a major in the army reserve who returned from active duty in Bosnia in September 1996, helped me prepare a document on that situation which reflects our shared feelings.

I always have been opposed to the sending of American troops to Bosnia-Herzegovina to conduct combat operations, but I agree with the current peacekeeping mission. The United States is the only nation in the world capable of bringing peace to the former Yugoslav Federation. The European community tried unsuccessfully for three years to create a meaningful dialogue for peace.

Only the United States, by structuring economic incentives and the use of force against those who are not willing to comply, can create an environment conducive to peace. When all of the combatants declared their commitment to peace, it was the United States that made sure this was captured in writing at the Dayton Peace Accords.

Once the accords were signed, America owed it to NATO and the world to lead the effort by sending U.S. troops to Bosnia to maintain peace. This role I fully support. Only America can provide the tremendous civil-military response necessary to accomplish this mission. No other nations could bring to bear the international resources required to accomplish peace.

This country has the most highly developed Civil-Military Operations (CMO) apparatus in the world. This unique force structure was developed over the last one hundred years. Some CMOs have been more successful than others. In the middle of the nineteenth century, Gen. Winfield Scott, known as the father of the CMO, successfully pacified the Mexican populace while occupying formerly enemy territory.

The occupation and reconstruction of the American South after the Civil War was the first nation-building operation of its kind, and it served as a model for the Marshall Plan, which was implemented in post–World War II Europe. Then there were our failures in Vietnam and Somalia. I think we sometimes learn more from our failures than we do from our successes. We must not put American armed forces in harm's way without sufficient means to protect themselves.

A significant armored threat existed in Bosnia. The United States responded with a well-equipped armored force. Why the United Nations Protective Force (UNPROFOR) did not take the same approach is not clear. It was done on a piecemeal basis, which ended up in humiliation for the UN force, with UN units being halted or captured. I believe there was a lack of resolve and confidence at the United Nations and in European capitals.

Peacemaking and enforcing can be accomplished only by making conditions appear favorable for peace in the eyes of the combatants. The first step is displaying a capable force that everyone recognizes is prepared to "force" peace. Once the fighting has stopped, incentives for peace are bestowed upon those parties who demonstrate the desire for it. Then, install price tags that combatants must be willing to pay in the event they believe war is a more favorable option. Economic aid, for example.

The U.S. is the only nation on earth capable of exerting influence worldwide. This is due, in part, to our holding the moral high ground and often more important, the economic high ground. The United States is by far the world's most generous country, undoubtedly giving more resources to world charity than the other nations combined.

It is important that we maintain that image in times of peace as well as war. The U.S. military enjoys a very positive image at home and abroad, especially in peace-starved Bosnia, where the mission is very straightforward—enforce the Dayton Peace Accords.

If hostilities erupt between the Serbs, Croats, and Muslims while U.S. troops still are in Bosnia, they should be immediately withdrawn, citing the condition of peace as a precursor to their presence. In the event hostilities are directed toward the peacekeeping forces, our troops must react quickly and decisively to eliminate the aggressor force as a partner in the peace process.

My bitterness about Vietnam boiled to the surface when former Secretary of Defense Robert S. McNamara's book, *In Retrospect: The Tragedy & Lessons of Vietnam*, was published.

One morning in the spring of 1996, while relaxing and enjoying the fruits of my retirement, I anticipated my day would be routine. I would go to the curb and pick up the newspaper, put on a pot of coffee, read the paper, go for my daily run, and then head for the golf course.

I opened the paper and found myself staring at a front-page article reporting that McNamara had acknowledged in his new book that he knew almost from the beginning that Vietnam was a terrible mistake and the war could not be won.

My insides turned to knots. I was angry, I was disgusted, and I was sad. I had not felt that low since the fall of Saigon on April 30, 1975. Few Americans can understand the impact that event had on most Vietnam veterans. The evacuation of Saigon and the level of anarchy surrounding our final withdrawal was surpassed only by the discouragement I felt while watching the pathetic scenes of the North Vietnamese Army marching victoriously into Saigon.

When I read the story about McNamara's disgraceful confession, all my emotions associated with the fall of Saigon came rushing back to me. In 1975, it took me several weeks to shake the discouragement I felt. On that spring morning in 1996, I did not go for my run and the coffee stayed in the pot. It took me a month to regain my enthusiasm for life.

Before my first twelve-month tour to Vietnam, beginning in December 1965, I could hardly wait to get there. As a soldier, I felt it was my place to be where the bullets were flying. I "marched to the sounds of the guns," volunteering for Vietnam not once, not twice, but three times.

On my first tour, I served as a Regional Popular Force advisor. I remember reporting to the Dien Ban district on December 30, 1965, full of energy and eager to take the war to the Viet Cong in my sector. I believed in our leaders, I believed in the principles of democracy, and I believed in America.

I returned to Vietnam for my second tour in March 1968. I had been in the country for only a few days when I became enlightened by the message traffic I was exposed to at the headquarters of the Military Assistance Command Vietnam, Studies and Observation Group (MACVSOG).

Based on the information I was reading in the daily Situation Reports (SITREPS), I began to lose confidence in the direction the war was heading. In my mind, I began questioning the methods we were employing in an attempt to gain victory.

I perceived that the Short-Term Reconnaissance and Target Acquisition teams (STRATA) we were putting into North Vietnam were not really effective, except for the possible psychological effect of causing the enemy to think that we could operate in his backyard at will. I suppose it made the people at MACVSOG headquarters feel as if they were doing something, but it led me to become dissatisfied with my own piece of the war.

The number of fragging incidents, where men kill their officers, that I saw in the SITREPS, the officer rotation policy, our assessments of enemy capability—all these things caused me to question our strategy and level of commitment.

I felt the fragging was the direct result of the officer rotation policy. Officers were sent to combat units, but they were rotated out to staff jobs before they could learn the art of killing Viet Cong. The NCOs and other enlisted ranks were exposed to the fighting for a full year before being relieved, while the officers punched their tickets and left the line after six months.

In other words, the NCOs and enlisted ranks were twice as likely to be killed or wounded as the officers. In my judgment, that practice indicated a lack of commitment by the officer corps. Also, it was unfair as hell. No wonder soldiers were angry.

An NCO cannot be created by sending him to school. He can be properly seasoned only through years of toil in physically and mentally tough assignments. By the end of 1968, the Army's professional NCO corps had disintegrated and was replaced by one that had been forged in a schoolhouse, not on the battlefield. All of the best NCOs had been killed, wounded, or had retired or separated themselves from the army out of frustration. The army leadership in Vietnam and those in the Pentagon had to see this.

The daily SITREPS also indicated an enormous amount of enemy sustainment and activity, regardless of where we bombed, how much we bombed, or how successful our search and destroy mission had been.

I also was greatly troubled when our leaders declared that the fighting in the Nah Trang Valley was an American victory, when it was a miserable defeat. That was another example of deception. I felt someone was confused, and I knew it wasn't me.

I had no idea that the war already had been lost in November 1965, when President Lyndon Johnson, at a private meeting in the White House, attacked the assembled Joint Chiefs of Staff for proposing bold measures to bring the war to an early and favorable conclusion.

Retired Marine Lt. Gen. Charles G. Cooper, who was present as an aide to Admiral David McDonald, wrote in May 1996 as part of his upcoming book, *Cheers and Tears*, that the Oval Office meeting took place only after the Joint Chiefs had argued long and hard for a meeting without McNamara present.

McNamara's position at that time appeared to favor a large build-up of American forces for a ground war. General Cooper writes that after the proposal of the Joint Chiefs, the president turned his back on them for a minute and then whirled to face them and exploded.

"He screamed obscenities," Cooper said. "He cursed them personally, he ridiculed them for coming to his office with their 'military advice.' Noting that it was he who was carrying the weight of the free world on his shoulders, he called them filthy names . . . and used the F-word as an adjective more freely than a Marine at boot camp. He then accused them of trying to pass the buck for World War III to him. It was unnerving. It was degrading.

" . . . He told them he was disgusted with their naive approach toward him, that he was not going to let some military idiots talk him into World War III. It ended when he ordered them to 'get the hell out of my office.'

"The Joint Chiefs of Staff had done their duty. They knew that the nation was making a strategic military error, and despite the rebuffs of their civilian masters in the Pentagon, they had insisted on presenting their views of the problem and recommending solutions to the highest authority. They had done so, and they had lost. So, too, had thousands of other Americans."

Now we learn that the secretary of defense was beginning to recognize the tragic error of his Vietnam policy as early as 1967, but he did little about it. His treachery against the Joint Chiefs was irrevocable.

He did not have the intestinal fortitude to stand up to Lyndon Johnson in November 1965. Nor did he have the courage to confront LBJ with his growing doubts in 1967.

Instead, he was content to write a pitiful little memo to the president, which Johnson ignored. Was this to absolve him from any responsibility for the war's disastrous outcome or for the loss of more than fifty-eight thousand American lives?

Some American historians are applauding McNamara for breaking his silence. I think some things are best left unsaid. To me, he simply is a coward, a man who was afraid to acquaint his boss with reality and who lacked the necessary moral courage to be straightforward and honest with his chosen military commanders.

McNamara apparently was more fearful of losing prestige with LBJ than he was about losing soldiers in Vietnam. Otherwise, he would have supported the Joint Chiefs and confronted the president with a unified front. He failed to realize that loyalty is a two-way street.

The secretary of defense could have gone down in history as the master architect of détente and the supreme strategist of the Cold War. Before becoming lost in the quicksand of Vietnam, as the French had before him, he had accomplished a great deal for America and the army.

It was McNamara who transformed our paper army into one with teeth by creating the readiness reporting system, and it was McNamara who skillfully maneuvered the United States through the formulation of our nuclear and Cold War strategy. Somehow along the way, he lost sight of the fact that he was a leader of men, not automatons or robots.

I could not believe that he admitted to the world that he had such little value for the lives of the American servicemen and women, that he sent them to a war that he knew could not be won. I felt betrayed.

On a more personal note, I lost my father and mother in 1980 and 1981 respectively. They had a hard life, but they knew the joy of living in America for many years. When Edith and I came to the United States in 1961, one of the first things we did was attend my brother Jan's wedding.

Thirteen years later, he was dead, killed in a horrible automobile crash. Jan died when an off-duty New Jersey state trooper, who was chasing another car, smashed into his automobile. Ironically, he lost his wife and two young sons four years earlier in a head-on collision. Those two events were the greatest tragedies in my family.

My brother Walter, who lived with me in Chicago before I joined the army, died there in 1990. He was only fifty-nine. My older sister, Pelagia, and her husband and two sons came to the United States from Poland in

1962. My parents spent a lot of money to buy their freedom from the Communists. They live in the Pocono Mountains of Pennsylvania.

My sister Wanda, who was the youngest of us seven, lives with her family in Brooklyn, New York. My brother Eddie lives in New Jersey and my brother Henry resides in the New York metropolitan area.

I had never had any desire or reason to return to the place of my birth. Our farm and everything my parents had owned became part of Russia after the war. Also, part of Eastern Germany was given to Poland.

On a beautiful sunny day in the autumn of 1996, Edith and I decided to look up George Kennedy in Harrells, North Carolina. Kennedy had sponsored the Gaweda family's trip to America. George McGill, the local fire chief, was gracious enough to take us around.

I recognized the old schoolhouse and Kennedy's home. We walked the field where our small dwelling was located. My mind was flooded with memories when I looked at the cement foundation blocks still in the ground. It was all that was left of our past.

Learning of my benefactor's death, Edith and I visited his grave, where we said a prayer for a good man who had helped to change the lives of the Gaweda family forever.

Edith and I have been blessed with six wonderful, second-generation American grandchildren, divided evenly between three boys and three girls. When my granddaughter Ginny was twelve years old, she wrote a school paper about me entitled, "People Who Have Overcome."

After ably summarizing my lifetime in two-and-a-half pages, she concluded:

"My grandpa has overcome so many hardships in his life that it seems he has lived many lives instead of just one."

You can't beat that.

Glossary

AA: All American, a nickname of the 82nd Airborne Division.
A-1: World War II model, single engine aircraft, highly maneuverable, known as the Skyraider.
ABN: Airborne.
ADC: Assistant Division Commander.
AFB: Air Force Base.
ARCOM: Army Commendation Medal, awarded for valor or meritorious service.
AK-47: Soviet-designed automatic assault rifle using 7.62 ammunition.
AN/PRC-25: FM field radio, line of sight transmission, usually limited to 25–30 miles.
ARVN: Army of Republic of (South) Vietnam.
ATT: Army training test.
AUSA: Association of the United States Army.
B-52: Heavy bomber spreading death and destruction across the land.
BAR: Browning automatic rifle, World War II vintage.
Blackbirds: U.S. Air Force C-123s or C-130s transport planes painted black with no markings, in SOG's 90th Special Operation Squadron.
C-119: World War II–vintage cargo aircraft, known by paratroopers as the Boxcar.
C-123: Twin-engine, propeller-driven, cargo/paratroopers drop aircraft.
C-130: drop aircraft known as Hercules.
C-141: U.S. Air Force first jet cargo/paratroopers drop aircraft, better known as Starlifter.
CFA: Combined Field Army.
CG: Commanding General.
CH-53: U.S. Air Force cargo/troop helicopter, better known as Jolly Green Giants.
Chieu-Hoi: Open arms policy. Program set up to encourage VCs and NVA to defect without fear of retribution.
CIA: Central Intelligence Agency.
CIB: Combat Infantryman Badge.
CMO: Civil military operation.
CO: Commanding Officer.
CP: Command post.
CSM: Command sergeant major (the highest enlisted rank).
DAI-UY: Captain Vietnamese armed forces.

DCG: Deputy Commanding General.
Dien Ban: Military district located 25 miles south of Da Nang.
DFC: Distinguished Flying Cross, fourth highest award for valor.
DMZ: Demilitarized zone between South and North Korea.
DSC: Distinguished Service Cross. Second highest award for valor.
DSM: Distinguished Service Medal. The highest award for meritorious service.
DZ: Drop zone.
Elbe: River in Central Europe.
EM: Enlisted man/men.
Enlisted grade and rank:
    E-1, Recruit
    E-2, Private
    E-3, Private First Class
    E-4, Specialist/Corporal
    E-5, Sergeant
    E-6, Staff Sergeant
    E-7, Sergeant First Class
    E-8, Master Sergeant/First Sergeant:
    E-9, Sergeant Major, Command Sergeant Major.
Eshwege: Nazi labor camp, located 90 miles Northeast of Frankfurt.
FAC: Forward air controller—pilot who flies over the battlefield relaying calls for air strikes or artillery fire.
FO: Forward observer—ground based director of artillery fire.
FOB: Forward operational base, with command and logistic elements, where SOG troops were housed and trained.
FTX: Field training exercise.
Gotha: Town in Eastern Germany
Ho Chi Minh Trail: NVA supply roads and trails running south from North Vietnam, through Laos and Cambodia.
H&I: Harassment and interdiction—artillery fire (pre-plan).
Hoi An: Capital of Quan Nam Province.
HQ: Headquarters.
IG: Inspector general.
Ilmenau: Town in the mountain ridge of Thuringin.
Iron Curtain: Dividing line between East and West Germany and other European countries.
JFKSWCEN: John F. Kennedy Special Warfare Center, Fort Bragg, North Carolina.
Kamien-Koszyrski: Town in Eastern Poland (pre–World War II).
Kurfurstendamn: Berlin broadway.

Long Thanh: Vietnamese Airborne/Ranger training center also SOG training center for STRATA teams. Highly classified operation run by SF Detachment B-53, the resident team.
LZ: Landing zone for aircraft.
M-16A1: Standard Army rifle, firing 5.56 mm ammunition.
M-1919A6: .30 caliber machine gun, used during World War II and Korea
MACVSOG: Military Assistance Command Vietnam, Studies and Observation Group.
MATA: Military Assistance Training Adviser Course, at Fort Bragg, North Carolina.
MC1-1C: Army standard steerable parachute.
MI: military intelligence.
MMFOB: Monkey Mountain Forward Operational Base.
MP: Military Police.
MREs: Meals ready to eat.
MSM: Meritorious Service Medal. Third highest award for meritorious service.
MWR: Morale, welfare, and recreation.
NATO: North Atlantic Treaty Organization.
NCO: Noncommissioned officer.
NCOIC: Noncommissioned officer in charge.
NCOA: Noncommissioned Officers Academy.
NCR: National Cash Register Company.
NKP: Nakhan Phanam, Thailand. (U.S. Air Force Base) SOG launch site for operations into North Vietnam.
NVA: North Vietnamese Army.
O-2: FAC–observation aircraft, twin-boom engine, known as Oscar-Duce.
O&I: Operation and intelligence.
OIC: Officer in charge.
OCS: Officer candidate school.
Officers' grade and rank:
    O-1, Second Lieutenant.
    O-2, First Lieutenant.
    O-3, Captain.
    O-4, Major.
    O-5, Lieutenant Colonel.
    O-6, Colonel.
    O-7, Brigadier General.
    O-8, Major General.
    O-9, Lieutenant General.
    O-10, General.

OV-10: Twin-engine, lightweight, armed reconnaissance aircraft, known as Branco.
PIR: Parachute Infantry regiment.
PSG: Platoon sergeant, ranking NCO in the platoon.
PT: Physical training.
PX: Post exchange.
RF/PF: Regional Forces/Popular Forces, all Vietnamese units, recruited from villages within district.
R&R: Rest and relaxation.
RTO: Radio-telephone operator.
S-1: Command staff personnel section.
S-2: Command staff intelligence section.
S-3: Command staff operations section.
S-4: Command staff logistics section.
S-5: Command staff civil affairs section.
SF: Special Forces.
SM: Soldier's Medal; the highest award for valor for non-combat action.
SOG: Studies and Observation Group.
Static line: 25-foot paratrooper lanyard that automatically deploys parachute.
STRATA: Short-term reconnaissance and target acquisition.
T-10: Standard Army reserve parachute, 24-foot canopy.
T-10C: Standard Army main parachute, 35-foot paratrooper canopy.
TASS: Tactical Air Support Squadron.
TOC: Tactical Operations Center.
U-2 Blackbird: Spy plane used by U.S. Central Intelligence Agency.
UH-1B: Small, troop-carrying helicopter, known as a Huey.
URC-10: Small emergency AM radio, voice and beacon signals used by all air crews.
USAF: United States Air Force.
USASMA: United States Army Sergeants Major Academy.
USNAD: U.S. Navy Advisory Detachment at Da Nang.
USS *Pope*: U.S. Navy transport ship.
Viet Cong: South Vietnamese indigenous communist guerrillas.
Wildflecken: The largest Displaced Persons camp in Germany for Polish refugees.
WP: White phosphorus (rockets or grenade) known as Willie Peter.
XVIII Airborne Corps: Military organization above Division.

Index

A

Abrams, Creighton 111, 130, 243
Adams, Arthur 215
Allen, Marie 211
Anderson, Michael 244
Aschaffenburg 26

B

Bahnsen, Doc 194, 195
Bell, John H. 245
Bell, Travis 234
Blough (Major) 89
Blue, Josigh 66
Boylan, Peter J. 206
Bradley, Richard J. 133
Brady, Morris 154, 155, 157
Brandenburg, John 157
Brown, Wilbert 163, 181–182
Burtrum, Clayton 98
Bush, George W. 138

C

Carter, Jimmy 215
Cavanaugh, Steve 107
Chamberlain, Neville 29
Childs, Leon 178, 182
Churchill, Winston 30
Clark, Charles 142
Clinton, William J. 113
Colombo (Major) 91, 133
Connally, William 184
Cooper, Charles G. 254
Craver, Douglas M. 144
Crocker, George A. 202

Cronkite, Walter 78
Crowe, William 229
Cummings, Clarence 124

D

Dabney, Fred 168
Dabney, Gina 189
Dacyszyn, Michael 65, 71
Daladier, Edouard 29
Danielson, Ted 68
Davis, Hugh 140
Dien Ban 80, 83, 85, 91, 252
Distinguished Flying Cross 105, 111, 194
Distinguished Service Medal 16, 242
Downing, Wayne 113
Dugan, Charles 103, 105
Dulles, John F. 58

E

Earle, Richard 178, 181, 182
Eisenhower, Dwight D. 30, 58
Eschwege 24, 43
Eschwege (town) 21, 22, 23, 32

F

Farris, Jack 213
Fischer, Hedi 32
Foss, John W. 16, 137, 220, 228, 229–231, 232, 235–236, 237, 238, 239, 240, 242, 244–245
Fowler, Franklin 204
Freitas, Alexander 151
Fulton, Tom V. 118

261

G

Garner, Alan W. 7
Garner, Joe R. 112–113
Gavin, Jim 199
Gaweda, Amy 116, 117
Gaweda, Antoni (father) 16, 22, 23, 40, 131, 255
Gaweda, Eddie 17, 18, 19, 20, 21, 22, 23, 25, 131, 256
Gaweda, Edith E. (wife)
Gaweda, George G. 61, 94, 116, 117, 128, 134, 172, 184, 245
Gaweda, Ginny L. 256
Gaweda, Gregory C. 63, 94, 115, 116, 117, 128, 134, 172, 173, 174, 176, 177, 184, 238, 239, 242, 250
Gaweda, Helena (mother) 17, 22, 26, 131, 255
Gaweda, Henry 17, 42, 131, 256
Gaweda, Jan 17, 62, 63, 131, 255
Gaweda, Peggy 117
Gaweda, Tadeusz (Command Sergeant Major)
Gaweda, Walter 17, 22, 26, 42, 131, 255
Glabik, Pelagia 17, 19, 22, 255
Gleason, John 208, 209–210
Glover, Charles 7
Goethe, Johann Wolfgang von 35
Gorbachev 176
Gotha (town) 25

H

Hargraves, James E. 145
Hay, John 123
Hayes, Douglas 151
Healy, Fritz 135, 225–226, 239
Hendrix, Charles W. 73
Hitler, Adolph 17, 18, 20, 24, 29, 30, 31, 177

Ho Chi Minh 81, 110
Hoi An 86, 88, 90, 91
Howze, Hamilton 64, 65
Hubner, Elizabeth 33, 34, 61, 171, 173, 174, 175, 176, 177
Hubner, Helfriede 32, 38, 173, 175, 176
Hubner, Klaus 32
Hunt, Joseph 206
Hutchinson, Jarold 145, 159, 233

I

Iacocca, Lee 227
Ilmenau 33, 34, 37, 171, 173, 176, 177
Inch, Timothy 166
Iron Curtain 30, 36, 54, 61, 172, 174
Ivey, Claude 220, 228, 242

J

Jackson, Stonewall 72
Johnson, Charles R. 65, 66–67
Johnson, Harold K. 189
Johnson, James D. 122
Johnson, James H. 197, 200
Johnson, Karl L. 247
Johnson, Lyndon B. 70, 73, 76, 111, 254–255
Johnson, William V. 185, 186, 187, 189, 190

K

Kamien-Koszyrski 17–18, 19, 20
Kellogg, Paige 205
Kendrick, Robert 76, 123, 124
Kennedy, George 26, 39–40, 48–49, 256
Khrushchev, Nikita 57, 58
Kitchens, Johnny 219
Kovel (town) 20
Krosen, Frederick J. 144

L
Lap (Colonel ARVN) 86–87
Law, Lawrence L. 53, 54
Lekson, John 67
Leonard, Kay 226–227
LePage, Lewis 129
Lindsay, James J. 144–145, 197, 211–212, 213, 214, 215, 216, 218–219, 220, 222, 225, 228–229, 233, 234, 235, 236–237, 242
Lindsey, James J. 135
Lloyd, Herbert 71–72, 72, 73–75
Lloyd, Trivett 244
Lupyak, Joe 182–183
Luther, Martin 35

M
MacArthur, Douglas 226
MacDonald, Hugh 73, 75, 76
MacFarland (Corporal) 74
Maher, Arnold 49–51
Malone, Cecil 66
Manfred (brother-in-law) 37, 38, 173, 175, 176, 177
Manfred 173
Markham, John 162, 164, 178
Marsh, John 243
Martain, Roosevelt 187
Matrejek, Wanda (sister) 17, 19, 21, 22, 63, 256
Mazur, Stanislav 41
McBride, William 52–53
McDonald, David 254
McDonald, Thomas B. 181, 185
McFarren, Jacob 247
McGill, George 256
McKinney, Gene C. 249
McLymore, Robert M. 245
McNamara, Robert M. 252, 254, 255

McNeill, Dan K. 145
Meadows, Richard 112, 113–114
Meredith, James H. 65
Merritt, Kenneth 159
Michalowski, Mickey 41, 42
Minitery, Louis 195
Murphy, Audie 245

N
Nance, E. T. Jr. 95
Needham, Thomas 240, 242
Nelson, Swede 169

O
O'Brien, Robert D. 143
Olchovik, Stanley 105–107, 108, 114
Olds, Bowman 205, 215
Orlov, William 190, 191, 192, 193, 195
Ornstein, Alvin 146, 147, 148, 150–151, 153–155, 156, 157–158
Ortega, Daniel 238

P
Palastir, Joseph T. 228
Palmer, Bruce Jr. 76
Parker, Harris 90
Patton, George S. Jr. 30, 146
Pitts, Joseph 204
Poole, James 89
Potter, Richard 119
Powers, Gary 58
Prehn, Robert 118, 129
Pupa, Joseph 42

Q
Quist, Francis H. 64

R
Ralstone, David F. 214

Ray, Roy 140–141
Reagan, Ronald 176, 202, 207, 217–218
Reiter (boss) 54–55
Ringler, Arthur 118–119, 121
Roche, William H. 146
Ruth, Henry 147–148, 149–150, 155, 156, 157

S
Sanderson, Alfred 97, 98, 100
Schroeder, Daniel 242
Schweinfurt 26
Scott, James T. 136, 200–201, 202, 203, 205, 206, 207, 213, 224, 225, 241
Scully, Timothy 198–199, 203, 216, 218–219, 241
Seigle, Robert N. 95–96, 98, 99, 100, 202
Seitz, Richard J. 98
Sennewald, Robert W. 193
Shalikashvilli, John 248, 249
Short, Kermit 164
Shukoski (PFC) 133
Sinkovitz, Michael J. 96–97
Smitka, Ernest 129
Somerholder, Robert 67, 68
Spell, Henry 222
Stalin, Joseph 17, 18, 30, 36
Stiner, Carl 126

T
Tackaberry, Thomas H. 233, 234
Thompson, Laverne G. 97
Throckmorton, John L. 67
Tower, John 207
Townsend, George 129

Trobaugh, Edward 207, 225
Trong, Ngui 81, 87–88, 89
Truman, Harry S. 40
Tucker, Gertrude 77
Turner, Joe 221
Twitchell, Heath 139–142, 144, 159
Twomey, Tom 124

U
USS *Muir* 26–27
USS *Pope* 43
USS *Upsher* 52

V
Van Autreve, Leon 129, 135
Vaught, James B. 185, 186, 187, 193, 195, 233
Vega, Alex 242
Vuono, Carl 241

W
Walter 26
Warner, Volney 143
Washington, Harold 209
Weinberger, Casper 136
West, Virgil 95
Westmoreland, William 83, 109, 111, 113
Weston, Freddie J. 151
White, Victor 145
Wildflecken DP Camp 25, 26, 40
Williams (Sergeant) 74
Winter, Maurice 80–85, 86, 87, 88, 89, 90, 91, 133
Wooten, Henry L. 48

Y
Young, Joe 140